Blue Mesa Review

Issue Thirteen

The Creative Writing Center
University of New Mexico

Blue Mesa Review
Department of English
The University of New Mexico
Albuquerque, NM 87131

Tel.   505.277.6155
Fax   505.277.5573
Email bluemesa@unm.edu

Blue Mesa Review is a literary magazine published annually by the
Creative Writing Program at the University of New Mexico. Funding is
provided by the College of Arts and Sciences and the Department of
English Language and Literature.

Manuscripts are accepted July 1 through October 1. For complete
guidelines, please contact the managing editor or visit our web site at
www.unm.edu/~bluemesa/.

Cover Art: Beth Love

"Six Persimmons" by Arthur Sze originally appeared in *Redshifting Web:
Poems 1970-1998,* published by Copper Canyon Press (1998).

Blue Mesa Review 13

Editor
Julie Shigekuni

Managing Editor
Maya Allen-Gallegos

Associate Editor
Charles Linsmeier

Poetry Editor
Gene Frumkin

Fiction Editor
Daniel Mueller

Technical Editor
Matthew C. Allen

Editorial Board
Ali Abd'Allah-Ellis, Tani Arness, Tamara Brenno,
Yvonne Gillam, L. Goeckel, Kurt Gutjahr,
Ally Hack, Ben Ikenson, Jody Ipsen, Lindsay Lancaster,
Andrea Remmer Merkx, Robyn Mundy,
Marisa Saavedra, Emily Sperry, Lauren Snyder

Editor's Note

I am reminded of my Japanese grandmother, who used to give each of us something on Sundays when we visited—a Parker pen for my father, dishtowels for my mother. Her gifts were simple. But I've come to think of Blue Mesa 13 more like a care package from my Jewish in-laws: her mandel bread placed beneath dehydrated orange sponges from William-Sonoma, an Ella Fitzgerald CD from him, clothing from designer outlets for my husband, my daughters, and me. Marmalade. Even though none of us has ever cared much for marmalade, my mother-in-law loves it, and we save it for her visits, tucked in the back corner of the refrigerator.

While writing can be a solitary, often private, act, the editors of Blue Mesa have discovered this semester that the production of a literary magazine, like a care package from my in-laws, is quite the opposite. Each week during the fall we came together as poets, fiction writers, artists, and students to produce what you see here as Blue Mesa 13. Those who've read past issues of Blue Mesa might notice that this issue—unlike its predecessors—has no theme. The reason is simply that we couldn't agree on one. Rather, the contents along with their organization and our new look reflect our disagreements, our differing aesthetics, sensibilities, and ideas—combined to give you what we think of as the best work available. Our promise is that inside you'll find something that someone loved, maybe even fought for—from the authors to the editors, and now to you.

We think you'll enjoy what you see here, and we hope to find you again next spring wanting more.

Contents

Fiction

Poetry

Creative Nonfiction

Interview with Arthur Sze

Contributors

All the Meanings Serious Can Have

Michelle Brooks

I have made myself uncomfortable for men, but there are limits. Right now, my boyfriend Austin is with his best friend, also named Austin, on an all summer canoe trip down the Brazos River, Brazos meaning the arms of God. In this particular case, God's arms are full of branches and snakes and old tires. While he is gone, I am stuck with Austin's 6'3" boa constrictor named Homey. I hate Homey and his glass tank and I especially hate that in three days I will have to feed Homey a live rat, which will have to fall from my fingers unless I can convince some stupid/brave person to do it for me.

The canoe trip is an excuse for Austin and Little Austin (which is not a witty penis metaphor, but rather the way to distinguish his short best friend) to share private time, which essentially means they've been on a running drunk for somewhere near a month and show no signs of coming home until the very last minute, that minute being the day they register for their last year at the community college where I work as a financial aid officer. Austin has called once, asking "Will you feed my snake? You're the only one who can do it," which would have been flattering if he hadn't been talking about an actual snake who eats living rats, something else I loathe. All his other friends have visited them on the river at least once, but I have not been invited. I am eight years older than Austin. On a good day, I feel wild and reckless and on a bad day, I feel like Bobbie Dunne, a two-hundred pound Mineral Wells legend who works at the Howdy Doody and tries to lure younger men into her bed by telling them she has a new air-conditioner at home.

Pushing the snooze button, I roll over hoping to wake up in time for work. Sometimes I think I make this stuff up, but there's Homey's cage. I see it every morning.

I wake up the second time, hot and sweaty even though I only have one thin sheet over me because the wall unit isn't able to keep up with the July heat. What's worse is that in three weeks I will have to leave this shithole rental house and find another that won't be too expensive. The landlord, a masseuse/aromatherapist named Claudine left a note on the door, telling me that my lease would not be renewed because the house she moved to would not allow her three goats inside the city limits and had fined her $100 per goat each month. Claudine suffers from the illusion that her problems interest other people in such a compelling fashion that her victims will forget that they are being sodomized without proper lubrication. I have looked at other places, but they all require expensive deposits or stink like cat urine. The one place I could imagine living sits above a used bookstore on the town square, but will not allow Homey.

It's Friday, and I think about calling in, but I've already used most of my sick days and will have to take vacation time for my move. I push myself out of my waterbed, into the shower, and out the door, trying not to think about the fact that I've got to get in a hot, smelly 1978 Ford Granada to drive twenty minutes to a job that doesn't pay me enough to get a new car.

The sunlight is so bright it hurts, and I decide to stop and get a Coke on my way. I figure I'm already running so late, what's another five minutes going to do? My brother says this attitude accounts for my credit card debt and that I must weigh every financial decision, even if the amount of money seems insignificant. My brother's one goal in life was to get away from this town, which he has already achieved by becoming a high-paid lawyer in Singapore. He offered to send me a check for $7,000 to pay off my debt, which try as I might, I can't seem to chip away because of interest and late fees. I wanted to avoid this fate, but finally called him last week and said, go ahead and I'll pay you back at $300 per month until nothing's left. Nothing, unfortunately, being the best I can hope for.

With money on my mind, I drive past the Brazos River Rattlesnake Farm, a place that announces itself with hand-painted signs advertising "Live Snakes, Next Exit." I'm wondering how much money they would give me for Homey, as they are in the business of buying rattlesnakes at $4 per pound, maybe more for exotic ones like Homey. When I mentioned this as a possible alternative for Homey in Austin's absence, Austin said he would rather sell his snake to strangers than see it sold to the rattlesnake farm where it would live out its days in a pit with many other snakes. Homey is special, Austin said, and I found myself in the peculiar and alarming position of being murderously jealous of a snake.

I have been to the snake farm once, years ago with my mother just after she got out of the hospital for an extensive operation to remove a large nest of malignant tumors and just before she overdosed on my dead uncle's morphine in an attempt to smother the pain caused by the operation. Dust had settled on everything in the shop—the stuffed snakes, the rattlesnake jewelry, the tanks—so much so that I couldn't tell what was living and what was dead. Upon seeing my fear, the owner saddled up to me and said, "Darling, you got nothing to worry about. The only living snakes you can't see are in those boxes over there." The boxes sat in the corner with a big rock anchoring them down, "Caution!" written across the front of the old cardboard. Mesmerized by the slight motion of the boxes, I nearly pissed myself when a kitten ran across my foot. Also charming: underneath a tank of copperheads by the cash register, two potbellied pigs slept side by side in a box, oblivious to the fact that they would soon be dead, which is probably a good way to be. You, of course, are free to believe anything you want.

Another time, Austin and Little Austin went to the snake farm in the winter and sat on a bunch of crates and talked to the owner for a solid half an hour before asking, "So where are the rattlesnakes?" Well, you guessed it, they were hibernating in the very crates that Austin and Little Austin were sitting on.

I do not know which is worse: the sound of the rattles or the hibernating menace right under you, silent and waiting for the spring.

After three hours of pretending to file student loan applications, I tell my boss that I have cramps and need to go home. It's the perfect excuse because they can come on at any time and disappear just as quickly. Nobody's doing much anyway because the summer drains all energy from the days, leaving the nights for mayhem. During the worst heat wave in the 70s, Mineral Wells had eight murders in one month. Things seem slower now, but who knows how long that will last.

One of the secretaries is reading people's tea leaves and telling them the future from the shapes the leaves make. You have to drink the tea, turn your cup upside down, twirl the saucer three times, and see what images have formed. As much as I want my future, I can't stomach the taste.

So I meet my best friend Stacey at El Matador. She doesn't eat, but if you can look past that, she's the perfect lunch companion. El Matador sits between the Salvation Army and JoAnn's Fabrics in the Golden Triangle Plaza, a run-down strip mall next to the Baker Hotel, a huge building that used to be a spa for celebrities many, many years ago. It's strange to imagine this town being a place that people wanted to visit instead of a place in which the unlucky manage to get stuck.

"Can't you get rid of the damn thing? Let him deal with his own snake for a while," Stacey says. Tired from the heat, she slumps in her chair. This makes her look like a little girl, even wearing what she calls her "Lois Lane" outfit for her job at the Mineral Wells Index. One of her responsibilities is to take pictures of car and boat accidents, something she likes for the metaphorical value, if not the actual activity itself. The actual work pains Stacey because her last boyfriend died in a motorcycle accident on Highway 281 a few years ago, and she can't see an accident without thinking about that one.

She shakes grains of rice off her fork and puts about three up to her mouth. If she ever ate everything that was on her plate, it would take hours. I don't know how she does it. If something is good, I tend to want more even if it ends up making me sick in the end.

"I can't. He's counting on me." Two tables away, a group of boys makes farting noises with their arms. I start to smile, despite myself.

"Don't those bastards ever die?" she asks.

"All I know is that I told Austin I would take care of him. He doesn't have any other options."

"That boy of yours ain't worth a kiss my ass," she says. She puts down her fork to slow down her eating. "You should sell the snake, take the apartment over the bookstore, and try to find a better job."

I suspect she doesn't like Austin because of his pornography obsession, which I also find objectionable, but not for the same reasons. Last Valentine's Day, I took him to New Orleans to see Jimmy Buffet, running up my last credit card with any room on it. He didn't get me anything because he'd just ordered nearly a thousand dollars worth of porn off the Internet and was broke. We stayed at a hotel in Baton Rouge, where he confessed that he didn't know if he could ever tell me that he loved me. If this story has a happy ending, I'll be as surprised as you are.

When we got back to Texas, I went to a Bible study with Stacey that night. Austin was going to a bar to watch the Dallas Stars play. I asked him which bar he was going to so we could hook up later. Sadly, the bar in question was Hooters to which I replied, "I've had enough of other women's boobs for a while," still pissed off about not getting a Valentine's Day present. On our way to the class, Stacey hit me over the head with the Good Book, telling me that I deserved better.

"Jackson asked me out for tonight," Stacey says. Jackson is the sports editor in her office. I met him once, a middle-aged guy without kids. He's left food on her desk for six months, snacks like animal crackers. Stacey enjoys these treats, but hasn't pushed for more. Unlike me, the more Stacey likes someone, the more reluctant she is to date him.

"And?" I ask.

"I haven't answered yet. He e-mailed me, and asked me if I wanted to see *Last Picture Show*."

"That's your favorite. Like in his house? Like alone for the evening?"

"I'm assuming. Unless you know of a theater that shows movies that are almost thirty years old." She's trying hard to be cool about this whole thing, but her face erupts into a smile.

I try to remember how long it's been since I was excited about a night with someone.

Then I sit and watch Stacey pick at her food as if it might hurt her and am reminded that I have to feed Homey soon. I wonder why the snake won't eat dead food. Perhaps because it cannot answer the question why it, the food, died. I also suspect that it only senses the food when it, the food, moves since snakes don't see the way we do. And therein lies the question: how do you distinguish between the living and the dead, the harmful from the nourishing?

—▬ ▬—

Riding through the decommissioned army base in town, I wipe sweat off my forehead and watch a tarantula run across the street. My mother used to collect them and freeze them and decorate the house with them in clear-cast molds. Stacey navigates the roads, trying to find her last interview for the day. She's supposed to talk to a man who needs a liver transplant. I'm along for the ride, hanging my arm outside her car window, feeling it burn. We pass an old tower that I used to go to with my first boyfriend to make out on the weekends. The ground is rumored to be littered with land mines, which only added to the adventure.

The liver man lives next to the petting zoo where I spent one junior high field trip.

I remember the guide telling us that if we put our fingers out, the calves would suck on them. When everyone had their fingers in the calves' mouths, one of the boys that worked at the petting zoo said, "They'll suck on anything," in a dreamy voice. Everyone tore their fingers away.

"You going to wait out here?" Stacey asks.

"Yeah. I'm going to circle ads and maybe we can go by one of the houses that allows pets." I roll down all the windows, lean back the seat, and start to look at one of Stacey's papers.

Stacey glances back one last time before collecting her notebook and camera. "You sure you're up for the heat?"

"I'm fine," I say, the same thing I said the first time I had sex with Austin on a large rock at Possum Kingdom Lake. Something felt wrong, but I didn't see until the next day that I'd been stung by dozens of little ants all over my back. By the middle of the day, I had a fever and chills. The bites left scars, distant constellations that I can see only when someone else holds up a mirror.

After a few hours of looking at places I don't want to live, Stacey drops me off at home. I get my mail, hoping for the check from my brother. Just when I was imagining how good it would feel to pay off all my bills, Claudine and her damn goats had to come screw up my life. Now I have to piss some of that money away on security deposits, pet deposits, and hook-up fees. The check from my brother is nowhere to be seen, but I find an envelope addressed to someone who used to live here marked child support information enclosed. A mailer stamped sexually explicit material inside is addressed to Austin care of me. He gets more and more of these packages in the mail, making me wonder what I'm doing wrong. The one thing that comes to mind is that he has only one kidney, which makes him kind of a lightweight where drinking is concerned and sometimes after four or five beers he can't get it up. This experience proves traumatic for both of us because he feels like an asshole, and I feel like an asshole because I can't do anything to make him understand that I don't really care. I toss the box aside without opening it, but I'm ashamed to admit that I've given into the temptation to look before, shocked only by the volume of breasts a man can see without getting bored.

The only other letter is from my gynecology clinic. I think back to my pap smear a few weeks ago. In the waiting room, I had a direct view of a retarded teenage boy sprawled on the only couch. He kept his hand down his pants and complained about the heat to his grandmother who read the paper and grunted. Now I'm wondering if there's something my insurance wouldn't pay, one more person dunning me for money. But it's a letter telling me that I have chlamydia and that I need to go back to the clinic and get the scrip for the drugs to treat it before it becomes something serious. I think about all the meanings serious can have, good and bad, before I set the letter aside in a pile with all my other outstanding debts, bills that keep coming. I'm not sure how I'm going to pay.

After a Dr. Pepper, I manage to get Homey into the small carrying cage in which he made his first journey to my house. I do this by coaxing him with a stick. I fear him, and I will not feed him. The phone rings as I close the door of the cage. Austin? Does he somehow sense what I'm doing? I let the machine pick up.

"Hey, it's me. You're right. I've decided to give love a chance," Stacey says. "I called to ask if I could borrow your necklace. I mean, what the hell. Call me if you get this in time."

Stacey sounds young and happy. I think that she deserves somebody nice, but I also want to tell her *be careful*. I put Homey in the passenger seat of my car and pray that the rattlesnake farm is open. The hours are erratic at best. That first and only time I was there, I clutched at my mother as we walked in the door. In the corner, a rattlesnake rattled and scared me and I grabbed onto my mother's shoulders, a woman five inches shorter than I am, a woman whose entire body had been decimated by cancer. It breaks me now to think about it.

My mother and I came to the farm because she was looking for a rattlesnake in clear-cast for a birthday gift for one of her nurses. The owner, a big old boy named Garland, told her that he didn't get too many of those anymore because a lot of people who used to do that had cancer from the acetone used to make the molds. There are so many terrible things that nobody tells you about. And I stood there thinking, the thing she loved is killing her and it's too late to go back and be careful.

"How much will you give me for this?" I ask Garland when I arrive, Homey in tow. Garland looks exactly the way I remember him, except he wears a sterling silver rattle around his neck. Homey and I barely made it through the door before the end of the day, but we're here and I'm going to make a deal.

"He's a pretty thing. You might be able to get more for him at one of the pet shops in Ft. Worth."

The thought of riding with Homey all the way to Ft. Worth is more than I can stand. "I want him gone now."

"Let me see what I can do," he says. He reaches down and picks up Homey's cage to get a closer look. I lean toward the cage, while Garland touches him through the wire bars.

"I can give you a hundred. Will that be enough?"

It's true that I'm clutching the handle of Homey's cage so tight that my hand hurts, but I let that son-of-a-bitch go.

Spinsters

Stephanie Dickinson

I like Ghislaine. We worked together before my bosses fired her. She drank five paper cups of water from the cooler every hour on the hour, and carried her purse to the Xerox machine. I have dinner with her here at Uncle Nick's. *The fish is clean. Very fresh,* Ghislaine says. We're both statistical typists with brown eyes. She's forty-eight, a virgin. Born in Casablanca, a midlife child of diamond merchants who fled Hitler. I'm just thirty-nine. Never married. I pull at my cramped panty hose. Moon sweats to the Chrysler Building's antenna as mounted policemen in helmet-masks clomp past, their horses' flanks like half-sucked chocolates. Ghislaine's afraid of men, especially uniformed. Her mother's fear of Death's Head SS. The hummus arrives. *A month ago I heard my sister scream in the night. I thought it was a bad dream,* she says, buttering a pita. She's staring at the next table, the girl with an older man. Flies. Flies clot the dazed bones of their entrees. *She had a massive coronary in her sleep. I don't think she saw herself dying. You can't call it a tragedy. Not like Princess Di.* Ghislaine says, eyeing the wet between the girl's breasts. *Sometimes I see her shadow. So I'm refreshing my closets and drawers.* The waiter glances at my legs as he serves the parmigiana. Legs, the last asset to go. I imagine myself as eggplant, marks of the grill on my back, the thumbs licked after touching me. I think of my one-night stands, men who stacked would reach to the ceiling. Their weird haircuts. *Women should die at fifty. That's when you turn dry,* my first lover said. I was sixteen. I tap the rim of my wine, signal the waiter. *Use only green tea,* Ghislaine says, ogling the girl as she leaves. *It's better for you than coffee.*

Whiskey-Rich

Stephanie Dickinson

She listened to the wind stop, then the vessel
creaked as it rocked. Her boyfriend led her onto
the docked boat. "Do you know where you are?
You're on Al Capone's yacht." She didn't believe

him. The first-mate, a man named Greek, showed
them around. He was the color of mildew. His
chest, matted with white hair, reeked of goat
cheese. His body, cut and overdefined by

exercise, looked obscene. He led them to one of
the cabins and left. "Do you like it?" her
boyfriend asked. "I had to pay more than you
make in a week to get us on board." The bed's pink

cushions smelled of dead shrimp. The bedspread
was pebbled with roses of faded rouge and a
lampshade swung with the same gold braid as a
stripper's pasties. The gramophone still spun the

disk of an RCA Victor 78 record. "Are you
game?" he asked. The woman shrugged.
She looked in the wavy yellowy mirror in front of
them. She laughed, "I bet that's really a window

Capone had people shot through." He opened
the mirror like a medicine cabinet and pushed in
another mirror. They peered into the next cabin.
She expected to see the ghost of Capone taking a

whiskey-rich piss, instead the Greek was
standing, his shorts at his ankles. His Mexican

girlfriend was on her knees. She was
undeveloped, no more than eleven. Her boyfriend

pressed his hand to her buttocks. "Like that?"
She no longer believed in the spiritual universe.
The air was squib and roasted garlic. Turdy,
earthy. "He bought her from Mexico. $125 dollars.

I understand she has five distinct personalities.
When she's Queenie she'll try to kill you."

The Safety of Geology Questions

Zach Schomburg

I am crawling out of the cave that I discovered
in South Dakota and up through the linoleum
in your kitchen pantry. There you are.

I see your bare feet from the one inch of space
underneath the pantry door. You are mopping
brilliantly to Brahms, wetting the floor in large

circles as if writing an elaborate message to the
ceiling in cursive. Then you bake your son some
peanut brittle because his scores were perfect on

his geology test for which you helped him prepare.
If you opened the pantry door to put away your
mop you'd scream. You probably wouldn't even

ask me any questions about my reasons for being
or about the reality of a body attached to my head,
or about how I burrowed through the concrete

foundation on which your house was built, or about
my motivation. Or about the readers reading this
poem in which you are featured and how they are

wondering if there exists a satisfying conclusion,
or how they have momentarily suspended their
disbelief in order to appreciate the metaphor, or about

their demanding voyeuristic habits, curious as hell
about whether you're going to feed your son the
peanut brittle when he gets home, despite his allergies.

The Sandwich Board

Zach Schomburg

She worked at this local and independently owned
deli and wore this sandwich board of daily specials,
soups of the day, that sort of thing, and she would
pace back and forth and smile real big. Everyone
loved her. I loved her. She would ring this bell
and shake a little in her two piece and yell *chicken
noodle!* really loudly with this sexy emphasis on *noodle*
and that would just drive the men absolutely crazy.
They went out of their minds, staring, eating
the specials.

One night I met her in a bar and we drifted back
to my small apartment and she was still wearing
the sandwich board. I asked her why and she said
she had her reasons. She said she may never take
it off and she asked me if I could blame her and I said no,
I don't suppose so. We made love the best we could
around the specials, kissing and crying, warm and cold,
arms extended and splintered.

Beekeepers, Astronauts, etc.

Zach Schomburg

It's as if these men have
been replaced—the beekeepers,
the astronauts, and so on.
Or as if they have escaped when
rest of us were staring
into our cereal bowls, chasing
with our spoons, frosted
flakes as soft as pond leaves.
Let's call for them by train
load, pack them into cars
and bring them back into
suburbia by the thousands.
From now on, let's have our
children settle disputes with
yard sticks and colanders
rubber-banded to their faces.
I know, let's teach Americans
to weld again.

Late Shift at the Clambake Afterlife

Zach Schomburg

It is my job to crank this bright moon replica to the appropriate height every night. My legs are shot. It takes about 4 hours of peddling on this old exercise bicycle. The key here is to make these ladies and gentlemen feel they are still a part of some mortal and earthly environment. That is what they want more than anything. When I crank the moon to the appropriate height for example, I have to peddle smoothly and slowly. The rising of the moon cannot be too jerky nor can it be too slow.

Once it is up, and at the appropriate height, it is bright enough for the gentlemen in the swimming pool to see and handle their martinis off floating drink tables. It is bright enough for the ladies sitting poolside finishing off the last of the baked clam and catfish. Usually they speak of their aches and other burdens. When they ask if they appear bony or pale I tell them they're crazy and so on. When it becomes late, I pick up the megaphone and make some wind noises.

Sometimes I make the sound of a few dogs barking. Sometimes I just scream. It doesn't really matter. They'll hear what they want to hear. Usually one gentleman in the pool yells let's go inside, a tornado is coming. A few more of them believe the noises I make are the sounds of approaching torpedoes and they hurry to their towels. Whatever it is, they put on their clothing and scatter. They find shelter. One woman, who always sits with her feet in the water, says make a run for it, it's cancer.

Deviants

Darrach Dolan

I suppose I was blind to the dangers of being labeled a mammy's boy or attracting attention for anything other than kicking a ball or throwing a stone. I say this because when my Ma decided I was old enough to do the messages by myself, I took it to be an honor, a sign that I was more responsible than the other boys on the street. This happened in mid-November, barely two months into my first term at the Brothers, and the time of year when soot balls dangled on the wind like baby spiders and fueled our Ma's fear of chimney fires and of the whole housing estate going up in flames. Every evening, I would set out through the dark lanes between our terraced houses, hum along with the lonely strains of John Cullen practicing the fiddle one street over, skirt Gray's vicious mongrel, and cut across the grassless park. All the while I held tightly onto the shopping list in a pocket of my brown windbreaker—a player in the adult world of commerce.

Donovan's Family Butcher on the Malahide Road was the farthest I was allowed to go and my favorite shop. From as far as the roundabout, you could see its fluorescent display window where gleaming steel trays of livers, kidneys, tripe, sweetbreads, and pigs' feet were separated by rows of plastic parsley. On Fridays, fish replaced the offal in the window, and they too looked good, although at that time we all resented having to eat fish.

"At least you know what you're getting at Donovan's," my Ma used to say, as if I needed convincing.

Donovan's was bright and ordered, with tiled walls and fresh pine sawdust strewn across the floor. A metal rail ran the length of the shop with the carcasses of cows, pigs, and sheep hanging from it. Leading up to Christmas, turkeys were added to the rail and hung from hooks over the window and behind the counter as well, giving the shop a festive air.

Occasionally, Mr. Donovan would come from behind the counter to sweep up and replace the sawdust that clotted under the rail or hoist an animal onto his shoulder and carry it back to the block, where he divided it into parts with surprisingly gentle strokes of a blade. I imagined myself wearing his bloodied white coat, making the cuts and saying a few words to every customer. I thought being a butcher was as romantic as any job on our street, except maybe for Mr. Humphreys'. Humphreys was a plumber, and, even though my Ma said he was as thick as bottled pig shite, he was the first on the estate to get a color TV.

TV aside, it was Mr. Donovan I admired most of all the men around. He was a huge man with hands like spades and nostrils as wide as his fingers. He smiled politely and asked how everyone was doing, remembering the women's names and enough about them to ask after their kids and husbands. But his manner was cursory and it was his wife who made a real effort with the customers. She was a short, thick woman whose face was caked with foundation, smeared with lipstick, and as flat as the back of a bus. She affected a sweet disposition and sat hunched over the register, just beyond the carcasses, in print dresses she made herself from the one pattern. Perched on her stool, she directed conversation among the knot of women who gathered around her in rumpled stockings and bright headscarves that depicted fox hunts and country scenes.

— ◆ ◆ —

Before I started at the Brothers, I wasn't allowed to leave the estate by myself and only went to Donovan's when my Ma took me with her. In her company I could stand unobserved among the women, smelling their talc-and-cabbage perfume, listening to their stories.

"I haven't seen poor auld Mary Gogherty in an age," Mrs. Donovan announced one day the previous August. Myself and my Ma joined the circle of women.

"Funny you should mention that because I met her only the other day," said a woman whose scarf featured the Cross at Glendalough.

"Really?" Mrs. Donovan replied. "Isn't it great to see them out and about at that age?"

"Oh, not a bother on her. Looks ten years younger since poor Bob passed on. God rest his soul," Glendalough said.

The women looked at one another.

"Terrible thing."

"Sure it was a relief…"

"They say he was a bit of a you-know-what towards the end."

Raised eyebrows all around.

"God rest his soul, sure he wasn't the worst of them."

"No better man ever walked the earth."

"We all have our crosses to bear."

"But anyways, I'm out doing a bit of weeding when along comes her nibs in a bloody great beige coat," Glendalough resumed. "'Hello Mary,' says I. 'Grand day, thank God,' says she. 'If it wasn't for the vigor of the weeds you could be forgiven for thinking it's in the South of France we're living,' I say, just being sociable like. 'Don't I know,' says she, 'but I felt a bit of a chill so I had to put on me new coat.' 'There's a touch of the summer flu going around,' I says, playing along like. 'Indeed,' says she. 'But there's nothing like camel hair to keep a body warm.'"

"Camel hair!" Mrs. Donovan shook her head. The others, including my Ma and myself, were just as outraged.

"Have you ever heard the like?" Glendalough feigned astonishment. "Well, I says to her, 'Camel hair? Is it not a bit rough?' 'Oh, not at all,' says she. 'Feel it yourself. Nothing but the best material.' Before I get to touch it, she pulls back and puts on a show of looking at her watch. 'Oh, look at the time! I'd better get going or I'll miss the nine o'clock,' says she. And off she goes to morning Mass to burn the ears off of poor Father Connor and the rest of the bingo crowd!"

"Well, I never..." Mrs. Donovan was speechless.

"Can you believe it?" Glendalough lifted her eyebrows to their highest and most authoritative arc, the make-up around her eyes and mouth flaking off. "Now I'm not one to say anything," she paused, "but it was all I could do to stop myself from saying: 'Fancy you getting a camel hair coat and you with a bloody great hump on your back like a camel itself!'"

My Ma laughed with the others and said it was a good one, although afterwards she told me it was scandalous the lengths certain women would go to and made me promise never to make fun of Mrs. Gogherty's hunchback.

But things changed after I began doing the messages by myself. The women took notice of me, and whenever I tried to join their clutches and nod my head, raise my eyebrows, and flare my nostrils in sync with them, their conversations stopped.

"Doing the shopping, are we?" Mrs. Donovan would say upon

spotting me inching into their circle. "Sure isn't it the grand little man that will do the messages for his mammy?"

The women would nod to each other and some of them would click their teeth as if to say that the same couldn't be said for every young fella they knew.

"And where are you going to school?" another would ask.

"Saint David's."

"That's lovely," they'd cluck. "You're a big boy now. Keep your nose clean and the Brothers will make a man of you. They're great men altogether."

That would get them started about the Brothers and the great work they were doing above in the school and how it was a blessing to have the likes of them around to knock a bit of education into the young lads. Those women were all for the clergy and it was common knowledge among them that God had a special place set aside in heaven for the Brothers.

———

The Brothers scared me. They were sinewy men who were quick to anger, and at the time I racked my brains trying to understand why God would want them in heaven with Him. My Ma toed the party line and said that they were God's disciplinarians and were as hard on themselves as they were on us.

Classes were held in a dour and draughty stone building with fifteen-foot ceilings and wide-planked wooden floors. We sat in pairs at desks with hard bench seats and ceramic inkwells, in rooms smelling of damp clothes and stale cigarette smoke. The toilets, concrete troughs and concrete stalls, were outdoors and roofless.

The Brothers, many of whom were holdovers from the days when the school was a combination borstal and orphanage, were great believers in the dampening power of a good march. Every morning we had to line up by class and march in with our teacher. At morning break we were marched to the toilets. At lunch and at the end of the day, we had to line up in pairs holding hands and the Head Brother marched all seven hundred of us past the chapel and graveyard to the gate on the Kilmore Road. The Head was bald, with sunken eyes and yellowing skin drawn tight over cheekbones and chin. In the failing light his eyes disappeared into the shadows of his sockets and his teeth showed through his thin lips, and he led us, at funeral pace, through wind and drizzle. Years later they sold the graveyard to a developer and we got to see men digging up the bodies of dead Brothers and putting them on lorries to be taken away. Everyone said the new shopping center they built near it was haunted, but we all shopped there anyway. It was called Artane Castle and was the biggest shopping center on the Northside.

As I said, I was scared of the Brothers, and that's why I kept my head down and always did what I was told in school. The one time I got in trouble was when I was among a group the Head caught talking on the march to the gate at lunch break. He marched us round and round the playground until he knew we had just too little time to run home, eat our dinners, and get back in time, but not so little that the grumbling in our stomachs and the fear of our Mas wouldn't send us racing home anyway. Of course my Ma didn't understand the deliberateness of it all. She made me finish my mince stew, and lectured me on the starving children of Biafra and the sin of wasting good food.

She wasted some more time writing a note excusing me for being late. The Head was waiting for the likes of me. There were five of us in all, each with a nice young mother who wore paisley blouses and platform shoes and believed that things in the country might turn around. I gave him the note and he smiled tenderly before leading us to his office to give us six of the best with a leather he had improved by putting pennies between the layers.

The boy before me pulled his hand back and earned himself three extra for his trouble. I closed my eyes and held out my hand. The Head stroked my palm with his fingers a couple of times to make sure it was flat and level. It tickled. The crisp swish-and-crack was followed by a moment of calm before a bolt of pain shot through my body, almost knocking me out of consciousness. The next swish-crack brought me around and another bolt shocked me. I thought I would stop breathing, the ache in my chest was so great. In class, I couldn't stop my body heaving nor my lungs gasping, and my face was swollen and salty with tears. The other boys snuck glances at me and sniggered. Brother McMahon, our teacher, took a deep drag on his cigarette and didn't say anything when I couldn't lift my pencil to do the sums.

John Cullen befriended me the next day. He had curly hair and wore horn-rimmed glasses that were held together on one side with plasters that he was always having to replace when they lost their stickiness or when boys punched him. He was spindly and restless and had a way of bobbing up and down and flailing his arms that reminded me of a bird about to take flight. I knew him because he lived on our estate in a house that backed onto the lane behind ours, but I hadn't seen much of him until we were put in the same class and even then, I had never spoken with him alone.

"I don't care about the others calling me specky four-eyes," was the first thing he said to me. "I have a lazy eye so I have." His hands fluttered to his eyes as if I might not know what he was talking about.

He went on in his jerky, over-eager manner as if we knew each other well. "If you rub roisin into your palms it doesn't hurt as much when they leather you."

I was surprised to hear him say that because he, too, was a nervous boy and always did what the Brothers said. That was one of the reasons the other boys didn't like him. I was obedient, too, but didn't wear glasses or have anything that made me stand out.

"I have some roisin at home that I can give you. I have it because I play the fiddle and that."

We all knew he was a fiddle player because we used to hear him practicing while we were running through the lanes, searching for wood to light fires or playing tip the pole. He was the only boy on our estate to play a musical instrument and we felt sorry for him, and perhaps that was another reason why we hated him and spoke about kicking the shite out of him. However, other than one or two of the older lads knocking the glasses off him or making him carry their bags home, it was all talk.

"I sometimes hear you playing," I told him.

After school we walked home together so he could show me the roisin. His Ma was older than my Ma and a lot fatter, but she was nice and the house smelled fresh and clean like the Byrnes' car with its air freshener. She made us tea and brought us buns that she had baked herself. I hadn't really thought of him as an only child until he showed me his bedroom and another room he practiced the fiddle in. No one I knew had their own room let alone a second one. I shared my bedroom with three younger brothers. Naturally I didn't tell John that. Even his wallpaper was normal and new looking. Whereas we had the racing-car paper we had always had, even though it had been ripped in many places and the babies had scribbled all over it with crayons and markers.

"I'm going to be a scientist or explorer," he told me. He had a whole shelf of his own books and he pointed out the ones that were on inventions. He had a collection of maps of other countries that he kept in tubes. The whole time I was in his bedroom, he was talking and showing me things. He opened a wooden chest and took out boards with mountains and houses glued onto them. He had made the mountains from papier mâché and had bought kits at the hobby shop in town behind Clery's to make the houses and trees. He told me that the boards fitted together to make two towns with mountains between them, and he used this for his train set. But he didn't actually put it together because he had so much more to show me.

After a while, he asked me what I did for a hobby. I told him that I liked bird-watching and that I had noticed that none of the common songbirds came to our estate. All we got were sparrows, blackbirds, and starlings. As soon as I said that, I remembered that they were all common types of songbird, but he didn't seem to know that, so I didn't correct myself. I had not told anyone about my bird-watching before, as much as anything else because it was in reality just looking out our back window on rainy days after I was given *The Common Songbirds of Ireland* as a present. But it got him all excited and he climbed up on a chair and took down a leather cylinder from on top of his wardrobe.

"It's a telescope." He opened the cylinder and took it out. He handed it to me. It was black with brass rings at either end and I was scared I might drop it. I wanted to try it out, but of course it was already dark outside and there would have been nothing to look at. We decided that in spring we would go bird-watching together.

That was the only time I got to go to his house, and I couldn't stay long because he had to practice the fiddle and I had to do the messages. For the next couple of weeks, we spoke in school and sometimes walked home together. He said he would bring me into town if my Ma let me. He'd been going into town by himself for years because he got fiddle lessons there — so he knew his way around. I thought that John might become my friend because I found it easy to listen to him talk about his hobbies and his adventures in town, and he listened when I talked about Leeds United and the gossip on the estate. But each evening, after I'd done the messages, I'd put on my Brazil jersey and go play football by streetlight with the others. They always let me join in because I was a good dribbler of the ball and was always good at setting up goals for others. We played until our Mas called us in. While John practiced the fiddle alone, I ran with the pack and was popular enough on the street not to stand out.

Two weeks after John spoke to me he was forced to leave the school. In truth, I was glad he left because I wouldn't have been able to speak to him after the accident and I was afraid that he might approach me in front of some of the others. The accident occurred because the teacher who taught the class next door to ours was out sick. That meant our teacher, Brother McMahon, was in charge of both classes. McMahon was proud of his reputation as a hard bastard and was eager to acquaint the other class with it. Confident that we wouldn't dare get out of hand, he gave us work to do in the morning and left the door open while he spent most of the time with the other class. We heard him bellowing at boys to read louder or give their answers. We imagined him calling them *gombeens* and *amadáns* while he chain-smoked Players and slapped his leather threateningly against his thigh. Every fifteen minutes or so, he'd slip quietly back into our class to check on our work and make sure we weren't acting the maggot. He'd go around the class and look at what we'd written in our copies. Because we had enough sense to do our work, he had no complaints, although he did rap a couple of boys on the head with his knuckles for good measure. We behaved all morning, and after lunch he told us he would let us go home early if we kept up the good work.

That was incentive enough, and each time he checked in on us we were all working away. He was obviously in a rare mood because he didn't rap anyone on the head or hold a boy's copy up by the corner as if it was contaminated and drop it into the bin. He even told us a Paddy Englishman joke and said that the other class were a bunch of bowsies that didn't hold a lick to us. On one of his spot checks, John raised his arm and said, "*An bhfuil cead agam dul go dtí an leithreas?*" because we always had to ask to go to the toilet in Irish.

"*Níl!*" McMahon said, but he was smiling and that reassured us he was still in good form and would let us out early. "Sure aren't you just back over an hour? Next time you'll remember to go when you're out."

John put his hand down and returned to writing in his copy in case McMahon decided to make more of it. But the next time McMahon came into the class, John put his hand up and asked to go again.

"Didn't I tell you, boy, that you should have gone when you had the chance?" He winked so we would know that he was only messing and would let John go after playing with him a little. We all laughed along with this joke at John's expense because we knew that when McMahon was in the humor for kidding around he could be very nice and might even let us off with no homework.

Suddenly there was a crash from next door, followed by scuffling and some shouts. McMahon clearly hadn't gotten the message across to them yet. We watched the broken veins spider across his face. He dropped his cigarette to the ground and crushed it.

"Please, sir. *Más é do thoil é*," John said.

"Shut up, you pup! Take my advice: do your work or you'll know all about it!" He looked around the class, his leather gripped menacingly. "And that goes for the rest of youse too or there'll be all hell to pay!"

His footsteps echoed down the corridor and were followed by the sound of leather hitting hands, legs, desks, whatever he could strike. They were really getting it, and we were glad. Now that they knew what he was like, they'd have more respect for us.

We put our heads down and worked furiously, giving up on the idea of getting off early. McMahon would now be in a mood for blood, and the best we could hope for was to give him no excuse to take it out on us. It was because I had my head down that I didn't notice anything until the boy beside me elbowed me and said that John was going to get murdered.

I looked up and saw John pacing back and forth at the top of the class. We all watched him with grim fascination, waiting for the moment when McMahon would return.

At first, John restricted his pacing to the top of his row, and I prayed that he had the sense to run back to his place as soon as he heard McMahon coming. But the longer it went on, the more brazen he became, and it was clear that he had something else in mind. He began pacing the width of the class, going to the window, looking out, then approaching the open door and peering into the corridor before retreating. Each time he peered out, we held our breath, thinking he was going to make a dash for it, and exhaled a collective sigh when he pulled back from the unthinkable. No one had ever openly disobeyed a Brother, but it looked for all the world like little John Cullen was about to do so. Back and forth, back and forth, he took us with him on a journey that exhilarated and terrified us.

How long this went on, I don't know. Certainly long enough for the muscles in my face to begin to cramp from grinning so hard. When I looked around, I saw that everyone was grinning madly, even John. It was all we could do to contain ourselves. Some began holding their hands to their mouths while others quietly shook with laughter. That really got John going. He began to ham it up for us. First he took a piece of chalk and dragged on it the way McMahon dragged on his smokes. Next he began pacing on his tippy toes, bouncing up and down with every step. He stepped out the door and back in again, looking to us for the approval we readily gave. He did a sort of pirouette, swinging off the door handle and landing in the corridor before leaping back in and bowing. We had never seen the like.

By this time we were all rooting for him. Flight suddenly seemed possible. But we were cowards and we wanted him to make the leap for us. I thought of Steve McQueen in *The Great Escape*, and how he went for it even with the Germans shooting at him. Though he ended up pierced by bullets and impaled on the barbed wire between Germany and Switzerland. We began a quiet, insistent chant. "Go, John, go."

Then we got the smell and knew he had done it in his pants. He stopped pacing and stood facing us with that silly grin slapped over his face. Boys began to laugh openly at him. There was a viciousness in the laughter now, a need to punish him for taking us so far and letting us down like that. He looked at us with the defeated expression of a man who knows all is lost and, as if making one final futile gesture that might give meaning to the loss, he lay down and began rolling across the floor. The shit squeezed out the top of his pants and stained the boards. We became animals howling for revenge as he rolled faster and faster in an ecstasy of fear and relief, his stupid face bright with happiness.

Only after McMahon burst into the class did we stop shouting and banging our desks. McMahon lifted him from the floor by his hair and was propelling him through the door before John's expression changed to one of dismay. We were deadly silent as we waited for a sign or a sound that would tell us what had become of him. But there was nothing, and we forced ourselves back to our copies, desperate to finish the work we had been given.

We were working away like that when McMahon returned alone. He didn't say a word, and we didn't dare look up. He walked up and down the rows, looking into copies and smoking. Then he left and didn't check in with us again until the bell rang at the end of the day and he came in to tell us we could go. We walked past him, heads bowed lest he catch our eyes.

I found a partner in the line, and for once we had to wait for the Head to arrive. When he finally showed up, he had John in tow. Together they led the school out. I was near the back of the line and when I got to the gate I saw John standing beside the pillar facing us. The Head had forced him to stand there, his arm outstretched holding a clear plastic bag with his soiled underwear before him and his other hand holding his nose in an exaggerated imitation of repugnance. We all marched by and out to freedom. I ran away home with the other lads.

John wasn't in school the next day or the day after that. His cousin told us that he had had an accident with paint and couldn't get it off and that was why he wasn't in school. But he never returned, and after that I didn't see much of him. On the way to the shops I sometimes heard him playing the fiddle. The rumor was that he was going to another school.

———•——•———

I continued as before, helping my Ma with the messages and the babies and playing football on the street. One day we were playing tip the pole because girls were playing with us, or because no one had a ball, when Francis from the Crescent told us that Mrs. Dunphy had caught John Cullen in the bushes with a telescope. He told us that there was talk on his street of going over to have a word with his parents. We abandoned our game and ran to the lane behind my house. We were hoping to hear him playing the fiddle, but his house was in darkness and the only sound was the furious barking of the dog that chased cars around the park. Someone suggested lighting a fire against the Cullens' gate. We gathered some papers and piled them against it, but no one had matches. After a while we gave up. Though it was unclear to me what he had done wrong, the fact that all the women on the estate were scandalized made me wonder. It even got to my Ma and she asked me if I knew the Cullen boy. I told her he had been in my class.

The last real contact I had with him was several months later. It was shortly after my Ma had read somewhere that you could never tell what scraps or bits of fat lying around, not to mention meat that was going off, went into the mince that butchers put in their trays. So she forced me to order a pound and a half of round leg beef cut into cubes, and just as Donovan was about to wrap it up, I'd have to ask him to mince it. This didn't please him, and it embarrassed me. But what could I do?

Anyway, one evening in April, I had ordered the beef to be cubed as usual, and Donovan and I were carrying on as if we didn't know I was going to ask him to mince it when I heard the women talking about John.

"There goes that young Cullen now," one of them said.

I looked through the window and saw him walking towards the bus stop across the road. He wore the brown duffel coat he always did and was carrying his fiddle case and a roll of sheet music. He put the case down at the bus stop and turned to peer in the direction the bus would come from. His glasses kept sliding down his nose and his free hand would flutter to his face to readjust them.

"That isn't the young fella that...?"

"The very one!"

"It's the mother I feel sorry for."

"Isn't that the way it always is?"

"Sure, wasn't I always saying there was something queer about him?" a large woman declared angrily. "But who'd listen to me?"

"He looks harmless enough," another prompted.

"It's the ones you'd never imagine are the ones to look out for, if you know what I mean?" Mrs. Donovan said, drawing them in closer by lowering her voice and forcing me to strain to hear what she said next.

"You might say to yourself that the Brothers up above in the school can handle anything you care to throw at them. And you wouldn't be far off the mark in thinking that. Aren't they the same men that raised orphans and took charge of delinquents for the state?"

The women nodded.

"It's many the gurrier that entered those gates only to come out at the end of it with a trade and a healthy respect for the laws of this world and the next. And more than once a lad they said was incorrigible would be handed over to the very same Brothers and in the end wouldn't he find he had a vocation! But then there comes along a case like your man there, with a telescope his own poor mother bought no less, and it's enough to throw the Brothers into despair and think there's nothing they can do anymore to stop this country slipping into the gutter."

They turned to look out the window at the boy who stood at the bus stop tapping rolled sheet music against his leg.

"The depravity of that young lad there might well be the straw that breaks the camel's back, so to speak!" The women shook their heads. "I'll tell you his story once, and I'll tell it no more!..." She noticed me edging into the circle and stopped talking.

At that moment Mr. Donovan called me over and handed me the meat, already wrapped, and before I had asked him to mince it. This threw me into confusion, and I wavered between asking him whether he had minced it or taking the chance. He smiled at me and started on about the atrocious weather we were having and how spring looked like it had given up on us. I agreed with him, searching his eyes for a clue, but there was none there.

I turned to pay. But Mr. Donovan's diversion was just long enough for me to miss what Mrs. Donovan told the women. All I know is that they stared at John through the window in disbelief.

"I saw him shit his pants," I said to the women. The large woman took a step towards me. Her lips moved as if to say something but the words never came. The others folded their arms across their breasts. "He was in my class. That's all. I don't really know him."

Mrs. Donovan banged the register and the drawer shot open. I handed her the wrapped meat and she rang up the total. My face burned with humiliation.

On my way out I heard her say, "Ah, go easy, Betty. Sure he's just a bit of a mammy's boy is all."

When I got home, I handed the messages to my Ma. I wanted to tell her what had happened, but she hushed me, handed over the baby, and told me that whatever I had to say could wait until she got the dinner on. I watched her unwrap the meat and saw, to my relief, that Mr. Donovan had minced it. I realized that I could not speak of John to her nor to anyone else. My stupidity frightened me.

I put the baby in the pram and strapped her in before my Ma could stop me. The baby began to cry, but I pulled on my Brazil jersey anyway, and ran out to join the other lads on the street. I was sorry I couldn't help my Ma anymore, and I prayed for forgiveness and for the strength to keep my head down until I was old enough to escape on the ferry to Holyhead and take the mail train to London. I sat on the curb watching the others play and waited for the call to join in. I imagined myself in London, all dressed up in a gray suit and hailing a black taxi. I imagined the women talking about how well I'd done and how I'd paid for my Ma to go on holiday. I was happy. I believed that I could simply play football in the evenings and hide out among the others until I left them behind forever. I didn't know that every one of those boys kicking the ball on that street would leave the country, too. I didn't know that, no matter how far I traveled, the hollow sound of a ball slapping concrete or the smell of soot in the air would take me back to a child who played the fiddle by himself and a child who ran away.

A Theory of Marriage

Emily Spiegelman

The light switch has been moved again to a place high above my head, so high that I have to float to reach it. I reach with one hand to flick on the lights, and with the other, grab onto the lines painted on the wall paper to steady myself. The glass bulbs hum with electricity and the kitchen is flooded with darkness. My mother stands in the middle of the room in her big winter coat covered with coffee stains and her knee-high lamb skin boots. She holds a black garbage bag open with her hand and when she turns to look at me, the tinkling sound of broken glass escapes the wide dark mouth of the bag. She has a crazed look, half-terrified and half-gleeful.

"I thought you were Dad," she says.

My brother Ben sits at the kitchen table, watching with a huge grin on his face. More bottles into the bag: brown bottles, frosted bottles, clear, green, and a slender blue one like a model sky scraper. Crash, crash, crash, one after the other, as the bottles hit the bag spread out on the kitchen tiles.

"No more bottles of booze on the wall," Ben chants, "no more bottles of booze." Crash, says another bottle. Crash. Ben is cheering, laughing hysterically.

"Allison!" my mother snaps. "You have to make him be quiet. Tell Ben to stop. It's a secret, Ben, this is a secret. Your father's in the closet, he's in the bedroom closet with his ties and you'll ruin the surprise, Ben, you'll ruin it." She drops the garbage bag and does a few twirls with a bottle of peppermint schnapps and a waltz with Irish whiskey. For every bottle she takes from the cabinet, two more appear, teetering on their round edges like children's toys. When she goes to throw them out, she misses the bag altogether. She showers the crumpled dark plastic and the tile floor of the kitchen with liquid and shards of brilliant glass and shrieks with delight.

"Do you think he won't notice?" I say to her. "Do you think he won't see that you've emptied the entire cabinet?"

"Get Ben!" she shouts at me. More quietly, almost whispering, she says, "Make Benjamin stop his racket or your father will hear him. You can hear everything when you're in the bathtub."

Ben is slapping his bare feet on the floor, clapping them down on the jagged pieces and when he lifts them again, the bottoms of his feet are ragged and bloody. He grins at me, and starts his song.

"No more bottles of booze on the wall, no more bottles of booze!"

"Come on, Ben," I cry, "help me find something to cover this with. We have to cover it!" I dig frantically in the refrigerator and pull out handfuls of soft brown banana peels, empty of their fruit. They'll stop us from cutting our feet, I think, and I scatter them on the floor in front of my mother.

"She thought you were Dad," Ben says. "You don't look very much like him, though. Ha! She thought you were Dad!"

Crash, as my mother sweeps bottles onto the floor with her arm. I move toward Ben to put my hand over his lips and keep him quiet and he bites me, his teeth like the jagged edges of wood. Outside the kitchen, the ambulance is stuck. My mother tells me, as she empties three bottles out of the cabinet to make room for six more, that its tires are flattened from driving over broken glass. I hear the siren, loud, steady, constant, and motionless.

I come up into my head in the middle of my five o'clock alarm. It cuts clean through the silence of the house and clean through me, leaving my blood pooled and humming in my ears. My body is slow and heavy, but my mind is working like I have been awake all night. It's going to be a warm morning out on the river by the time we're finished practicing; I can tell by the way the light from my windows is bouncing off the collection of blue glass bottles I have on my bookcase in dark, hot circles. Some of them are my dad's booze bottles, but some of them were presents, bought just because they looked nice and not because they actually held anything all that well. It's just like my mother, I think, wiggling my toes under my blanket: even in a dream, she's afraid that someone—anyone—my father especially, will hear her do more than creep around her life in soft-soled shoes.

I get up to brush my teeth and walk past my parents' open bedroom door without looking in.

I think the weirdest part about my parents' marriage is that they still sleep together. When my brother and I were little, we didn't think much about when our parents went to bed, or how, or whether they went to bed at all. What mattered was that, in the mornings, when we would run into their room and hurl ourselves onto their mattress like rockets, we'd find them still curled around each other in their sleep. I can't even remember when that stopped and when the new routines began. What I know is that, when you get old enough to watch your parents go off to bed together, both of them lumbering up the stairs at the same time, when they turn out the light in the kitchen and you're still up watching TV, the whole world changes.

Now, my parents don't even sit at the dinner table together and the silence eats more in a day than they do. At night, my mother crawls under the covers of that bed long after my father has fallen into a heavy sleep well on his side of the mattress. Careful, she must say to herself, don't touch his back, don't let your toes brush his. I wonder sometimes whether they can't help gravitating toward the center in the middle of the night. But for all the times I've wondered about how they share a bed without touching, and for all the mornings I'm awake before they are, I stopped looking in at them a long time ago. I don't have to anymore. I know that when I come home in the afternoons the bed is never made as if the whole thing — the tangle of sheets, the indentations in the pillows with the little loose hairs rubbed in from sleeping heads — is too much for either one of them to bear, like they're afraid to take it apart. The bed sits there instead like some artifact too fragile to touch. But I'm pretty sure that they both crawl right back in at night because I never find anyone sleeping on the couch when I go downstairs for breakfast. And as far as I know, the number of words they exchange in a given day isn't enough to equal "please go sleep somewhere else."

My mother has forgotten to go shopping again, so I take one of her bananas for breakfast. I've already eaten it by the time I get my shoes and extra sweatshirt into the back of the car. I don't know how she lives on these things. They're like appetizers for me. They only make me hungrier. Then again, I've gotten used to living in a household where everything is an extreme: hunger, thirst, touch, speech. My mother doesn't eat at all, and my father drinks as much as he possibly can. My parents sleep in the same bed without touching. We don't talk to one another in any kind of way that would disturb the peace. It seems strange, but then again I'm convinced that the whole concept behind marriage is strange, and one more thing in this world based entirely upon extremes. What is it that makes people decide they want to spend the rest of their lives together? The whole thing strikes me as totally unnatural. I mean, it's one thing if you go through a traumatic event with someone, you know, like sitting through a piece of really bad performance art. Or you hear those stories about people who help each other out during something terrible like a war. And suddenly, when the war ends, you find out that person is the only thing left standing. I read once about a man who stole food for a prisoner of war he thought was beautiful. Every morning he would meet her at the gate and pass her slivers of apple and bread through the tiny gaps in the iron. When the war was over, they found each other and decided to be together forever. I could see getting married after something like *that*.

But what I want to know is what makes people wake up in the middle of a completely normal—even boring—life and decide that they are going to slide a shaped and polished fragment of metal onto someone's finger and ask them to spend the rest of their living days with them? I imagine it's a feeling something like being awakened by the growling of your stomach. Maybe it's like eating a banana—the growling only gets louder, you can only think about what more there is to eat. But I swear there must be some love-equivalent to eating breakfast that doesn't involve a life-time commitment.

The city is never as still as it is at five in the morning; the streets are empty of cars and, suddenly, you begin to hear things that you can't hear during the day, like the way the air sounds as it rushes through the spaces between the brick buildings all clustered together like they're trying to keep one another warm. There's this weird pact, I think, to preserve the silence between all the people who are awake at five in the morning. All the joggers who go running along the river path before work smile at one another as they pass, or gently breathe, "morning" as they go by. But no one calls out or shouts. Even the joggers who run in pairs don't seem to want to ruin the quiet; they whisper while they jog, or talk in low voices like they're afraid of waking the bums who have fallen asleep inside their garbage bags along the bank.

At the boathouse, all the girls on the team stretch together before we take the shells out on the water for practice. We crouch down low and stretch our groin muscles, still stiff from being locked in sleep. We stand on one leg, the other pulled up behind us so that we look like a bunch of exotic wading birds. We lie on the cement and do sit-ups until our spines are rubbed raw through our cotton T-shirts. We do all of this in silence; nobody groans about feeling tight. Nobody bitches about having to get up so early. There's only the sound of the river gurgling in its bed, and our limbs cracking and popping in their joints.

While my parents are rolling over in bed, careful not to touch each other while one of them reaches out to turn off the alarm clock, I am on the river with the girls. We are crouched over our oars, shooting back in our seats, dragging our oars through the water and pushing ourselves forward again, gliding over the river. There are new sounds, the splash of wood catching the water, the hum of our seats as they roll backward, the coxswain with her rhythmic bark, *Row! Row! Row!* We drive hard with our legs, boring our eyes into the back of the girl in front of us.

I sit behind Katie Burlie who has been the stroke in our boat since I started rowing at the beginning of high school. For four years, straight in front of me, her back is all I have seen while I row, the muscles under her shirt knotting themselves together and untying in a single fluid motion. Sometimes, in the middle of a long piece, rowing hard and steady like we are part of a bigger machine, I float right out of my seat and hover just inches above the water, watch my arms and hands coming in toward my body and pushed out again, fast and smooth, following Katie's body in its back and forth as if she were a magnet. I hear sounds coming out of my mouth—my breathing hard, almost grunts, groaning, anguished answers to the things our coxswain screams at us. She is a little girl, maybe half my size and she has a voice that comes up from the roots of her toenails. She bends forward, adjusting our direction in the lane with a simple flick of her wrist, her hand gripping the rudder. *You're rushing your slide! COME on, you're rowing at a forty, I want a forty-two in ONE, TWO.* She can't know from where she sits how badly it hurts to row this hard, how the air stops coming into your lungs, how your legs refuse to go anymore but your brain is shouting not to stop. I scream back at her in my head. Sometimes it's just me; sometimes all of us scream in unison. Finally we reach the Boston University bridge, our finish line, its sides covered in red spray-paint graffiti. I can hear the water slapping against the support columns, gurgling around the metal and sinking into itself. The sun has risen and it's almost hot by the time we reach the bridge; I can feel the cool dampness of the steel pilings as we approach and I tell myself to go, keep going until the boat slides into the shade of the overpass. Done. My body won't stop shaking. Katie turns around to ask me something but I'm numb. I don't hear what she says. I can't breathe enough air to answer back.

After morning practice, when the shells are put away, Katie and I sit on the edge of the dock and hang our feet in the Charles, where the water is still cold enough to make our legs ache. Katie pulls her long blond pony tail over the strap at the back of her Harvard lacrosse cap. "I'm gonna cut this thing off right before I go to college," she says, pulling it over her shoulder. The way she strokes it—like it's animal fur—I don't believe her. "How short?" I ask. The dock is starting to splinter; sharp little shavings of wood are coming off in my hands.

"Probably like yours, chin-length," she sighs, lying back on the wood. I sprinkle shavings from the dock onto the light blond hairs on her arms. Either she doesn't notice or she ignores me. Her face is turned away, looking down the river, and her voice sounds quiet. "We're gonna have to keep each other in shape over winter break," she says. "We should really come running here every morning. If I don't have you, I won't make myself do it." Something about the way she says this makes me think how little time there is before we leave, how little time before we come back again from somewhere else. It hits me hard, even though I feel like I've been counting the days.

"A few more months," I say, and the words make my stomach knot but I can't tell whether it's excitement or something else. Katie sits up and a few slivers of wood slide off onto the dock. She turns her arm over and brushes herself off like she's shooing bugs.

"Do you realize that we'll be meeting people who *don't know* what it feels like to live in this city and row on this freezing cold fucking river?" I nod, grinning. "For the first time in our *lives* we won't really even live here anymore," she says.

"Visitors in our own houses," I say. I think about saying that I already feel that way, but I pull my feet out of the water and stuff my wet feet into the yawning mouths of my shoes.

"Thank God for that!" Katie whoops, throwing her arms up into the air. A few more wood shavings shower the dock. "I swear, coming back will be the best part about college." We both get up and stomp up the dock in our untied sneakers. I agree with her, about the coming back, but not for the same reasons. I like to think that there's something about coming back to what you've known all your life that makes you notice the good things. I remember coming home from summer camp and the way it felt to crawl into my own bed, my bed from when I was little, after sleeping in the bunks. Coming home from college has to be like that, like falling right back into the grooves you've worn into the mattress from sleeping in the same position for years.

Old mattresses, I think, are not all that different from marriage. There has to be a certain point at which people have been together so long that divorce is no longer an option. Divorce could have happened any time through sixth grade and I doubt I would have been too surprised. After sixth grade, divorce started to happen to my friends' parents less and less. I knew one person whose parents separated when we were in high school, but his mother had been having an affair that I swore even our school nurse knew about. I figure that by the time I arrive at college in the fall, everyone whose parents weren't meant to be together will already have split up. I can sit in my bedroom and practically count it out on my fingers: eight people in second grade, one in high school, none in college. By September, they will be safe. I will be safe. College is like the bridge on those race days so hot I'm surprised the river isn't boiling: hold out, hold out, hold out until the shadow of the finish line slides over my head and everything goes black.

Sometimes I'm sorry that the people at the boathouse started a rowing club for older women. It would be one thing if these women had been rowing all their lives and just wanted to have a little middle-aged fun and competition. But this is a club that can only live up to the name they have given it — The Ladybugs' Picnic. What a misnomer, my mother says, because rowing isn't a picnic at all. It's one of the hardest things my mother says she's ever done and almost as exhilarating as giving birth (which makes me think, why have babies at all, when you can have your time out on the water and come away without something extra to care for?). "Ladybugs" is supposed to teach crew to women who have never picked up an oar before, who don't know what it means to catch a crab or not to rush your slide, or to settle at 40.

After classes are over and Katie and I and the other girls on the team come back down to the river for afternoon practice, my mother and all of her little friends are standing around chattering while they stretch. They practice earlier than we do because there aren't enough shells for all of us. Thankfully, Katie's mother has taken up rowing with the Ladybugs' Picnic, too, and we make a game of walking past our mothers and pretending we don't know who they are.

"Crazy old ladies," Katie says to me.

My mother is loud when she's at the boat house; she and Mrs. Burlie call after us in shrill voices, pretending to be old and feeble. Then they yell things like, "We'll see you at home after practice, girls," so that everyone will know those old ladies are our mothers. We shake our heads and stride past them to the dock where the rest of our team is already shoving off onto the river.

But I don't think Katie is really ashamed of her mother the way I am. After we've pushed ourselves away from the boathouse and are gliding out to where we can start to row, I can see my mother standing on the dock. She has her eyes shielded from the late afternoon sun, but I know she's watching me in my boat. She's watching to see how I sit and how I hold my oar and how smoothly I move, gliding up and down slowly on my seat as we warm up our legs. Katie thinks it's nice that my mother cares so much about what I do and I know I should love the way it feels to know she's watching me and sometimes I tell myself she's thinking about how much I've grown up, how strong I look, how sure of myself I am out here. But there's something strange about how closely she watches, like she thinks I have something to teach her. Because underneath all the nice, motherly things and the way she shouts and plays on the water or in the boat house, she has taken to knocking on my door when I get home.

She comes in to talk to me mostly about crew. I've been rowing since I started high school four years ago. I plan to row in college. I was recruited by Yale and Stanford and Boston University. For a long time, B.U. is where I thought I'd go because my high school crew team shares the river with them now and I'd have as much of a home court advantage as you can have when you row. I know the river and the way the currents work better than anything I've ever learned in school. But since the silence in my house has gotten bigger and since my mother has started coming into my room to pretend she doesn't know just how big it is, I have been thinking about Stanford and California and how nice it would be to be that far away.

Most of the time, she just wants to tell me how much speed and strength her boat has developed since they first started, how her coach told her that she's pulling her oar in too high on her body and that's why it keeps getting caught in the strong flow of river and boat. She says that her coach is thinking about working the Ladybugs up so that they will be strong enough to send a boat to the Head of the Charles Regatta — older division — in October. She says I'll come back from wherever I'm going to college with my new rowing team and she'll stand on the bank and cheer for me and then I can cheer for her. It's weird, but when she comes in to talk to me about this thing that all of a sudden she's made us have in common, I feel like I'm one of those commercials about drug awareness, where a mom comes into her child's bedroom and tries to act all hip and cool and ends up alienating herself. And, of course, the point is that the drugs never get discussed. The kid clams up and the mom leaves feeling like she's accomplished something huge.

It's hot on the river in the afternoons, hot enough for us to take our shirts off and row in our sports bras. When the men's crew boats from B.U. and Boston College and Harvard and M.I.T. row by, they hoot and holler.

"They spend an awful lot of time teasing us for being high school girls," says Katie as they drift past, their two and four seats rowing and their one and three seats leaning over their oars to balance the boat.

"But the truth is, we're not all that far from college. If we showed up at some frat party, they'd be all over us. Fresh blood."

"Freshman blood," I say.

"Nothing wrong with that," says Katie, grinning.

Katie is dating a guy from Harvard. They met at a party thrown by an alum from our high school who started at Harvard last fall. Katie's boy plays lacrosse and sometimes on his way back from practice he stops to watch us row. He stands on the bank on the Boston side of the river with his great big shoulder pads. Sometimes he's busy cradling a ball when we pass. I'm not supposed to look out of the boat when we're rowing a piece so I wait until we've rowed down river and raise my eyes just enough to see whether he's standing there twirling his white plastic lacrosse helmet on the end of his stick. His name is Christopher. Christopher with the gold eyes. Christopher with the long thin fingers and the bent thumb, because he broke it in a high school lacrosse tournament last year. He waits for Katie at the boathouse where he talks to Mrs. Burlie, calling her Ma'am, because he's from the South. He's very polite, and always says, "Hello, Allison," when practice is over and the shells are put away in the boathouse.

Katie puts her finger on Christopher's chest and runs it down to his belly like she's drawing a line.

"Hey, how was practice?" she asks him. She slips her hand into his and they start to walk out. They walk like they always do, wrapped around each other. They remind me of wire figures, both of them long and thin and Katie almost as tall as he is.

Maybe Katie feels me watching them as they leave, to go have dinner in the Square. Maybe it's one thing for me to watch her back when we're rowing and another thing entirely when we're off the water. In any case, I heard Katie talking to our coxswain at the beginning of practice about how she and Chris are having sex. It's funny that she doesn't talk to me about it. We joke that my oar is my most constant companion, but before she dated Chris, we made a game of kissing the same boys on the same night without them knowing. I can handle hearing about sex. I'm not as ignorant as she thinks; she's kept Chris around longer than most of the guys she's dated. I would have to be stupid to think she wasn't getting something good out of it. But I never sat her down and acted girly and demanded to know what she was up to, or acted like a jealous friend who was losing her to another relationship. I figured she would tell me in her own time. And she did, today, the only way she could—she told our coxswain—loud enough for me to hear—that she's discovered that orgasms have everything to do with your asshole.

"I'm serious. Any time Christopher puts his finger anywhere near it, I come ten times faster."

When I come in from practice, my father is folding laundry. I close the front door and drop my keys on the table before he comes rushing out of the laundry room with a pair of Ben's pants in his hand.

"Jesus," he says to me, "I thought you were Benjamin. Where is he?"

"Not my brother's keeper, Dad," I say and turn to go upstairs.

"You might be interested to know that I found this in his pocket when I went to wash his pants." He's holding up a slim silver pipe. Ben usually stashes it in a sock at the bottom of one of his drawers. I shrug my shoulders.

"Don't know, Dad. You'll have to ask Ben."

"Don't you children even speak in complete sentences anymore? 'Don't know'?" He shakes his head at me like he's surprised how far I've gotten in life talking the way I do. He plants himself on the couch with his glass and Ben's pants and waits for his prey to walk in.

My little brother has a better sense of humor about our parents than I do, in part because he's appointed himself the great Defender-of-Dad, almost until it's painful to watch. Ben's the only one who talks to my father while he sits drunk on the couch in front of the TV. Ben asks him about work and does commentary on the news personalities while they listen to the headlines.

"Heather Kahn's a hottie, huh?"

"She's pregnant, Benjamin," my father mutters.

"Dude, you totally can't tell, the way they've got her all hidden behind the desk like that. That's right, Heather, honey, shuffle your little papers. Damn, what a tease."

Occasionally, he gets my dad to laugh. Things only really go wrong when my dad asks Ben about school. Dad likes to turn the joking into something serious as quickly as he can. I've seen how it works because he's done it to me: pretend to be light hearted, turn to someone and, smiling, ask them the question that hurts them the most. He does it to Ben while I sit and try to watch the news over him, his long sixteen-year-old body sprawled on the floor in front of the TV

"Have you heard anything back from your teacher about the test, Ben?"

"What test?"

"The one you took two weeks ago? How long does it take to grade a multiple choice test, Benjamin?"

"Nope. She hasn't given it back yet. Next week, she said. She's teaching a lot of sections this term. It takes her a while."

"Well, how do you feel about it?"

"Feel?"

"How do you think you did, Benjamin? Generally, when you take a test, you walk out of the room, you have some sense of how you've done."

"I guess. I was tired. It was two weeks ago. Don't 'member."

"You don't remember? Jesus, Benjamin, you float through your days with not a care in the world and you have no concept of responsibility! No self-awareness! You don't give a shit about…"

It goes around and around like this until my dad yells things at him about how important it is to establish a work ethic now, before Ben has to start applying to colleges, because no one's going to sit on his shoulder and pleasantly remind him that he has a paper to write or a test to study for when he goes away to school. He goes on to say that should Ben get anything lower than a 3.0 during his college career, my father will stop paying tuition. Ben, because college is a full two years away and hardly a threat to the comfort of his lifestyle, says something about the lucrative field of exotic dancing, should my father cut off financial support. This only enrages my father. He stands up and stumbles over the couch, like he's forgotten it's there. My mother is careful to steer clear of such battles, disappearing silently upstairs on the soles of her wool-lined boots with her diet soda and banana. The truth is, Ben lies to my parents about his grades. As far as I know, he hasn't passed a math test yet this school year.

And even though he can't get algebra to save his life, he's got Dad all figured out.

"Dad has an illness," he says. "Alcoholism is an illness. It's like a disease. He can't help what he's doing because he doesn't even see that he's doing it."

"What about Mom, then? What's wrong with her that she can't tell him?" I ask.

"I don't know," he answers, standing in the doorway of his bedroom. "Mom's your department. You let me know when you've got a working theory."

Upstairs, I open the door to Ben's room. He's not home; it's the only time I come in here whether Ben's around or not. It smells musty because he keeps the door closed all the time. He bought one of those signs that restaurants and shops stick on their doors that reads *Shirts Required*. His clothes are heaped on the floor and some have fallen behind his fish tank, which bubbles peacefully in the corner across from his bed. When I sit down on his comforter, a soft odor of smoke — tobacco, pot — drifts up into my nose. It's a warm smell, it reminds me of the insides of boys' jackets where I feel comfortable and safe at cold, outside parties, and suddenly I realize how old my brother is. That there's probably some girl out there who tucks herself into his coat and soaks up the heat from his body and smells his smoke and feels good, warm, protected. I look around at the stuff lying on his desk, thinking maybe there's a picture of that girl, but I find an old math test instead, and a *Rolling Stone* with some woman I don't know on the cover. There's an article in there I might like to read some day, but I leave it there, closing the door behind me.

My own bedroom is right above the kitchen. When I was little, I used to be able to hear my parents washing the dishes after dinner. I could lie right here and listen to them talking — no words or real conversation, just the ups and downs of their voices as they told and asked and debated and agreed. I never needed a night-light or music to go to sleep by — just the talking. Later on, the stairs would groan — I could hear them coming upstairs to bed. I remember the way my mother used to tuck me in. I would lie in that half-asleep place I was in when she entered my room every night and sat down on the mattress so that I rolled toward her. She would lay her hands on my cheeks and I could smell the Oil of Olay skin cream that she used on her face at night to make the fine lines and wrinkles disappear, she said. The smell got stronger when she leaned in close to kiss me on the forehead and whisper, like she was describing me for my father, "A sleeping baby." The skin of her hands was always cool, and her gold wedding band like a sliver of ice against my face.

When Ben comes home, I can hear him through my bedroom floor while he talks to my father. He tells him he was keeping the pipe for a friend. Ben's an idiot sometimes. He forgets that he's dealing with

42

a man who excuses his own drinking habits on a daily basis. I sit on my bed, holding my breath, and wait for the screaming to begin.

"Allison?" My mother is calling from the other side of my door. I must have fallen asleep. The sound of her voice outside my door makes me ashamed to realize that I have been dreaming about Christopher and Katie. It's wet, a little, between my thighs. While I get up, the blood rushes to my head. I'm trying to forget the image of Christopher sliding his fingers between the pale halves of her ass. "Al? I need you to help me for a minute. Can you come out here?"

When I open my door, she is standing with her right hand cradled in her left but it's her face that looks wounded and tired.

"What's wrong?" I ask. Instead of answering, she holds her hand out to me. The skin of her palm is raised in a giant blister, taut and full of fluid.

"Look," she whispers. She tilts her flattened palm to one side; small white flecks inside her blister—fat pads—float across the bubble in her skin.

"Yeah," I say, "those hurt. Want me to pop it for you?" She nods, grinning nervously. I move past her and into the bathroom where I have an array of safety pins stuck into a bar of soap. I'm washing my hands when she comes in, still holding her hand against her chest like it needs to be protected from the light.

"I need a match," I say. She finds one in her bedroom and watches while I strike it and hold it up against the sharp end of one of the smaller pins. I hold out my hand to ask for hers, and she places her palm in mine. The skin on her hands is growing callused from the rubbing of the wooden oar handle, but it fits almost perfectly in mine, still cool and dry like when she used to tuck me in at night. Her fingers, lightly freckled, are bare. I press the pin firmly into the taut skin and watch as the clear fluid oozes out over the pin and drips over the edge of her hand.

"Ew," she breathes.

"Yup, pretty gross. Doesn't hurt the way you think it will to pop it, though." She takes the Band-Aid I offer her and follows me down the hall. She stands there in the doorway, watching me climb back onto my bed with my history book, as if I'm going to do homework. My father's voice floats up through my floor, accusing Ben of throwing away his education and participating in reckless activities.

There is something strange about her expression and I start to feel guilty for trying to look busy and distracted. I feel sorry for her; at least I think that's what I feel. Sorry even though she's brought this on herself as much as my father and his drinking and the silence and Ben and his forced indifference.

"You can come in," I tell her.

She sinks down on my quilt and pops open her soda can. She takes a long drink, tilting her head back and I watch the muscles of her throat working hard, like she can't take the stuff in fast enough. I pick at a loose thread, wrapping it around my finger until the tip turns purple while I wait for her to finish.

"Wow," she says, then sits silent for a moment. Something about no sense of respect for his parents and teachers, something about financial obligations and *how much money have you spent on this shit?* drifts in under my door. She turns to look at me.

"What happened with your brother?" she asks, swallowing. She's about to put the open can on the carpet when I tap my bedside table.

"Dad found a pipe in his pants. Ben said he's keeping it for a friend."

She smiles strangely, as if it hurts the corners of her mouth, and she reaches across to find a place for her drink; I clear a circle next to my phone. Her eyes get stuck on a picture I have there: my mother took it at the Head of the Charles regatta last year, and all around me the river banks are full of people in a thousand different colors. There are boats passing in the background and I'm standing in my racing clothes holding my oar straight up in the air. It is twice as tall as I am and looks like a skinny armless man. I have already submitted the picture to the high school year book committee with the caption, "Allison's Significant Other."

"Do you believe him?" she asks me. She doesn't look up.

"Don't know," I answer. Then, "No." She turns her face toward mine suddenly brightening.

"I think we old ladies may be ready to row in the Head of the Charles in the fall." She beams at me. "If we can keep doing what we did today, we may be ready to take your boats on in a couple of weeks."

"You can try," I say, "but we wouldn't want you to hurt your backs."

"You should be more concerned about your own. Hey, you hungry?" She rubs the blisters on the palm of her hand. I think about asking her where her ring is. She has to take her wedding band off to row because the blisters from the oars would only get worse if she wore it to practice. Her first day out on the water was the first day in all my eighteen years that I saw her without that ring. She still puts it back on after her shower, but I know what it feels like to take off a ring that you wear all the time. Your hand feels lighter. Naked. Exposed. Ever since that first practice, I think she got addicted to that weightlessness. She lost all the roundness she had carried on her hips and through her middle since she'd had Benjamin sixteen years ago. She stopped being a normal mother size. She got skinnier than all of her friends. She's gotten smaller than me.

"Yeah."

"Well, see whether maybe you can interest your father or Ben in some dinner. There's stuff in the fridge you could throw together."

"What about you?" I ask, though I know she's already devoured her banana. She eats them in the bathroom while she waits for the shower water to heat up and leaves the peels in the upstairs trash so that the hallway always smells warm and sticky like bad suntan lotion.

"I'm all set. I've got paper work to do before tomorrow, anyway. It'll probably take me all night. But send your brother in to see me when the battle's done down there."

She gets up to go, but lingers for a while in the doorway of my bedroom, looking into the far corner like she's hoping to find something she lost in there. My father is shouting about the addictiveness of things, how you can get hooked without even knowing. Ben answering, who the fuck are you to know about addiction.

"Mom?" I ask, and at the same time that I don't want to ask, I can't stop the words from coming. "Do you want to stay in here tonight?"

She looks up from where her gaze has been fixed and her mouth is surprised, the corners turned down, lips pursed like she's going to answer. Instead, she shakes her head, smiling at me to apologize.

"Thank you, baby. No."

I'm relieved she doesn't say yes.

When she closes the door behind her, I turn out my lamp and lie back on my pillows. My father and my brother swear at one another, yelling back and forth until my brother's voice cracks with tears. The noise they make is startling in this house full of quiet. It permeates everything. Lying in my bedroom, I think I can hear the china plates in the downstairs cupboards squealing against one another, the delicate cracks in their shiny surfaces growing deeper, reaching out like tree branches or a river and its tributaries on a map.

"Shut up, Ben," I whisper, "Shut up, shut up, shut up." I dig my fingernails into my palm. And then it hits me so hard I feel like I've been dropped onto the river from the top of the B.U. Bridge:

The most amazing thing about racing is that despite everything that flows through me, I never lose control. My hands don't slip on the oar, my legs don't stop pushing me backward in my seat. Somehow my body works in spite of my brain; my body knows that if I stop moving or stop following the rhythm of Katie's back, everything beautiful and synchronized about our boat will crumble: the gentle backswing that happens as we all slide forward on our seats to take another stroke will suddenly stop, the rumble of oars turning in the oarlocks will grow irregular and come to a halt, our breathing will come in broken, panicked blows. We'll lose the race. I have seen women knocked unconscious by the handles of their oars when the paddles get locked in the force of the shell's motion on the water. Slowing down, or stopping altogether, is dangerous. And the more I think about it, maybe that's the way it is for my mother. Maybe it's more the fear of chaos and the destructive force of uttering those words *I want a divorce* that allows her to joke and shout in the afternoons by the river and still come home at night and say nothing at all.

For Lynda Hull

Millicent C. Borges

You smile at us, in folding
chairs. *Fiat Lux* and *Chiffon*.
The syllables curl into insignificant
worlds.

Turban-headed, hands gesturing,
you barely stay afloat at Duttons.

But this was before icy roads,
and missed stops.

Before shattered ankles and nights
awake. The crutches of friends.

How absolutely young we sat
while you searched the audience
for ex-lovers, joking like a bride.

For water, asking politely.
Between poems, between
the memory of a hospital bed,

a girlhood friend with AIDS,
drunk conversations in a walk-up
in China Town, a woman on a fire
escape — wearing nothing but stockings,

stretching her back into the worlds
far away from the dark city
you were between.

She

Millicent C. Borges

for Helen Keller

Was
taken to cold
startling wet
poured through narrow
fists forced
open
by teacher

Above
massive palms
measured itchy
letters between thirst
and
words

Voicy
fingers
closed around language
like a blanket large
enough to bounce
a girl

in
its center.

The moving
lips and jaws
working.

Birds.
The trial
and error
of beating
      wings above.

      Around
her face,
the warm breath
on her neck at night.
      Soon.

they told
her. When
the music comes,
      You should.

Seeing Fellini

Millicent C. Borges

The second man lights up, and smokes
a cigarette next to a pool of water.
He walks around a fountain.
An apple stem twists its way
between my fingers through the alphabet
to the first letter of the name of a man.

There are people dancing
to carnival music like a parade.
There is a painting of an egg yolk and women
in heavy robes, a carousel with a British flag.
Lost in the distance, a frog prince tosses
a golden ball.

There is an ocean and sand and
soldiers' boots. A green globe
of movie lights with a community
of trailers, a drummer and seagulls.

A row of carpenters leers at a woman
with a bare midriff who is jumping
on a trampoline. A third man
checks into a hotel in Arizona
and apologizes.

There are lollipops and fudge
and cougars and breasts
and penises, and fences and
a lot of ice and stairs.

The wind is everywhere.
Long curtains billow
through the open windows
like Rapunzel's hair.

Some people are crying;
their make-up drips black
pancake into white. Down
the steps of a cave and into dark
canvas stars, my eyes follow a man
walking.

A flute player in a polka dot suit
gallops a clear-cut circle around a fire.
And some people are laughing and pointing.

And now everyone is holding
their side and making up the punch line to a joke
that started with the opening of a door
and a frantic search under the bed.

The staccato of double tonguing
a musical score. Military conscription.
Orders that trample the conductor's baton

before the open sheet music where a stray
note in the margin is a hand to hold,
a moment in time, a room where anything

can happen.

A room where I collect someone else's life.
The rippling fire of something better than light.

For Myo Myo: Horsecart Driver #142

Willa Schneberg

Bagan, Myanmar, 1993

She doesn't know why Myo Myo got her on the bus
off limits to a rucksacked tourist with a Lonely Planet guidebook,
since government greed has made it criminal not to fly.
Maybe he wanted to be subversive without dying for it.
Maybe he was still enraged at a government
who gave him a week to clear out of his hometown.
Perhaps, he hoped she would contribute
in dollars towards the house he builds in his mind
of light and dark thatch
on the banks of the Irrawaddy River,
when his horse is out of commission from hauling foreigners
who want to see Pagan, its name and glory erased
by Ne Win who rules based on what his astrologers declare
unlucky.

Burmese women passengers wearing *longyis* and
paste on their faces from the bark of acacia trees
peek at her when they think she is sleeping
or when her head is down, as she digs dirt
out of her nails with a tiny knife.
They all go into a cafe for the umpteenth time
for a fix of thick coffee with
long strings of condensed milk in cracked cups,
as the bus mechanic yanks something out of the engine
that looks like a ginseng root,
so the old vehicle can continue to stagger along through the night.
For twelve dollars in *kyats*,
seated in a place of honor behind the monks,
she is on her way to Yangoon and home.

Phnom Penh as Still Life

Willa Schneberg

*The expulsion of the population from Phnom Penh is a measure one will
not encounter in any other country's revolution.*
 — Communist Party of Kampuchea document

They have even kicked us out of the hospitals.
Our bewildered loved ones carry intravenous bags
as we push them in their beds.
Weeping fathers hold our daughters
in bedsheet slings around their necks.
We hide rubies in the bottom of our cookpots
stuffed with sticky rice and green mangoes.
We carry our homes
on our heads
or dangling from bamboo poles
and begin walking on wide roads
going east, north and west.
We could be standing still
we walk so slowly.

In Phnom Penh geckos hide in the walls.
Offerings of lotus flower, mangosteen and salak
waste on small home altars.
Gold leaf Buddha heads disappear
in the debris of *naga* decorated *wats.*
Ravaged *cyclos*
their wheels and bicycle seats pried off
curl up on their sides.
Cold coal irons pine to glide on white cotton again.
Hammocks tied between coconut palms wait motionless
for the bodies they have caressed
to return…

Lost River

D.N. Baldwin

Twenty years had passed since my brother eloped with the woman I planned to marry. I was away at the time, studying art, unaware of any bond between them but through me. With those years came notes and calls, engraved invitations requesting my presence at this or that ceremony or a family gathering; but with each summons I demurred, deceived when pressed — steadfastly maintaining my status as exile. Then my mother died.

Since I claimed the authorities had revoked my license for driving while impaired, my brother met my flight from Philadelphia. I had long ago stopped seeing red flashes when I thought of Harlan Day. I no longer wanted him broken or quartered or dragged behind a car, but in the air over Maryland I downed a breakfast of scotch and milk to face him, to travel home once again, uncertain about a renewal.

In front of the terminal I found the red Cadillac Seville he had described, though I hardly recognized the bald and lumpy driver, a chestnut-size growth on his neck as if something had lodged in his gullet. He wore a Western suit and shirt with horse-head stays, string tie and boots made from Iguana hide; and I took him for an aging and solemn Elvis impersonator who wore hair pieces when he performed, or maybe someone coming to grips with his sexuality in middle years. He was an inspector with the Highway Department, rising from flagman, made around fifty grand over the table, maybe another ten, in food and liquor, under.

"That you, Harlan Day?" I said.

"Nobody else, Fisher." He nodded, staring ahead at the taxis and limos and shuttle buses slanting in and out of disorderly lines, the weekend travelers swarming. I tossed my garment bag in the back seat and glanced around. Never known as a smoker, Harlan drove a nonsmoking conveyance, and I would have to wait for the cigarette I now craved.

We sped away, covering distance like an auctioneer covering words. "Gotta pee or need something to drink just say so," he said.

"No thanks, Harlan," I said, having no intention of prolonging this trip.

Heading west we passed fields of Angus cows and untroubled horse farms with endless white fences. Patches of early autumn color began appearing, the varnished-greens shifting to pyrotechnic reds and yellows and blends thereof, a poverty of browns and tans. The season brought back images of two teenagers swigging hot chocolate or homemade tomato soup in a deer stand. Fisher and Harlan Day Polk, as inseparable as a tramp and an open road. In those days, we called him Hairline or H.D.

We climbed, the Caddy gliding through the scored rock passes with bands of rust and gray slate, the way rising, falling, a modest cedar house or mobile home set here and there in hemlock or maple and white oak. Ascending and descending until, accompanied by an unnamed country ballad, we crossed into West Virginia and the road meeting the wheels of our touring sedan changed pitch. It struck me how far along the mountain flora had advanced toward dormancy here, the dazzling colors in decline, much like the last slope before we leveled out and crossed the Lost River, then turned with it to the south. In the valley a mist of wood smoke hovered low over the resting fields, the hay cut and bundled like jellyrolls, the cattle with a lazy start on the day.

Growing up, we ventured from this valley only for movies or sports or to a spot where the railroad ran along the Potomac's southwest branch. There, at a frog in the track a brakeman had many years earlier fallen before his very own train. His ghost roamed there still, the story went. Nights with the right conditions brought sounds of bail against eyehole in the lantern's frame, a terrible light thrown in all directions. Lovers parked there, Marietta and I with them, though we never saw or heard evidence from the other side. Only later did the tale grow suspect, a ruse for engagement in that frightening air, I believed.

Marietta had undergone a double mastectomy last year, about the time she and the brakeman began reappearing in my dreams; and those dual themes of love and resurrection had portended this day, I now understood, crossing the last bridge and entering the town. My purchase on composure slid away as we passed the General Store/ Post Office, and I saw in the distance the cafe my great-grandfather had built with gambling proceeds he brought back from World War I. My parents ran the place when we were kids, Harlan Day and I drafted into the business when the old man fell dead one night, like the bowling ball he had just guttered at a seven-eight spare. We worked after school and weekends and gave up sports and hated the place for what it took. Eat Dirt Cheap was a promise still dispensed in staticky neon.

Early Saturday. A cat yawning in a window. A man in overalls washing down a fire truck, the canvas hose sluicing water streetward, the Caddy's tires slapping at the stream as we slowed. "We got cakes and deep-dish shit people brought to the house, you want something to eat," he said. Climbing out, he slammed the car door hard enough to make the chassis sway.

I climbed out myself and immediately lit a cigarette, crumpled the box and stuffed it away in my pocket. Smoking, I caught the early beams of sun playing off the flow of water between us, some crows in a nearby field undercutting the hush with their call.

"Thanks for the ride, Harlan." Looking at him, I thought of an engine that had seized up; his head ached, his eyes burned, I was certain. He rose before dawn to do this bit for the family, and no doubt believed I had scheduled this early shuttle out of pure meanness.

He pointed across the street to the house where my high school math teacher once lived. "There's your bed and breakfast," he said. "Kate's Bed and Breakfast now. Check in's at one. Until then, you can leave your bag in the car."

I looked at Kate's, looked two doors down to the cafe. Two women sat at a window table — one covering her face with a mask of Madonna, the other a mannequin — their arms bent in the same unnatural fashion, pointing off vaguely.

"She whiles away her days there, opened or closed. She and the dummy," he explained. "Got the mask when Mama died."

They seemed focused on the table's edge, as if distracted by something inconsequential, an ant or grain of salt on the tablecloth. Their vacant manner reminded me of those confined to institutions, and a ripple went out over my skin. Suddenly I wanted no part of all this and felt like a vagrant, standing in the street between the house I no longer knew and the cafe. I listened to the crows, the faint rush of water from the fire hose, the river that would earn its name by simply disappearing in a rock face at the valley's north wall.

"Go on over," he urged. "She's been looking for you. So's your mama, but I guess she can wait."

"Is everything all right?" I said.

"As far as I'm concerned, the goddamn place can burn down, her in it."

"That's great, Harlan Day. Just goddamn great."

He turned that shopworn smile of reproof, mimicking a face rationed out to the alcoholics in the family — my father and me. "Why don't you get yourself a free beer. Drink all you want, the place is yours now, half of it anyway. Take what the hell you want," he said, starting toward the house where he and Marietta had lived with my mother, where my mother lay for a viewing. I wanted to run after him, to bring him down and pound him, scrape away his smugness in the asphalt, but turned instead and started toward another portion of what had come and gone long before.

Only eyes behind the mask moved as I approached, eyes the only animation, an option precluding a wave or friendly gesture. I heard neon arcing through the same tired turns of tubing, eyed the same tired mortar and brick and picture window with minor distortion fronting the street. On the white crepe-paper trim, a squadron of mummified flies lay randomly, the bleached shell of a bee. A grease board next to the entrance announced Friday's lunch special: pork cutlet, bean soup, fresh rolls, and kale.

I put out the cigarette beneath my shoe, noticed the door shade half-drawn, a Dr. Pepper sign swung to *closed*. My fingers danced over the door's brass plate before I pushed, my heart pounding like that in a puppy. Long-forgotten scents swept past me, a breath of boiled greens and coffee, cigarettes, and foods deep-fried. From the kitchen Puccini's *Madame Butterfly* beamed, and against Cio Cio San and her maid in the Flower Duet, I made a sweep of this lost place as if sweeping the interior of a shrine. The updated fixtures, frieze carpet and alabaster walls, then Harlan Day's mounted sixteen-point buck maintaining his vigil, overseeing with glassine eye the tables set with the same steelware and tour-guide-of-West Virginia place mats. A corkboard with business cards and Polaroids of pickups and dogs and men in camouflage with weapons and their kills. The faces new, but the bears and deer and ungainly elk seemed unchanged.

"Marietta," I said tentatively, bringing her and the mask around. She wore a loose-fitting robe over jeans and a tee shirt with Mozart's bust, the towel on her head like a burnoose.

She stared through the other face—her eyes a dark slough of appraisal, and I wondered if we would conduct our reunion in the manner of those along the Grand Canal during Carnival when she faced her companion. "Well bless my soul, Lucy. Death and roses, mysterious lights, nights with visions, fantasies and newspaper photographs, *only* time I ever see him. But which is he now, real or imagined? Past or present? Thin as his boyhood self; that self you don't remember, Lucy. But graying some, I see. And such a serious face. My, my."

"Let me look at you, Marietta."

She stood and bowed and cast aside the cutout, Marietta overdoing it with a flourish to present her back, then her front. How outlandish to be in her presence again, I thought, as wobbly and unsure as a man set down on a distant world. Like the brakeman's legend, she endured. Her beauty—matured and saddened—endured.

"How are you getting on?" I asked.

"Well, the boy who delivers bread is late, my meat refrigerator won't get below forty-four and a half, and there's a pencil stopping up the toilet in the men's room," she told me, her tone matter-of-fact, as if she were relaying this to hired help or to Lucy.

"And you? The kids?" With visits from my mother came news, though she tended to be stingy on details involving Marietta.

"The boys are both in Morgantown; Harlan Junior finishes next year, wants to be a mining engineer. I don't know why. A.J.'s a year and a half behind. He's a poet, but majors in education. Both fine, both survivors, Fisher. They'll be back for the funeral, and you can see for yourself. Meet your nephews…Me, I'm like an apple brought up from the root cellar in winter, not as much to look as in the fall, but some substance left, I suppose."

"Everyone alive has that much, Marietta."

"Okay, I'm what you see. Older and wiser. A few pounds thicker, a few more wrinkles than you. Hair thinned some with the chemotherapy. Coming back in now though," removing the towel and shaking down the tresses as if to document her claim. "And it's okay if you stand there like you're afraid of offending your eyes. I get that a lot nowadays."

I started toward her, the damp scent of her hair like the feminine dampness after a swim, sprigs of gray invading auburn. "You're as easy on the eye as ever."

"Listen to you."

"I mean it."

She pulled a brush from the pocket of her robe, began brushing her hair. "Trip okay?"

"I was no sooner in the air, and we were landing. The drive from the airport took longer than the flight."

"Lucy and I were just talking about what you'd do when you arrived—whether you'd come over here first or to the house."

"What'd you pick?"

She looked down, looked at the brush in her hand. "Want some coffee?" she asked as dutifully as a waitress.

"The beer cold?"

She squinted, regarding me from a place where we once experimented with caring. "This early?"

"No early or late when there's no schedule."

"Well, sit down. I'll get you a glass, that and a ham biscuit, if you like."

"I'd handle road kill for a ham biscuit, Marietta."

She stepped around me, avoiding my eyes. "Don't try to disgust me. I'm past disgusting, Fisher." Watching her proceed, weary arms at her side, I thought of tribes who insured survival of the group by quitting their weakest when food was scarce.

Sliding back the cooler door, I freed a long-neck Bud, twisted off the cap and added a shake of salt. With the first swallow came images of an adolescent ripping off beer for a date, images of me and her, her and Harlan Day.

I took a seat beside Lucy—her wig near Marietta's auburn, a wedding band on her plaster finger. She remained serene as the opera faded, as if purged of emotion. I watched a car arrive, an older couple walking solemnly to the house. Harlan Day glanced over, admitting them, then shut the door.

Marietta backed through the kitchen curtain with a lacquered serving tray and I noticed the ring-free hands as she set a mug and plate before me. She sipped coffee from a spoon, watched me lift the biscuit and breathe it in, watched my first bite. "Mama waited for you, said you were coming, said she could feel it."

"She was right. I'm here."

"Twenty-one years, three months removed."

"How was it toward the end?" I asked.

"She never wanted anyone to know."

"When she came to visit last year, I knew. She was philosophizing."

"She was generous with everything."

"Thanks for caring for her, Marietta."

"She wasn't any trouble, but there's some things I can't do any longer. Running this place with her sick got to be too much. Harlan Day was no help, him and that damn job that takes him all over. We almost closed down. Then Sarah Milford, the black soprano in our choir, pitched in cleaning and cooking. Said the Lord directed it and wouldn't take a dime."

"He might have cut her a better deal."

She studied me, sipped from her spoon. "It's hard to believe."

"The Lord?"

"That you're here. So much has changed, yet nothing. I got your card, that and the fruit. I couldn't write a thank you note, but you were in my thoughts."

"And you're all right now?"

"I'm still a little tender, numb in places along my arm, can't lift half what I used to, and bad dreams plague me as if I was a visionary."

"I'm sorry, Marietta."

"Sorry that they're gone? You never liked them anyway," she said. "They were always too small."

"I don't remember complaining about size, only access." I remembered layers of lingerie, bras with catches that would confound magicians.

"Well, maybe I can buy them back or barter for them in some after-death bazaar, that or turn up a fresh pair."

"You look fine."

"They're implants, Fisher. Hard as tea cups."

"The follow-up's okay?"

"That's what they tell me, but with every scratchy throat or bit of nausea or headache..."

She looked away.

I wanted to hold her, but did not. I drained the beer, rose for another. I bought a pack of Marlboros from the cigarette machine, and at the table she reached for them before I managed to free the golden pull band. "It's what kills that gives you a better sense of mortality," I said.

"I only smoke when there's things to examine," she said, sliding an ashtray between us. "Then I'm as addicted to them as I am to life." With her first deep draw of smoke, she closed her eyes and acquired the look of someone who had broken out of rehab.

"What are you examining now?"

She looked at me, her eyes misting over. "Be staying long?" she said, exhaling a plume that lifted an edge of Lucy's place mat.

"I'm not sure. I took a room at Kate's."

She raised her brows. "Gonna paint while you're here? Paint for therapy? Paint the hills?"

"I only brought a few changes of clothes."

"A.J.'s kind of impressed with what we hear about you. Mama kept your letters and the clippings that said you were being shown in some gallery in New York or elsewhere. Key West. Moving around, skittish as ever…She was real proud, said I should've ended up with you."

"You've done just fine, Marietta, raised fine children."

"They are fine and I love them dearly, but maybe I wanted yours."

"I nearly accommodated you." She had offered love with few binders, but I filled with dread when she talked of settling in this town, seeing my future die in a haze of grease and cigarette vapors. She never understood my departure for Philadelphia, never comfortable those first few months when she came up on weekends. *So many loonies staring at you, you feel you're about to be devoured.* The city proved threatening, loud, my art like a rival woman.

"I see us as kids, Fisher. I see us in the back seat of your Fairlane or us skinny-dipping. We laughed, went places, even peed together. Over the years *funny* withered." Her cigarette became a dart that she aimed at the ashtray. She tapped away as if reluctant to release the stub.

"You've raised two boys. Made the restaurant go. That's not funny stuff."

"What happened?" she asked, though not for the first time, I realized. When she was clear of me, I had wanted to know myself until I learned my way around questions.

"Your heart was always here."

"I couldn't move as far and fast as you," she said.

"I've slowed some."

"But never married."

I mashed out my cigarette, thought about another, thought better. "I liken it to looking for a kidney, Marietta. Never found the right match. Besides, there's compatibility in alone."

"But you're around women."

"Sure. Other painters, gallery people, students and such."

"Maybe the women you see, the ones who pose for you or those in your classes, bore you because they're naked all the time. Maybe you've become desensitized."

"I'm far from being desensitized by nudes, Marietta, and models pose without clothes only rarely. They're expensive, city scene's free. And if someone does pose I never take liberties or cross lines. Fun's fun. The creative process is spoiled when you get into your subject matter."

"I picture you with models, Fisher. Arm and arm, confident, spanking about in fancy places."

"If I do go out, it's with friends mainly, dinner now and then, or just hang. The work consumes most of my time, owns more of me than any person I know." I wanted to tell her that I had lived with a standout figure-skater for nearly six years and we fought over — what? — I never knew fully, maybe distance. I wanted her to know that I remained dissatisfied, unfulfilled, despairing in my lowest inebriate states that I might never know love.

"Models, they get immortalized in those paintings, don't they? They get fixed in a photograph or on canvas at their most beautiful moment, stay there forever."

"That's what it's all about, Marietta," inclining my head to study her, wondering how I might render her in this piss-poor light — light that has her projecting too sullen and sad a mood.

"You enhance them even."

"I set down an interpretation of what I see, an idea. Put me into what I see."

"Sounds sensual."

"It is."

"I remember the exhibits at school or the fair, your devotion to beer joints and old barns, folks in doorways or windows, but never me, clothed or otherwise."

I wanted to tell her that she was the prototype for much of what I put to canvas, she the source I borrowed with most frequency. "I couldn't have steadied a brush had you been nude, Marietta."

She turned to the mannequin. "Do you believe what you're hearing, Lucy? Men can say the most flattering things when they're drinking."

"Besides, I wasn't a very good painter then. I couldn't do you justice."

"As you got better, I got older though, and I don't see paintings of women my age."

I finished my biscuit, took a pull of beer. Was this the church-going mother of two that I was hearing with sound ear? My sister-in-law? "What do you mean?" I said, though I knew full well her meaning. I began moving lines around, doing an abstract of her, drawing on memories — the graceful slope of her legs and buttocks and back, her neck arched, a pouting, near arrogant air about her.

She pushed aside my plate, looked at me. "Do you take commissions?"

"Architects work on commission. Commissions limit their expression, their risks."

"But you'd take one if you had license, the outcome entirely in your hands."

"I have."

"How much would something like that run?"

"I can't do what you're thinking, Marietta."

"Why? Because I'm old, starting to sag? Because I'm doomed? Or you don't want to put you into me?"

"I'm involved with you in the wrong way."

"You're involved with me?"

"Of course, I am. To you, this town, this place. And even if we'd never known each other, you're married to my brother."

"It was never a marriage, Fisher; it was a moving violation. Maybe because he never felt entitled to me. Maybe because you were still here, like this building's shadow. I tried though, but he bullied me, cheated on me from the beginning. I felt guilty and thought about leaving, becoming a hooker and punishing myself that way. After the operation, when I was lowest and feeling abandoned, I accepted an invitation from a snack salesman and told Harlan Day I was going for a check-up. He never noticed, never cared."

I sat there stunned, studying my box of cigarettes, a million images cruising.

"Why'd you come down here?" she said finally.

"You know why I came."

"Nothing else? Curiosity? See what I look like now? How I've been bearing up?" that thought restoring her somewhat.

"Out of respect for *her*, the family plot, my father. Curiosity? Sure."

"To see how the rest of us are getting on?"

"I don't give a damn about the rest, Harlan Day or the cafe, if that's what you mean. But I loved Mama and you, especially you. I cared so much that thoughts of you occupied entire years and intruded on everything I worked at, you want the truth."

"You thought about my body?"

"A woman is more than her body."

"Until she loses it."

She was mostly right; men were mostly drawn to trophies. I rose and stretched, caught for some reply. The processed beer began weighing in with discomfort. "Okay if I use the bathroom?"

"You got to ask me to use the bathroom?"

"I mean, you said a pencil was stuck—"

"With no customers, the ladies' room's not much different from the men's."

——

When I returned I found Lucy sitting alone, Lucy staring on as vacantly as ever. Reaching for another beer, thinking how I might smell when greeting mourners, I caught in my side view a snatch of motion and turned. At the entrance to the kitchen stood Marietta, the curtain a sheathe around her. Her clothes lay neatly stacked on a nearby stool, Marietta like someone about to make a strip-show entrance. "Look at me, Fisher," she said, allowing the curtain to fall away. The sudden thrust of flesh jolted me. My eyes cut to the front door. "They sliced me from arm pit to arm pit, Fisher, and he never gave a good goddamn. Hardly anyone gave a good goddamn."

Once in Independence Square an alarm sounded in my head as a pair of men approached from my rear and I ran for my life, the desire to make that kind of exit overwhelming me as I set the bottle on the counter. "If he were to come in here, he'd kill us both," I said. "Is that what you want?"

"I want you to look at me, goddamnit! I'm being outed."

Disoriented for a moment, intent on the street, where in blurred vision cars seemed to mass. I envisioned my coffined mother, Harlan Day bent in prayer, tearing up. "What are you trying to prove with this?"

"You look at me or I'll come over there, Fisher, for God and everybody to see."

I turned slowly, and I felt my insides rock. She was an angel, disquieting and fetching as a mirage. I swung back, steadied myself against the humming cooler, wanting to not want her.

"Is it such a horrible sight?"

"No, goddamnit."

"Then look."

"Someone will pick this instant to come for us," I warned, long a student of irony.

"I don't give a damn who comes."

"I didn't come home to fight or die, Marietta. I came…"

"Pay your respects to the living, Fisher."

"You don't know what you're doing with this," I said.

"I know I never had to ask you twice."

This time I did a slow long take of her, marveling at the site of her again, at the effort the surgeons had made. I felt weak. "Why?" I wanted to know.

She regarded me evenly, then changed her tone. "So you'd understand."

"When I heard, I destroyed a canvas. I almost came here I felt so down."

"I don't need that," restoring the curtain part way.

"I was down for what you went through, for what got away."

"Bring it back then."

"You're more than any portrait I could do, Marietta." I wanted to yank the curtain away, throw it out with the paint rags. Have her hold a towel instead. Marietta, a wood nymph—affecting surprise—stepping from an outdoor bath. Old men looking up lasciviously from a card game.

The tone of her skin required a touch of green to liven it. Highlight her with a floral background, some sky and willows with catkins. To lend vitality, a tint for hair that reached her waist as it once had. Whorls of pure color for the face. With a sable brush I'd purse the lips, accent them, warm her mood. High-key her. Make her less somber, perky. As sensual as the women in those old men's dreams.

"You're leaving and you're not ever coming back. I can hear you figuring."

"We've got to get up to the house," though the house was the last thing I wanted, knowing I couldn't face Harlan Day or my mother.

"They can wait."

"Where in the hell is this going to get us, Marietta, besides dead?"

"I wanted to be honest."

"You wanted to see my reaction."

"What was your reaction?" she said.

"You *saw*. Lucy even saw without looking. And now we can return to our lives."

"There is no other life, Fisher." She rotated, showing me her back, and my legs weakened. "Is there any hope?"

"For what?"

"This body. Could you do anything with this body?"

"This isn't the place, Marietta, and I don't do home delivery."

"I'd be on a Greyhound bus this afternoon if you wanted me up there."

Twisting off the bottle cap, I finished my preliminary of her. "You can't ride a *bus* in your condition, all the way to Philadelphia for something perhaps out of our grasp."

"A plane then."

"What would everyone do without you?"

"Only way they'd know I was gone was when the cafe didn't open for breakfast. State troopers and truckers from the chicken plant would be scratching their asses and peering dumbfounded in the window there, their stomachs growling so as to be heard clear to the bank's drive-up teller. Then they'd know." She wiped her palms on the curtain.

"What are we saying, Marietta..." The notion was so deliciously insane I took a pull of beer to check an adolescent giggle.

She said without pleading, "Take me with you."

I felt the jump in my heart rate, the gain transferred to my temples, my feet. "To South Philadelphia?"

"If that's where you're going."

"You're crazy."

"Crazy's the only thing that's kept me sane."

Lost in her again, I watched her work into her camisole and panties, into her tee shirt and jeans and shoes, leaving behind the robe. I pictured Marietta readying herself for a bed where I waited. "You'd really let go of all this?"

"When Harlan Day left for the airport, I wanted to hide. Then when I saw you I knew it wasn't any use, that you were where things don't get hidden."

"That includes your husband, you know. He'd come looking for us. Gun us down like a rival gang in a drive-by."

"He'd never look further than the dining room."

No moral battle raged in me, no brotherlove, though I countered with, "Wouldn't it be fair to wait for the funeral, talk this over with Harlan Day?"

"We haven't got time."

"Out of twenty years, what's a few hours?"

"We act now because she'd want it that way."

"You want to do this for Mama?"

"We're doing this for us, mainly. But having us together would make her happy, give her peace. She wants us to understand that ceremonies are for the living, that for us, time apart, any time apart, is time squandered."

"Is she going to help us get out of here?"

"We'll take his Cadillac."

"Marietta, Jesus. He'd have a seizure." The idea had appeal. I began to laugh.

"Rightly the car's half mine, but it's like driving a goddamn semi."

"So we just ask Harlan Day for his keys, and he hands them over."

"I've got a set," she said. Forefinger to her thumb, she gave her wrist a half turn, moving toward me, her fragile scent lessening the bracing effort of my knees. I felt like a ship leaking ballast. Lightheaded, aimless, with no fix on anything I knew. She touched my face, my lips a butterfly harvesting nectar from her fingers. "You remembered." I remembered too her scent, the essence of her that had undergone no change.

We kissed full and deep, and I realized she had never kissed Harlan Day in this same way. While I still had my hands under control, I guided them over her body.

"We'll take back what we misplaced," she whispered. "I'll screen out the rest of this, his name."

"And your kids. What about your kids? Will I be their father?" The idea troubled me.

"Youngest one never got along with his father. He reminds me of you. He'll understand and come to visit. Harlan Junior, I don't know."

"But how's something like this going to affect them?"

"I told you, they're survivors."

"The neighborhood is old, sometimes noisy, crowded, and the people no better than when you were there last. My studio reeks of chemicals, and the rest of the rooms look like a street gang holed up there. I eat out, that or microwave my meals, drink too much scotch."

"We're survivors, too."

"What about this place?"

"We'll sell out."

"And your clothes?"

"Models don't need clothes, Fisher."

Returning to the table, she gave Lucy a peck, promising to have A.J. bring her when he came. She cleared the table and wiped it down, washed the dish and cup and glass, set them to dry. She bagged a cold six pack of Bud, emptied the cash register of everything paper. She locked the cafe, trading that set of keys for one in the zippered recess of her purse, keys with a Cadillac fob.

We paused, listening to the organ my mother once played, each to our own silent prayer, our soft visions. I thought about transitions and I thought about time, the empty space that gave solids form. Poised beneath a sycamore, where the sun made dapples over its body, the Caddy seemed to wait conspiratorially, as clean as the fire truck after its wash, a warm blood sheen to it. I knew I wouldn't keep the thing, that I'd leave it in long-term parking if we weren't arrested, mail the coordinates to Harlan Day. A car that fine would never survive Philly anyway.

Opening the door for Marietta, I wondered what I might say to him if he should rush from his vigil to confront us. "I'm leaving you the cafe? Trading my share for your wife? I'm commandeering your Caddy." Harlan Day, the balding, aging image of Elvis, maybe spying on us now, I thought, making the big engine come alive. I checked the gas gauge, shifted to Drive and pulled away, the cafe in my mirror. As we crossed the bridge, Marietta turned on the radio and started a beer, the act reminiscent of times when after a movie or a ballgame we headed for a rendezvous with the ghost light, understanding after so many failed tries that we'd never get so much as a flicker out of the damn thing, only what passed for love.

The Warp is Even: Taut Vertical Loops Between Our Father and the Earth

Luci Tapahanso

Today I began anew:
in the gray pre-dawn, the air is moist.
As I walk, my footsteps echo in the still morning.
Damp, fragrant circles appeared overnight on the cold driveway,
soon they will vanish with the sun's first rays.
But now, I breathe the sweet dampness.
>Suddenly I miss my father so:
>how he savored such mornings.
>He would have spoken to the solitary dove
>that sits on the edge of the red tile roof.
>Its long, delicate coos are the rhythmic pauses of desert
mornings.

Today I began anew:
this afternoon, after phone calls and class preparations,
I sit in the bright sunlight, and twist, then loop
The edging cords along the bottom and top of the loom.
My fingers move easily between the turns of yard — such needed
>slants of rain.
"It hasn't rained here for months," I tell the loom.
On a clear, quiet afternoon last spring, my mother said slowly,
"It's hard to weave now; my eyes are getting weak."
It seemed that she had been thinking of this for some time.

Today, the tightly spun dark red yarn falls into place evenly.
I began anew for my mother, and some things
she remembers as she looks at rugs:
>The long afternoons decades ago when the children slept,
>The soft tamping of her batten comb echoed in the small
house.

The intricate double-sided rugs her mother-in-law wove.
Even now, 80 years later, she marvels at the saddle rug
Náli Aszdáán made for her husband, my father.
I began anew for my mother's memories.

Today I began anew:
on the mantel is the small basketball my grandson left
when he last visited. I look down the bright hallway
and recall his bubbling baby laughter.
His dark, shiny eyes glitter with delight.
I easily remember the warm tautness of his little body in my arms.
His black, thick hair against the bend of my elbow.
He lets me carry him as if he were an infant.
> I sing old songs and he watches me.
> He watches the huge, blue sky overhead.
> I sing songs created for him, "Whose little boy are you?
> Said I am Grandma's boy, Grandma's little baby boy."
As he listens intently to the songs,
and watches the skies of his homeland,
I memorize every thing.

I wish for such moments every day.
Today I weave the first four rows of black yarn
For my little grandson who inherited my father's name: Hastiih
    Tsetah Biihsoi.

The warp is even: taut vertical loops
Between our father and the earth.

Ablution

Elizabeth Ann Winslow

Waking in his bed, I stretch under the airy comforter. Like him, it has a light touch. After a full year, I still can't get used to sharing Mohamed's things that are so weightless, and white with the trust that no stain would dare discolor and ruin them. But his rugs and furniture, his walls and window frames: when he is not looking, they are sure that I will be the spoiler.

My muscles are stiff, aching as I move. They are punishing me for getting old and breakable. They cannot forgive me, and I foresee a lifetime of increasingly painful mornings pulling out in front of me like a rubber band that might snap back at any time. Since why should I assume my life will be long? Just because it seems long behind me?

The woods of Mount Carmel are encroaching on the window, but out of sight I could hear, if I tried, the soft rush of the Mediterranean. It is the dry cold of October and I feel it in my bones. In the night, we passed from having sex into making love. A fine line, yet perceptible. This still does not answer, for me, the question of whether it is love and my life a love story. I search my mind, not my heart for that answer. My heart already knows and is never complicated. Not that I am so concerned; not every question needs an answer to feel fulfilled. Making love is on one side of having sex, and fucking is on the other. Now we have done all three.

Arching my back, I see him watching me from the doorway. If he had a cocked hat and a dark cloak, he could be a private eye. He comes and sits on the edge of the bed, white undershirt and boxers on the white comforter. It is all becoming dingy despite his best efforts. Even blueing will not remove the wear of time. Like fancy cosmetics to smooth out your face, as if only the past, and not the future, is full of wrinkles. He tries to make his life stainless and pure: for this reason he has invested in a washing machine and dryer, which he keeps on the enclosed balcony. I would have thought he was too old for such nonsense. Certainly he is too old to have retained any kind of real purity. Yet he manages to stay somehow boyish and clean while my soul gathers hidden soot. Shame is the grime that comes off on your fingers. Shame will not rub away from the fingers that have touched it.

I knot my hands above my head. There is something very alive about pain; but I do not always want to be so alive, first thing in the morning. I like to wake up as I imagine the dead come into heaven: a swimmer resurfacing, cushioned by warm water which gently pushes me into the air. The elderly must wake most mornings like that, seeing the ripple of sun with calm surprise. Together, Mohamed and I have eighty-four years. Perhaps I have the eighty and he has the four. But no: we are half and half when split apart.

If I were eighty, I might die in my sleep. Instead the pain wakes me roughly, like those who have died too soon and must be revived with electric shocks to the heart.

Mohamed smokes, knocking the ash from his cigarette onto the hardwood floors. A *muezzin* cries out in the valley and we turn towards the sound. The lone voice echoes through the *wadi*, with no comfort except itself, returning. I wonder how many people are prostrate this morning. It has been a long time since he has prayed. Ramadan has passed and with it feelings of piety and compunction. The singing is rife with sorrow and longing, but it is like the lost dreams of one's ancestors, and does not concern us.

He turns back to me, stroking my neck and bare shoulder. I roll to face him, and my cotton nightgown twists to bind my legs. His eyes are wet and bloodshot, staring and open. He has not slept well. Lately he has been an insomniac, sleeping fitfully and pacing like a cat. I cannot stay awake, even out of empathy. His right hand plays with the strap of my gown, his fingers thick and calloused. He builds staircases so that people can control how close they are to Allah, and to each other, on horizontal and vertical planes.

"You should go to a doctor," he says.

"It's not so bad."

His pinked brown eyes roll away from me. "I worry," he murmurs, blankly. He is too tired for inflection, pressing his fingers against his eyelids, as if trying to pop his eyes back into his brain.

Breakfast is last night's lamb, cold and chewy. The spices have soaked in further during the night, committing themselves more. He clears my hair from my shoulders and rubs my back. I push my plate away and drop my head to the cool wood table. He kisses the back of my neck behind my ear. Someone bangs their fists against the front door.

It is my brother, Sa'id. "That was some climb!" he complains, slapping Mohamed on the back but watching me warily. I am still wearing my flimsy nightgown. I pull the straps back onto my shoulders and poke at my food with my fork. Sa'id is a young man. He is the youngest of my brothers — only twenty-six. It amazes me that I could be sister to someone so young. We have never lived in the same house or had any part in each other's lives.

"And how are you?" he asks.

"So the word has traveled!"

Mohamed pours the coffee. Sa'id is chagrined, "Well, what do you expect!"

"I'm fine."

"She's worse all the time," Mohamed tells him, like I'm a sick pet. "She won't go to the hospital. She'll be the death of me." He smiles at me but I don't smile back. When it is just the two of us, he likes to say, "Who will take care of you, if you worry me to death?"

But he does not want to remind Sa'id how my family shirks their duty. And Sa'id must get a full report for the village. They will want to know how Allah is punishing the daughter who left all sanity and modesty to live with a man, catching them all off guard in her forty-first year, when they were too tired, and perhaps liked her too well to kill her for bringing such profound dishonor at such a late age. My family trusted that I could control and account for all the nebulous currents of my life. My father's last words to me were: a strong tide will only wreck such a weak boat. All harbors are unfriendly now. And my mother cried as if her heart broke open like a glass genie lamp. My brothers and sisters were silent in the horror of their own possibilities.

Sa'id looks at me closely as if my wrinkles are abstracted scripture, my face the face of a mosque. "Do you know what it is?"

"Who cares?" I say. "We are all going to die."

The two men watch me in silence. They drink their coffee and feel weak and skeptical. It is because they can't control it that they feel their own weakness. But a woman never controls her own life and so she is always strong. Sa'id has my mother's face but without her kindness. I leave them sipping and go into the bathroom, yanking the ill-fitting door shut behind me.

The tap water is scalding and the tub is rusted and old-fashioned. Mohamed found it for me, over the objections of the landlord. He towed it up the seven flights with some of his friends. It has its own feet but has not yet learned to walk.

I remember that day. The landlord threatened to kick us out for our wastefulness. I was afraid, but Mohamed just laughed. He was building all the staircases in the landlord's new developments, and so the man could not afford to throw us out. "There are plenty of tenants," Mohamed said, "but not so many good carpenters."

Later, we had sex in the tub while it was still filling with water. I had bought a jar of bubble bath, and as a joke he spread it on his chest, the purple swirls changing to foam that clung to his curling hair. Then he spread it on my legs.

"You like those French movies," he said. "Let's always be like that: like a movie. Just the happy ones, never the sad."

The water frothed up around us like the tide.

The steam from the tub makes my head ache, and I realize that I am still dehydrated from sleep. I turn the tap to C, burning my fingers, and drink out of cupped hands. I am hiking, as a girl; I have found a cold spring. I wash my face with the water, which drips down my gown and onto the floor. I am hiking, and it is not that the troop has lost me, but that I have lost myself from the others. The front of the gown is drenched and I peel it off, my arm muscles complaining sharply. My muscles only like to be still nowadays. They are like my grandmother, who has become so sedentary that she will not even rise to relieve herself and must be cleaned off like a baby.

I pull my limbs into the tub, like a puppeteer with a stiff marionette, and the pain makes me angry and impatient: it is a ridiculous pain, with no reason or dignity. It tantrums like a child. Does it expect me not to walk, bathe, make love? Does it expect me to go to bed, but not to get up again in the morning?

In the kitchen, Sa'id and Mohamed murmur about how everything is getting more expensive. They would like to talk about me, but the apartment is too small. The water bites into my legs: this new pain is welcome and distracting. It burns my skin up to the waterline, a pinkish brown that reminds me of Mohamed's eyes. His insomnia is for my sake but does me no good. It is as if I have inherited his sleep, and am never awake. If only I could sleep his sleep for him. For a long time now we have been dreaming each other's dreams, as lovers do.

"Sleep," I plead. "You're so tired." I rub his back and sing him sad village songs. But the massage makes him horny and the songs make him laugh, reminding him of his childhood. He pulls me close and I start to cry.

"What?" he says, letting go. "Did I hurt you?"

His rough fingers are careful and delicate against my skin, always kind and strangely grateful. I can't tell him why I'm crying. One of these days he will fall asleep in the danger of the construction site, and then I will, as he says, have worried him to death.

The water burns and burns, up to my neck. My father always twisted the bottom lips of his horses, to distract them from the pain of shots. It would often calm them mysteriously. For the first time all day, I am not conscious of my body.

Mohamed raps his knuckles against the door, quietly. "Fatima? I'm going to work."

"Is my brother gone?"

"He's waiting downstairs. We'll walk together."

So they will get their chance to talk, after all. "You can come in, if you want."

He opens the door and leans, as he did in the morning, against a doorframe, watching me with that same air of careful detection. But my naked body gets the best of him and he comes over to perch on the edge of the tub. I lay my hand on his knee, leaving a wet handprint. He takes my hand and kisses the fingers. We have had sex in this tub many times and I haven't forgotten any of them. Instead, my body has forgotten me. It has stopped clanging a constant painful reminder. I don't want him to go to work. I want him to stay. "You can come in, if you want," I say again.

"This is serious," he says. "We're going to the hospital when I get home. I wish I could take the day off but I can't."

I dunk my head into the water. It sears my skull and fills my ears. He places his hand on my forehead. "You're getting gray, old lady."

"So are you. But on you, it's becoming. It makes you look very wise."

76

He smiles, tensely. "I'm taking you to the hospital tonight—I'm sick of this nonsense. It's worrying about you that is making me gray."

He leans over the tub, the curls on the top of his head still thick and black. I play with them admiringly while he dips his hand in the water, peering at but not touching the dark spot on my thigh. "What's this? Did you bruise yourself, banging into something?" His fingers brush it lightly. I cringe. He looks up directly, suspiciously. "Where did you get this?"

"I banged into something, like you said. I tried to close a drawer in the kitchen with my hip and it didn't want to go. But it's all right now."

"You're bruising very easily lately. I don't like that."

"Never mind. I've always been clumsy—don't tell me you're just noticing now?" I smile and pat his cheek. "Is my brother still waiting downstairs?"

"You're right, I better go. I'll be back early—at two. It's the best I can do."

We kiss.

"It was very sweet last night," I say, quietly. The change was perceptible to him, too, but we haven't talked about it. He kisses me.

"You are what made it sweet," he says.

Lunch is couscous and a tomato salad. I begin thinking of what to make for dinner. I have been out of work for a month, and cannot find another job. The schools do not need teachers mid-season. And now there is this constant body-ache, and Mohamed does not want me to work. "They will think that I can't take care of you if they see you limping around," he says—as if that is his real concern. So I am a housewife, like my mother and my grandmothers, and many of my sisters. But all of my training is for other things. I am not educated in cooking, cleaning, taking care of the needs of a grown man. The apartment somehow seems dingier than when we both worked, its former clarity fading like an old Polaroid. Sa'id will report all of this, and my family will conclude that Allah, the All-Merciful, is gently nipping at my heels like a heavenly sheepdog. Though of course they would never speak in such terms. They do not think He has a sense of humor. I myself am beginning to doubt it, lately.

Yes, if I had married early, or even late, I would know how to keep the apartment from being submerged in this lackluster shabbiness.

The afternoon has exhausted me and I make my way back to bed. I am dreaming about Mohamed, building houses that we will never own, when a key turns in the lock. Soft footsteps enter the apartment and for the third time today someone stands looking at me from a doorway. I squeeze my eyes shut. I know it is the landlord. I am not surprised.

He approaches the bed and my heart patters like little feet chased by a much larger predator. I pretend to be asleep but he saw my open eyes when he entered the room. Even if he hadn't, he would know that no one sleeps with such extraordinarily tense unhappiness. My muscles jerk, as if I will leap up, but are useless. Quickly, he gets on top of me, holding my wrists in his strong fists. He does not have a light touch, and I will bruise. I try to fight him. I always try to fight him. But my body only wants to be still. It is tired all the time and hurts less when it is still. He is not such a big, heavy man, but he seems to be made of muscle, like a lean and nasty dog. He laughs at my wriggling. I am the fish and he is the fisherman.

This is his ritual. Not a ritual like prayer, but a ritual like sacrifice, like the ancient bloodletting of the smaller animals. Did they bleat like I bleat, when they were bound and saw their futures?

The first day, I fought so frantically that he slammed me against the wall and I had bruises down my back. Mohamed was away. That was when the pain began, the aching. Now the landlord feels bold: it is enough if Mohamed is at work, and he never worries about leaving marks. Somehow there is still the terrible sharp pain, of this thing which is not even fucking. Somehow I am always weak and full of tears, like a useless sac of liquid, waiting, waiting, to burst and flow. He sweats while I cry, the sweat almost a complaint, as if it is hard work for him. Today he is rough and angry.

He knows that I am ashamed and will never tell. He may even know how this shame began when I left my family and extends like a metastasizing tumor south from my heart.

"Don't even try to struggle," he says, his shiny face close to mine. "We both know you are too weak. The word is all over town of your strange illness."

He yanks me from the bed with the quick pull of weeding. My bruises will be green like weeds and the pain stringing down my muscles like rot striking roots. I have taken half the comforter with me, in my fist. My whole life is leaking out of me, in drips. The color has bleached out of the walls, the sheets, the curtains.

The front door opens and Mohamed calls my name, gently, as he whispered it the previous night: rippling with a love that like the love of my parents will surely expire at the sight of a soul, so full of holes in a consuming sea. He comes to the doorway and stands, a picture of my own horror, in an ashen frame.

He wails and the sound goes over me like a wave and I am under water. The landlord cowers and whimpers. He is a coward in the face of what he cannot control. So are all men. The dog is off the cat but the cat does not feel better. I close my eyes. But women...

I wake in the sickly and yellow evening. Cushions are propped around me, so I might mistakenly think I am sleeping on a cloud. Mohamed has begun packing: my things, his things, in confusion. My nylons dangle from one side of a suitcase, his socks, the other. The bathtub will not come with us, unless it can learn to walk on its own. It is essential to walk on one's own. I'm afraid that it will not come.

Mohamed is bowed at the window, a low form on his shabby rug. The voice of the muezzin comes over the valley and pauses at our square of light. "Praise Allah, Allah, Allah," Mohamed sings softly, as if in response. His voice is penitent and sad. It blends and is lost in the customary swelling sadness of the muezzin. "The All-Merciful, Merciful, Merciful."

His face is taut with the bitterness of prayer.

I remember the previous night. Mohamed's bare skin as sweet as honey.

"Marry me," he said.

And he thought it was pain that made me cry.

Spaceman from the Eastside

Ada Limón

Three quarters of a foot
typically lie between
the average car seats,
where your hand sometimes falls,
where the stick-shift stands aloof.

I like to call it space.
I named it after you.

Three quarters of a mile
across a wet metal bridge
with a statue tied up
in origami cranes, I sometimes
stop before crossing.

Even two halves of a whole
are suspended when smoke
beats up against itself and we stay
silent. Space between my belly
and my spine. Space between
finishing this drink
and starting the next.

From five o'clock in the evening
when the light is almost gone
and the cold is settling in colder
on to the time early when I wake
and ice linoleum floors remind me
that it is winter and this is a tomb,

I like to call it space
because I've named it after you.

Mother Dream

William Greenway

I'm asleep in my old bed
when I'm wakened by ghosts—
the covers have risen above me
and twisted into white shapes
in the dark. It's static
from the TV screen
in Mother's room.
She's broadcasting
one of her moods.
She comes in weeping—
two of her old friends
have died. I stand
to hold her clumsily,
her tears wetting my T-shirt.
This never happened in life,
and she had no friends.

I go back to bed
and watch for a while
the blue light from her room
flickering in the hall,
as once again my covers rise
and twist into shapes,
like handkerchiefs at a funeral.

Services Rendered

Rosalind Lieberman

"Your father can't stay here," I'm told.
"He walks the hall without his pants.
Leaves his door open, stove flame on.
He'll cause a fire, kill us all."
It's noon, a hot mid-August day
I come straight from the airport,
Find my meticulous father
Smelling of urine and excrement.
"*Mamalleh*, put on the light,
it's dark in here," he says.
I lead him to the toilet,
help him shower. He hides his
nakedness. "It's a disgrace,
what's happening to me."
I never heard him cry before.
He weeps without tears, dry barks
of helpless rage, harsh ragged sobs.
I help him dress, give him a shave,
a bowl of soup, a Kaiser roll.
The doctor could be daddy's brother—
blue eyes and even whiter hair.
He says (as gently as he can)
"The trouble is behind the eye."

Wire

Janice Robertson

In Beulah that day, Stepchild did something he never had before. Normally, to get anesthetic, he would unlock the back doors of vet practices at night as easily as he might unlatch a dog kennel or a hen house. He would steal one or two vials of Detomidine at a time and no more clean needles than he needed for one procedure. He kept suspicion down across the region that way, and also kept the DVMs to unsophisticated locks on their doors, latches that left a half inch of air between the jamb and the door so a knife could be inserted through the crack to lift the hook off its eye. But this day, Lou Bracken had called him without the usual notice, and Stepchild knew a horse would not be able to tolerate the pain of the wire up his ureter without anesthetic.

That day, behind the Beulah Veterinary Clinic, the girl had started screaming as soon as Stepchild picked the bloodstained bandages from the dumpster. She screamed louder when he wrapped them around her head, and she tried to claw them off of herself. The bandages were not brown with dried blood, but bright and damp with it. With his large hand, he pressed the bandages to her forehead and busted into the Beulah Vet Clinic waiting room, the little girl in his arms. A woman sat with her German shepherd. Startled, the dog barked and lunged at the screaming girl, choking himself with the chain around his neck, and hauling his owner out of her seat.

Stepchild addressed the receptionist, a young woman in a white smock who had dropped the phone when the girl and Stepchild entered.

"Please. Please. Give me anything to help her before we get to a hospital. Where is the nearest hospital?"

Again, the little girl tried to pull the bandages off, but the father grasped both her hands in one of his.

"I hit her with my car and I had some bandages in my first aid kit, but you've got to give me more. Please give me something to soak up all this blood."

The receptionist ran back into the examination room, and Stepchild with his girl followed her. The vet—white-haired with red suspenders under his white lab coat—stood still at the girl's screaming. A litter of snow-white kittens crawled over each other on the steel table.

"Move!" Stepchild cried. "Please! Bandages or anything bulky enough to compress this wound."

The vet spun around, opening his top cabinets. He took down three boxes of sterile gauze, ripping the cardboard apart to get at the rolls. He unwound the gauze and moved to wrap it around the soaked bandage pressed to the girl's forehead. But with his free hand, Stepchild grabbed the wad from him.

"More," Stepchild said. With his fingertips he pressed the fresh white gauze into the bright blood beneath, hoping it would seep through. "Don't you have more?"

"In the back. There's more in the back," said the receptionist, and she disappeared past the waiting area with the doctor close at her heels.

The girl had stopped screaming. She snuffled softly and watched the kittens on the table. Stepchild mashed his fingertips more forcefully against his daughter's forehead and cradled her in his other arm. He flung open a cabinet. Swabs, culturettes, Detomidine. He liked Detomidine for its fast-acting effects and pocketed the small vial. A kitten spilled off the edge of the examining table. He heard the hard running of the doctor and the receptionist returning, and he concealed the white, bloodless gauze wrapped around the bloodstained layer of bandages with his broad arm. He shifted the contents of the cabinet around to search for another vial of Detomidine. There were none. He quickly closed the cabinet door.

The vet, fury in his eyes, stopped breathless at the door of the examining room. He held out a stack of towels. "Get her out of here! Go! Take U. S. 31 south about 50 miles until you see the sign."

And Stepchild rushed out of the waiting room with his daughter and only enough horse tranq to sedate a 60-pound dog or lamb.

The 1968 Pontiac Catalina strayed over the white line of Orchard Highway, dipped into the ditch, then heaved back out. Stepchild held the wheel with his strong arms. He struggled against the force of the wheel, his rolled-up white shirtsleeves flashing with each jerk of his shoulder. The front right tire piece flapped against the road, rolled up under the wheel well, and then flapped out again like a tongue.

The tire was blown; most of the rubber had blasted away a few yards back, but Stepchild had kept going.

"We can't wreck the rim, Porkchop. We have a long drive ahead of us tonight. We're going to see the ferries," he told his daughter.

The little girl sat in the front bench seat alongside her father and wiped the blood clean off her bangs and forehead and eyebrows with a sterile alcohol pad. "It didn't really hurt, but I screamed good," she said.

"Yes, you did, Porkchop," the father answered. "You screamed like a good girl. And you're not afraid of the bandage anymore like a good girl." On the back seat, its green cloth covered by plastic, lay blood-soaked gauze bandages, and next to those sat a wadded pile of unwound white gauze and a stack of folded white towels.

"Now we can do the other horse," said the girl as she tightened the elastic band of the ponytail high on her head. She rubbed her pant legs. "It's hot, but I don't stick to the seat because of my jeans."

Stepchild was not a vet, but he had gone through two years of veterinary training at the technical college up north in Marquette. Only a few horse owners knew of him, and they called on him when they wanted the insides of their horses examined without the cost and risk of exploratory surgery. Stepchild charged $125 for every internal examination he performed on a horse. He had a limited collection of equipment: an endoscope without a video monitor, and a twitch for strapping around a horse's upper lip to control it instead of anesthetic. Rarely, Stepchild used horse tranq, and when he did it was because he had taken the risk to steal it. He was useful to horse owners mostly because he could search a horse's cavities with his endoscope for much less money than a fully accredited DVM, and most of the time he didn't find anything, so there was no need for a follow-up visit from the professional. And when the horse owners did need to call out the veterinarian with his brand new endoscope and video monitor and surgical skill, they knew they weren't wasting their money because Stepchild had already confirmed a problem. Because of this, the horse owners around the area—from Cadillac to Manistee to Onekama—kept quiet about Stepchild. They paid his $125 fee even when he found nothing malignant or foul in their horses. They didn't ask where he got his equipment, and none of them spoke a word to their regular DVMs about Stepchild, even if the DVMs complained that they had found their clinic door latches off their hooks and undone again and two or three vials of tranquilizer missing from their supply.

Without the video monitor to let him actually see inside the animal, Stepchild had developed a sense of blind feel, a feel for lesions on the bronchial tree, blockages in colons, clutches of worms in tracheas; one time he removed holiday tinsel from the duodenum of a two-year-old mare. He knew, when the retrieval forceps crunched through what felt like a chicken bone in a trachea, that the horse had a web of cancer in its throat. He knew when to push further, through foreign matter, and when to stop, to readjust the path of the scope so as not to tear a membrane or puncture healthy tissue. Stepchild kept his endoscope airtight: the bending rubber was without holes or wrinkles; the angulation cables were firm; the distal tip was quick to respond to any movement of the angulation control knobs. The only problem was that the stainless steel grasping and retrieval mechanisms were dull and much less nimble than when he had stolen the scope from the veterinary hospital in Cadillac five years back, the same year his daughter was born, and the same year he began stealing anesthesia and sterilizer and cleaning solution from DVMs across northern Michigan.

And the same year his wife had left him. She'd left without any following word, but Stepchild knew she'd taken the Greyhound from Cadillac to Detroit to get a job at a peep show. He knew she'd choose some upscale joint where men paid ten dollars to enter a closed booth and after a few minutes the partition would lift to reveal snatches of his wife's body on the other side. The partition would tease back down after a few more minutes. His wife had often talked of "dancing" professionally. To her, stripping was dancing and she talked of it as some girls talk of one day landing a spot in the Joffrey Ballet. Mornings, when Stepchild came down for breakfast, she would be straddling one of the kitchen chairs, shimmying her shoulders, her movements sharp, as if rehearsing a routine. And she wouldn't stop when he entered the kitchen, the stovetop cold, the toaster smoking with Pop Tarts. There were no legitimate strip clubs in northern Michigan, only deep woods shacks Stepchild had heard about where women took down their halter-tops in exchange for beer or Schnapps.

Sometimes Stepchild couldn't clean the scope properly for lack of solution. And now, after years of improper care, he knew his endoscope could no longer serve him. This would be his last examination. He needed the money to get him to Charlevoix, to sustain him and his daughter until his first paycheck arrived from the ferry company. He had heard of an island further north off Charlevoix, Beaver Island, where ferries ran twice a day. He knew how to repair diesel engines; he'd built the engine of his first car. And in a few years when his daughter was old enough to know how to make change, she could collect ticket money. In the meantime, she'd stay by his side, watching him; he wanted her to learn some work before her hands lost their childish clumsiness, so they could grow deftly into the skills of a trade.

The little girl clanked the metal parts of her lap belt together, snapped them fastened, then pressed the button to free the two straps. She held the metal parts in separate hands, twirling them in circles by their limp straps. She licked one of her thumbs, squinted her eye, and held the thumb up, aimed out the window, above the horizon line cut by the tops of pear trees, up to the blue sky. "*Sun down, you better take care,*" she sang at the setting sun.

"It's a flashing tongue," she said, holding up one of the buckles for her father to see. Her hand made a fist around the alcohol wipes.

The buckle was orange from the reflection of the sun, and she tilted it so the glare skipped over his face and neck and the white of his shirt. She stood in her seat and rubbed the smooth metal over the patches of whiskers on his cheek. His arms and shoulders braced the steering wheel. The girl walked back over to her side — her blue canvas tennis shoes denting the plastic seat cover — and looked over the dashboard to try to see the split tire.

"It goes *thwap, thup. Thwap, thup,*" she said.

"Sit down and drop those wipes." The father slapped his little girl's behind, and the steering wheel jerked to the right; once more the car swayed over the white line. The little girl sat down, and with her lips pressed together she looked at her father. Past him, out his window, she saw the horses.

"There are the horses for the needle, Daddy," she said.

Stepchild saw a girl older than Porkchop standing motionless by the red barn, her hand around the wire fence. A Palomino stood next to her, straddling the ground, his back legs spread, his penis hanging. The horse drew in his back legs, then again struck them out; still no stream of urine to the dirt. The girl's fingers unclasped the wire fence stiffly, as if released, and she tripped and fell backward.

Next to the barn were a manure pile and a hitching post. A man in a heavy brown suit and hat appeared from the barn. He said something to the girl and she got up from the dirt.

Stepchild stopped the car at the side of Orchard Highway. The little girl sat down in her seat and pulled one of her father's heavy flannel shirts from the back of the car. She settled it about her shoulders as an old woman drapes a cardigan without putting her arms in the sleeves. She threw the pink alcohol pads on the floor next to the bloodstained bandages.

Stepchild said, "I'll be back, Porkchop. This one might take a while, so lie down and go to sleep."

The little girl lay down on the plastic-covered seat and shut her eyes tightly. The father grabbed his metal toolbox from the backseat and locked all four of the doors. He crossed Orchard Highway to the barn and horses.

The man in the brown suit stood by the hitching post. He called out, "Stepchild?"

Stepchild answered, "Yes."

"Hal Stricken. Lou called you out here as a favor to me. I'm one of his boarders. My girl and me have been waiting for you most of the afternoon, since I left the office. This is my girl Maeve," the man in the brown suit called back from the hitching post. "I see you got some trouble up there."

His girl stood next to him in a baby blue shirt with pearlized snaps and jeans and stiff cowboy boots, the toes and heels of which were trimmed with silver. She had short brown hair. She held her palm up, as if to drain away the pain, and Stepchild saw her burn from the electric fence.

"I had to tag back up to Beulah and get some anesthetic, then the tire blew on the way down here. Lou up at the house?" The white frame house stood back in the pine trees, beyond the barn. A fallow field, white with sand, lay between the pines and the barn.

"No, checked earlier," Stricken answered. "You got a light to change that tire with? By the time you get done with the horse, you'll be out of daylight."

Stepchild shifted his toolbox to his other hand and looked at the horse. Its penis still hung out from its sheath. Its back legs were no longer spread, but close together with one hoof raised up at the tip, the horse's weight on its sturdier leg. The knees bulged with arthritis.

"You ride this boy?" Stepchild asked.

"Copper don't go fast, but I take him around the yard," answered Maeve. "I take him around like the barrel racers." In the field beyond stood two rusted oil drums.

"She doesn't ride him," Stricken answered. "She's too afraid to ride him. She just comes out here and brushes him all day, combs out the tangles in his tail." Stricken reached for the horse and ran his hand along the light orange rump.

"I ride him like the barrel racers," Maeve said quietly.

Stepchild saw the western saddle and bridle on the dirt next to the hitching post. The horn, the pommel, the cantle, and the stirrup leather—most every piece of leather—were covered with silver trim. The leather was not yet flexible or worn, but as rigid as it must have been when it came in the mail from the Sears catalogue.

"Why did you call me out here today?" Stepchild asked. He knew why, but he wanted to hear the man say it.

"He's hanging all out there," said Stricken, irritated.

"The boy can't piss?"

"No," said Stricken.

"When was the last time you saw this boy take a piss?" asked Stepchild.

"I don't know. My girl isn't out here but on weekends, and I'm out less. Lou was the one who called me up and said I'd better get somebody out here."

"Did you turn the fence off?" Stepchild asked.

"Yes," answered Stricken.

Three more horses stood behind the wire fence in the shadow of the barn, all dark bays. Two swished their tails in the third one's face.

"Well, turn it back on so the others don't break through. What's Lou going to do if he comes home to these others broke free?"

"My girl keeps shocking herself," said Stricken. "We have to leave it off or else she gets burned. Show him your burn, honey."

Maeve stepped closer to Stepchild with her upturned palm. It looked bruised instead of burned; a singed black line as slim as the wire ran across the center of the palm.

"Quit grabbing the fence wire," Stepchild said.

"I don't grab it," Maeve said, smiling at the attention. "I brush along it, forgetting, and the pulse pulls my hand on." Her hand didn't drop, as if she wanted him to examine it.

Stepchild laid his toolbox on the dirt. "Halter Copper and hitch him to the post." He brought out of his toolbox a twitch and syringe. For this one, he'd need the Detomidine. He hooked the flat chain loop of the twitch under Copper's upper lip and quickly twisted it tight with the attached stick. The horse's eyes grew large and his long yellow incisors showed as Stepchild held the stick of the twitch high and twisted it once more to tighten the chain, lifting the upper lip off the teeth.

"Hold this," he ordered Maeve. Maeve took the stick end of the twitch and held fast. Her burned hand hung at her hip.

"He don't like this," Maeve said. She stood on tiptoe as the horse bobbed his head high, and the chain's twist slackened.

Stepchild wrapped his broad hand over Maeve's and jerked the horse's head down, the tension of the chain now crumpling the upper lips, scrunching them down like wadded velvet over the teeth. "Keep his head down, then. Hold it tight. Make him think about the pain."

"I'll turn the fence on," Stricken said, and he turned for the barn.

Stepchild reached under the horse's belly, and quickly, as if throwing sand on a fire, he swabbed the tip of the horse's penis bright red with antiseptic. He cast the bright swab to the ground and stamped it into the dirt. Stepchild heard the electric fence wind up and drone; he inhaled the dry metal air. Copper swished his tail and tucked a hind leg inward.

"Can I let go of his lip now?" asked Maeve.

"No," answered Stepchild. "Hold him extra tight. Give him another twist on the chain."

Maeve turned the handle of the twitch; the chain on the upper lip tightened and the horse flung his head up once more, but this time Maeve, with her slim arm, yanked it back down.

Stepchild stuck a syringe into the glass vial of clear liquid. He drew the plunger up, pooling the anesthetic into the hollow barrel.

Stepchild ran his hand along the spine of the horse as he moved his way from the withers back to the hindquarters. He stopped, slipping his hand off the backbone, down between the stifle and the sheath. He felt the smooth damp fold, and swabbed it with the alcohol wipe. He dug the needle through the skin.

The rubber bulb of the syringe hit the Luer-lock tip. "Relax him a twist now," he told Maeve, and he withdrew the needle.

He picked up the endoscope, removed the insertion tube.

"Is that pipe for plumbing?" Maeve asked.

He didn't answer her. He attached a fine flexible wire covered with rubber in place of the pipe-like insertion tube.

"Stricken," he called. "I need you out here."

At the white frame house, lights went on. Stepchild saw Lou's wife at the window.

Stricken emerged from the barn before Stepchild finished his words, standing with his legs apart and his hands on his hips, as if he had known he would be summoned. Sweat ran down the sides of his face from underneath his hat.

"I need you to mind his hindquarters," said Stepchild. "Keep him still. Keep him from swinging from side to side."

Stricken walked to the horse and spread the fingers of both hands on the horse's rump, his brown suit jacket draped against the horse's coat. His head stuck up over the horse; he looked toward the hill, to the Pontiac Catalina barely visible in the fading light, and the black bank of pear trees beyond it.

"You're going to need a ligh…"

The horse buckled his back legs as Stepchild drove in the wire.

"Twist him another turn," Stepchild ordered Maeve. She dug the chain around the lip once more and held the twitch with both hands.

The horse swung his back end, ramming Stricken against the hitching post.

"Goddamn you," Stricken said to Stepchild. "Goddamn it."

"Is that what you want? For the boy to do you like that against the post?" asked Stepchild. "Brace your weight against him. Keep your hands flat on his rump."

Stricken pushed the horse off of him, and its back end swung out from the hitching post. He pushed his jacket sleeves up over his white shirtsleeves. He propped the butts of his palms against the horse's ribs. He stiffened his elbows, and trenched his heels into the dirt, bending one knee as a runner does before the start of a race. The top of his hat dropped to meet the horse's belly.

The horse was still again, except for the swish of its tail. Stepchild probed the wire further. Maeve held the twitch tightly.

"Kidney stones," said Stepchild. "They're in the ureters and probably the bladder." In one long pull he dislodged the wire.

Stricken lifted his head off the horse's back. "You're done?" he asked.

Stepchild wiped the wire with sterilizer and remantled the insertion tube.

"Aren't you going to remove them?" asked Stricken.

"Relax the twitch," Stepchild told Maeve.

She untwisted the chain and rubbed the horse's upper lip. It bobbed its lip against her palm as if scratching an itch.

"I can't remove them. I don't have enough anesthetic to keep him numb," Stepchild answered.

"Well, go get some," said Stricken.

"Get someone out here tomorrow. This boy is in pain and he needs those stones taken out." Stepchild coiled the endoscopic wire and placed it in the bottom of his toolbox.

"That's what you're supposed to do," said Stricken. "That's why we had you come out here."

"I just come to diagnose the problem," Stepchild said. "I'm sure Lou told you my fee is one hundred twenty-five dollars cash." He took the twitch out of Maeve's hand.

"I could've told you he had a problem," Stricken said. "I don't need someone to come out here and for one hundred and twenty-five dollars tell me he has a problem."

"My fee is one hundred twenty-five dollars cash," repeated Stepchild. He lifted his toolbox. He couldn't see across the horse to Stricken's face, but saw his shoulders and hat in dim outline.

"Dad," Maeve said, "my hand hurts."

"To hell with you," said Stricken. "I won't pay you anything unless you remove those stones. Who the hell are you?"

Stepchild ran his hand along the horse's spine and walked around behind the animal. He passed Stricken and climbed the dark hill to his daughter.

"Who are you?" Stricken called out again.

At the highway, Stepchild turned around and saw Stricken leading the horse into the lighted yard of Lou's house, his hand grasping the strap of the halter, his daughter following behind him.

Stepchild opened the car door and light flooded onto his little girl. She lay on the seat, sleeping, her legs bent to her chin, the flannel shirt around her small shoulders.

Stepchild picked up the flashlight from the seat. "Get up, Porkchop," he said. "Get up and hold the light for me." He shook her ankles.

The little girl woke. She sat up and put her arms in the sleeves of the shirt and slid across the seat to climb out the driver's side door.

"Will we go see the ferries now?" she asked.

Stepchild opened the trunk of the car and its light popped on. He removed the jack. "I need the light over here," he said as he walked to the front right tire.

The little girl followed behind him. She held the flashlight in both of her hands, aiming the beam at the broad back of his white shirt. The red plastic of the flashlight projected what looked like a red-hot coil onto the center of his shirt. The daughter didn't say anything. Her hair had fallen out of its ponytail. She wiggled the light over her father's shirt as he lay down on the dirt, his head underneath the car, his hand feeling for the notch on the car's frame to insert the jack head.

"You look like a movie," she told him as she shook the light from side to side over his boots and trousers.

"Underneath here," Stepchild instructed her, pointing. "Get the light under here."

The daughter crouched to the gravel and shone a steady light up the belly of the car. A snap sounded as Stepchild's hands locked the jack head into the frame's notch.

He stood up, the red coils still flashing over his shirt and legs, and looked out to the pear orchard.

Porkchop shone her light into the trees: dim gleams of yellow on the heavy pears.

"What do you see out there, Daddy?" she asked.

Stepchild picked up his endoscope and gripped it tightly.

"I looked him in the face," he said.

"Who?" She shone the light into his eyes.

"At the vet's face. I looked him straight in the face to make sure we'd have to leave tonight," Stepchild said.

"Will we go see the ferries tonight?" Porkchop asked.

"Yes, we're going to the ferries tonight," he said.

And he cast the endoscope into the dark trees and turned to reach for the spare tire.

Letter to Grover from Billings

Fredrick Zydek

Dear Laura: This road is long as life.
There have been sweeps of Mack-trucks
and valleys enough to lose the senses.
Everywhere I breathe freeways and dirty
rest rooms bloom like monsters from the id.

All the way to Vantage I worried
about the petrified trees waiting
for us to carry them home in our pockets,
and dreamed of Moses waking to find
Egypt masting her sails and rigs

against the rising sea between us.
A row of snow topped pines
stood silent as Nuns all the way
through Missoula. Some caught
what there was left of the sun in little

eyes enough to warm both mind and brow.
One big surprise is that Billings stays
open all night. One can buy an apple
or an Eve within walking distance of this
Motel. There are even boys for sale

across from the all night book store.
They wave promises of tempests
and jockstraps just like in Seattle.
Some even have the balls to go in drag.
I've drunk a second bottle of summer

wine, and caught my reflection full
of frown and furrow and time. I'm
locked in the sudden worry there will never
be enough of what waits in the spaces
between to sustain the rest of the journey.

Letter to Blaski from Brunswick

Fredrick Zydek

Dear Steve: Ever notice how some poems
want to be prayed? There is a homing spirit
to such poems. They want to make their nests
at the core of mysteries I don't even know
how to write about. Pity me. I have never
been bright enough to understand these things.

The older I get, the more I seem to retreat
into a vast carelessness about the upkeep
of everything except my lawn. Strange how
mowing has become a religious act for me.
I spend more time with my yard than I do
any person I have ever known. Is that maturity?

Sometimes I think I was born to go among
the unnoticed. The retarded boys I brought
into my home so many years ago have become
my closest friends. Even the dogs we lug
between the city and this farm were all
abandoned and abused by someone.

I am drawn to the weightless and things of no
color. And for all the places there are
to be on earth, I have come to prefer a small slice
of geography no one visits except me and a few
squirrels. It takes me most of the summer to see
what others claim is not there. I can prove it.

I hope someday you can put aside your fears
of returning to Nebraska and come for a good
visit. We can spend a few days alone at the farm.
We will talk about the sacred pleasures
of gathering, and I will walk you to a place
where poems wait to be picked from thin air.

Commuting

Nick Hundley

Red chimneys cough blue smoke.
"Lord knows which tree this fell from,"
She whispers to each fire hydrant,
obliviously tossing peelings in the path
of a pedestrian wearing a three-piece suit.
The Thursday morning air echoes of pastries
and dogs eagerly waiting behind glass doors.
The patients walk to the candy store,
their gowns flapping in the breeze.
Those who got no sleep last night
buy plane tickets for a different hemisphere
daydreaming of gondolas descending
through timber. The children
slowly rise from their tiny beds
and use the furniture for kindling.

Listening For Worms

John P. Baum III

I walked into the house but didn't make it past the foyer. The divorce papers, unfolded, signed, and tucked under a vase full of dried flowers, were sitting on a small coffee table. I put them in my back pocket and walked out the door.

Across the street from Chatham's house, the Tanner boys were playing basketball. I stared as they hurled the ball at the goal countless times and I thought how their son-of-a-bitch father needs to show them something about the game. They finally turned around to face me as I stood in the street with the carton in my left hand, sloshing half-full with vodka and juice.

"You boys got a shovel?" I yelled it slowly so as not to slur any words. They disappeared into the garage and returned, running across the street, each holding one end of the shovel like a mobile limbo bar. Thomas, the older one, handed me the shovel and the younger one shuffled his feet. "Are you and Mrs. Chiles still fighting?" he said.

"Her name is Ms. Rogers," I said. No such thing as personal or private business existed in this neighborhood.

"Shut up, Morgan," said Thomas, the older one.

"We're doing fine. Ya'll want to help an old man out?" They nodded and I said I'd call them when I needed them.

I worked gradually, digging for hours. The hole was three feet wide and five feet deep. I measured. The beer helped out a lot; June with no breeze and the dirt, dry and dusty, lodged under my fingernails and seeped into my lungs. Using my shirt, I blew my nose several times, producing a thin blob speckled with black. I hated to dig a hole in the yard that my neighbors had once compared to the fairways at Augusta National but I knew I had to. It was still my yard. Chatham did nothing with it, yet I knew that somehow this would evoke pity, rage, embarrassment, or something at least, that would reach her.

The Tanner boys gave in with smiles when I offered them forty dollars. I settled myself into the hole, standing with my hands by my sides and eyes closed as they shoveled the dirt back in around me. "Pack it tight," I said, "maybe use some water." The dirt cooled me, starting with the feet; when it hit waist-level Morgan brought the hose over and sprayed water around me. I watched the water disappear almost as quickly as it struck the parched soil. I fit perfectly into the hole, smiling as the two boys, triumphant in their sweat, packed the last of the dirt beneath my chin and dribbled water from the hose, forming a slight mound around my neck. I could bend my head forward and touch ground level with my stubbled chin. "Perfect," I said, and they went home.

Saturdays are busy at the grocery store, and I knew Chatham would be at work until four. I sobered up and became thirsty; my tongue felt thick and coarse in my mouth and my throat throbbed for any cool liquid.

Nevertheless, I was proud. This took courage and confidence and I was really *doing* something about my problem. I felt the time was right to quit bitching. Hiding on the pine-flanked fairways at the club on an industrial mower, away from the real city and the yards and the people with whom I used to associate had gotten me nowhere. I talked to my boss, Mike, a passive man with no kids and no wife, and he always shrugged and tried to change the conversation. My friends from my days with Chatham had lurked back into the periphery of my world, becoming nothing more than names I knew and people I would run into occasionally. My livelihood flourished with my landscaping company and when that went under, so did everything else. Now I had made a concrete decision, determined to set things straight.

I began my career simply as a yardman which turned into a landscaping company: Chiles Landscaping. That actually went well until people's dogs started dying. The powder I used to kill slugs in gardens was doing it. It was the best kind to use because it wiped out slugs but did not touch the worms; they could crawl in it all day, sucking it up with the dirt but it wouldn't harm them a bit. And gardens need worms. The dogs licked the powder and died. I had used the stuff with every job. People complained and I ended up paying out the ass. My need for a divorce quickly followed.

After being owner of a company, I had to step down the ladder to groundskeeper's assistant at the Bamberg Country Club. Bills are bills and they have to be paid.

So I couldn't do any real yard work besides driving the tractor-sized lawn mower across the broad fairways at the country club, and that alleviated none of the pressures of all my problems that appeared immediately after I signed the divorce papers. The trouble was now I wasn't sure. In fact, looking at the yard, I knew I didn't want the divorce. My problems: If you lined them up against a wall, like soldiers at attention, you would have a disciplined regiment of well-trained, man-sized thorns trained to tear into my sides with exactness, spilling not guts like most people have, but a barrage of more problems forced down, compacted tightly below my stomach by the sheer volume of newer problems.

I heard the car door slam and I shut my eyes and began to call her name. I didn't hear her approach over my voice and I began coughing and spitting when I felt the dry skitter of dirt in my face. I opened my eyes and looked up, raising my eyebrows. My mind wandered and for a brief second I realized this was how a small dog sees humans. Her voice whined as if she were speaking to a child.

"Pulliam, what've you done?"

"I don't think I'm ready. I know I signed first but I don't think I'm ready."

"Too late. Didn't notice the date on the papers, did you? It's final." The divorce papers, however, were still in my back pocket. She kicked an empty beer can that succinctly rang with a dull *tin* as it bounced off my forehead.

"Two months I waited for you to sign those things. It gave me time to think," I said.

"You could've already gone, moved away and forgotten," she said and kicked another can, this one deflecting off my left cheek. "L.A., San Francisco, why not?"

"Jesus, what is going on in your head? Look at me. At what I've done to myself," I said. I nodded my head as best I could for emphasis.

"I know what you've done. You killed dogs and your career went down the toilet. Now you sit on lawn mowers at the country club and cry."

"What do you expect? I lost my business. I need something."

"You wanted the divorce and I agreed, only slower. I actually thought about it, you didn't. You just relied on your nanosecond intuitive decisions that usually get you screwed anyway."

"It's the yard, baby, I can't lose her." She laughed and said I needed a shrink.

I agreed and stared straight ahead at her feet, the smallest I had ever seen.

"Kill me," I said. "Kill me now. I'm in my element. *My* yard. It was all me."

"Who dug the hole, yard guy?"

I had gone over that yard on my hands and knees, pulling weeds too young to reach above grass level. Days I spent on bush placement alone. I was sober now, my throat hurt and I could feel a thin layer of dust on my face. I looked around and the sight crushed me. The grass was halfway mowed and a riding lawn mower, covered with dust, sat in the shadows of a verdant magnolia. The gardenias were now pared down to almost nothing. The holly bushes sagged and the oak leaf hydrangeas, dwarfed by several weeds, looked destitute, left for dead in the nothing that used to be my proudest achievement.

"I'm telling you, Chatham, kill me. Run me over with the lawn mower. Now. It's a rider, it'll work." Another quick resolution that felt right.

We used to drink bourbon on Sunday nights after I had finished work for the day. It was always our best time together. The company took up most of my hours during the week and she worked on weekends. But Sundays we would sit and drink and listen. She truly appreciated the yard on those nights and I adored her appreciation.

She left me in the yard and brought me dinner before it got dark.

"Here you go, sweetie," she said, placing one of our good plates on the ground in front of me. Steak, potatoes, gravy, a side of A-1, and a cold import beer that she opened with a polished church key. It was a spread fit for the fourth of July. She smiled as she kneeled in front of me; she pulled a knife and fork from her apron and carefully quartered the steak, displaying it's slightly underdone insides towards me. My throat was dusty, burning for the beer; I stared and it remained immobile, sweating in the faint reds and yellows of the dry June evening.

It was impossible for me to look at my watch but I figured it was around seven. The food was close enough for me to smell it. I could feel the heat from the potatoes, but they were just out of reach of my mouth, no matter how much I squirmed or waggled my tongue for a hint of taste. As the sun set behind the trees, angled beams of natural light moved slowly across the plate making the steak, a gorgeous cut cooked to perfection, glisten in the faultlessness of its medium-rare pinkness. Of course the glisten lost its luster as the flies set in until, finally, a neighborhood dog trotted up to the plate, sniffed me a bit, then loped away with canine pride, after having eaten the carefully cut meat.

Now the true hunger set in, and I began to squirm but all my muscles felt dead. The same position and no movement for five hours, with dirt compacted tightly against every square inch of my body, had rendered me useless. I knew that if I did succeed in getting out of this hole alone, I would probably flop around, like a dying fish, trying to get the blood to flow again and the atrophy would lead to injury.

The dark had settled in and the only light on the yard came from a window in the den. It fell in front of me in a stretched rectangle. From that point, only the edge of the trees that lined our backyard was visible, and I imagined, almost hallucinated, a buck crashing through the wall of trees and turning my face to jelly with its hooves and antlers, an uncommon look of rage in the round dark eyes of the normally tranquil animal.

I hated those beasts more than weeds or dandelions. It took me two seasons to figure out how to prevent them from eating my plants, especially in a town like Bamberg that is surrounded by forests. I tried everything: soap shavings, skunk juice, perfume, little hotel soap bars hung strategically in panty hose, until I figured out the solution: piss. A hunter friend told me they hate the smell of human piss so I began to pee around the yard, mainly in the woods by the garden but that only lasted a few days. Then I started my program. Whenever working in the yard and I had to go, I relieved myself in a coffee can; with that supply I filled smaller soup cans and placed them on a perimeter I had drawn on a map of the front and back lawn. That took care of everything, and my wife hated it with all her being. She called it primitive, disgusting, and embarrassing.

I could see one of the cans, ten feet away on the edge of the yard, rusted and turned on its side. No more program, I thought, and the deer are probably regular visitors again. A familiar ticking sound caught my ear and I almost cried at the sound: the sprinkler system.

Water ran down my face and I savored every drop that fell on my tongue, the salt and grit from sweat and dirt mixed in, but I reveled in it as best I could. The light from the den went out and the yard was dark. The sprinklers went off soon but came back on again. Dammit, Chatham, I thought to myself, don't you know you never run the timer past midnight. That screws up the entire time configuration and you have to spend an hour resetting the damn thing. But then I knew that she didn't know how to set it. Had she gotten someone over here to do it for her?

The sprinklers compacted the dirt more than before and removing myself from the hole was completely out of the question; they finally went off for good and I guess I nodded off to sleep somehow because the next thing I knew, Gabe Tanner, father of the boys who buried me, stood over me laughing, holding two drinks.

"You pathetic bastard," he said. I wanted to explode out of the dirt, but I gritted my teeth and looked away. "My boys told me about this earlier. I figured it was one of your yard projects. Luckily, you're still here."

"Just enjoying the night," I said. My throat, despite the relief of the sprinklers, was dry and my voice was not much more than a croak. I couldn't look at him directly. Our relationship had always been one of flimsy neighborly politeness behind which brooded the concrete jealousy and disdain that goes along with unacknowledged yet definite competition. Of course Chatham and Sherry, his knockout wife, were always close, forcing Gabe and me to at least speak to each other in a small talk niceness that we both knew was fake.

"So how is everything going, Pulliam? You doing okay?" he asked. I didn't look. I knew he was smiling, his baked bean teeth glinting slightly behind the full beard.

"Viewing the world from this point of view changes things," I said.

"Withdrawals from landscaping? Had to become one with the soil again. I understand." He was laughing.

"That's right. One with the dirt. So how's things on your side of the street? Your yard still keeping up with the brown patches that you made so famous? I could've helped you out, you know."

"I just never wanted someone I know to do something that someone

I didn't know would do for half the price. "I used to see him walking around his yard as whomever he hired tried to appear busy. He seemed afraid to get himself dirty in the yard, but he always talked about how good everything looked on his side, pointing to a hedge or new plant somewhere. He knew nothing about seasonal enjoyment planting and everything he tried ended up wilted. Of course we all knew, the other neighbors and I, that his yard guy suggested other stuff, but Gabe insisted on his own flowers, when and where to plant them. I offered several times to help but he just laughed it off, blaming the unusually hot or cold climate.

"It didn't take much to persuade your boys to get themselves a little dirty," I said.

"Forty bucks. How do you think I paid for the Bourbon?" I looked up. "Booker's," he said, "the best. The kind that comes in the wooden box. Thirty-nine, ninety-nine at Mannie's." He smiled and placed one of the glasses in front of me. In almost a child's voice, he said, "Want a little nip?" I looked at the glass and waited for him to do it, whatever it was, to torture me. He loved it. He leaned down and put a straw in the drink; a crinkle straw that he bent towards me so I could actually take a sip if I just stretched. I looked up at him, waiting on the *coup de grace*. He simply smiled, and I looked back at the glass. Innocently, it sat there sweating and seemed the most perfect drink of all time. A chalice. I heard Gabe clear his throat and I looked up; his cheeks blew out with that low grumble which accompanies the hawking that precedes spitting. He leaned over and with skill and marksman-like accuracy, a pecan-sized lugey dripped from his mouth and splashed lightly in the glass. A few drops of the cold bourbon flowed over the edge and I watched with rage as they rolled slowly down the side and into the ground. He laughed again and said, "I'll leave that in case you want it."

When I woke up again, an early morning fog gave everything a softly pallid appearance that I knew and was comfortable with. Morning was always the best with its damp coolness that too quickly burned away with the sun. You didn't think about wanting to finish your work when it was this early. The tumbler, inches away from my face, was still full to the rim, with all the ice melted. The ingredients had separated and the top part of the drink was a fuzzy lightness which bled into the darker brown of the forty-dollar bourbon, now stale. The acrid scent hunkered strong on my nose. I breathed through my mouth so as not to smell it at all, and it was this breathing I was concentrating on when I heard the door slam.

I heard her soft, barefooted steps before I saw her. She came into view and kicked over the glass. Her eyes were puffy and she wore her silk bathrobe. Although not a morning person, I loved to see her wake up against her will and stumble around the house in the early morning. She bent down to pick up the tumbler and the plate on which the congealed potatoes were stuck and I caught a quick glimpse of her breasts as she leaned over.

"Good morning," I said.

"You're still here," she said, shaking her head. "Persistent."

"Gabe stopped by for a chat last night."

"I heard. Ya'll woke me up so I invited him in as he was leaving." She said this without looking at me.

"Have you seen his yard? It's crap."

"It's not the yard that I need. Why does it all come down to that with you?"

"Gabe hires out work and then tells them to do what he wants and it all ends up dying. Even the grass." I couldn't understand the man's stupidity.

"I said I invited him in," she said.

"He doesn't know the difference between a shelf-style and a stair-style berm. What's the point of even discussing him?"

"I don't know the difference," she said. This I didn't believe. All those mornings over coffee I explained to her what it was I was doing with the tulip bed she had started. She knew the difference.

"It's all in the way you dig," I said. She went back inside.

As the fog burned away, I watched birds as they would hop around and then stop, cocking their ears to the ground; they were listening for worms. I resisted the need to blink as a tiny wren hopped within a few feet of me. A few bounces towards and then one away and then a few more until she was less than six inches from my face. I didn't breathe. She cocked her head and suddenly pecked the ground twice and held a wriggling worm from her beak. For a moment, she looked directly at me before flying away, as the worm frantically contorted itself.

—◆—◆—

"I would have done this sooner, but you always told me it was bad to mow the lawn while the grass is still wet," said Chatham. The mower was in bad shape; dust caked the entire body and pale blue smoke rose from somewhere in the engine.

"I told you to sell that thing if you weren't going to use it," I said. The nose of the mower, a two-year-old rider, vibrated with power two feet away from me. It looked as big as a tractor.

Chatham was wearing a green surgical mask, but the crinkle in the corners of her eyes gave away her smile. My face felt taut in the direct sunlight and the dry hot rush of wind from the underside of the machine made me cringe. Flecks of dirt pecked at my face and I closed my eyes. The sound of the mower drifted away and circled around behind me, moving from the left to the right side of my hearing, steadying there for a moment before the rhythmic noise of the engine ceased completely. The back door opened, and I heard Chatham's voice in bits and pieces, peppered with laughter.

Minutes later, Gabe appeared from around the hedgerow by the back door. He held a small cooler in his right hand and a metal folding chair in the other. He said nothing and did not look at me as he set up the chair at the edge of the yard, pulled a beer from the cooler, opened it, took a sip, and settled in the chair with his feet stretched out in front of him, one over the other. I heard the door open and close behind me. The mower started up again and the sound moved to the right side of me and finally came into view. She was still wearing the surgical mask but she had changed into her only bikini: a tiny blue thing she wore on the beach during our honeymoon.

I tried to get myself out of the hole, but the dirt, packed tight around my legs, kept me from doing more than cramping up my calf muscles. My stomach was tight with hunger while the rest of me seemed numb and that scared me a bit. I was sure my face was scorched by this time. Chatham steered the mower on the edge of the yard, looking over the side occasionally to make sure she was running it even. I looked over at Gabe and he was staring at Chatham as well, until he looked over at me and winked, finishing off his beer.

She was doing it all wrong, against the natural grain of the grass and the tendency to which it normally grew. I knew this grass and how it flourished and the best ways to make it look like a perfectly manicured fairway in a professional golf tournament. It was back and forth and *not* the outline of a square, an outline that, with each pass in front of me, was shrinking the space between my face and the mower. Each time closer and closer until I felt the heat and the flecks of dirt. This was not at all the way I did it, not the way it was supposed to be done. I began to yell, my throat burning with strain and Gabe, in his chair with a beer in his hand, laughed. He seemed to be staring at the shriveling space of uncut grass between the machine and me. The yard on which I had perfected the art of landscaping before going commercial, the *original*, was going to die and I knew it. Then she quit her pattern and turned the front of the mower towards me; the machine convulsed as she put it in reverse and then backed up to the edge. It shook again as she changed gears and headed for me. Wrong, *wrong*. Now Chatham was ruining her own pattern, butchering a perpendicular line through her set design of a square. At least keep it consistent, I thought with rage.

Within seconds the mower hovered above me and then a bright flash of light as the front knocked my head back. A brief second gave me a quick shot of the sky and then back again with the dusty black a blur in my eyes inches away. The heat, tremendous now, came at me in thumps. The bright flash again and wetness on my forehead. The sound pulled away again and ceased. I saw myself in the yard. *In the yard*. I sunk beneath the surface and like an underground snake, tunneled down, all of my muscles in sync, propelling me down and then up again into a new yard, one untouched yet perfect. There were more, I knew. Their smell dried my sweat and peeled the caked dirt from my body instantly. The pristine feeling of a hot shower that follows a day at the beach was nothing compared to this. I could float in this new emotion.

And then it was all gone.

Gabe's howling laughter emerged from the noise of the motor, as if it were winding down slowly after centuries of atrophy; a seven-second process as the belts and fans gradually came to a halt. I opened my eyes to a bluish haze that hung over the yard. Chatham straddled the mower, still wearing the surgical mask.

I did not want, nor did I need, an answer for anything. No resolution at all because the effort was unsurpassed. Of this I was sure. Few men, on a planet packed with billions, would go to these lengths. I still had the papers in my back pocket and I knew *nothing* was final.

"He was like one of those dolls that you punch but can't knock down," said Gabe. "Fantastic." He was right. You couldn't knock me down. This yard was mine. Then Chatham walked over to Gabe and kissed him. I looked away and tried to size up the level of the new cut. I squinted at the grass and couldn't believe that she had actually cut the yard on level three. That was too high for Summer; everyone knows that.

Deception

E.G. Burrows

A shaker of wind spills brant.
Dice in a cup rattle
and tumble across velvet water
until the small geese group
and grow silent, wary
of one standing on shore, hands
in his pockets, cap over his ears.

Does he think that they have brought spring
with such chatter? Have they carried
any warmth from the marshes?
He turns his back on them.
He feels the wind at his back.
They are too few, they lack
the proper clamor, and now
the loud rain is all that matters.

Laissez-Faire

E.G. Burrows

It was a summer's day
and the ooze of lassitude
buttered the way for houseflies
with samples of incurable plague.

A sanitary mind
might have prevented the influx
of those intent on lapping
the last sweet sugar of plenty

out of greed,
or a need to be cast in bronze
like the tyrant on his pedestal,
hairy and wild-eyed.

But I let the clouds drift by.
The air was full of chicanery
and the happy throes of backhoes
trenching the arboretum.

Track of the World, the Cup Holds No Crow

George Kalamaras

The wind moves the way a boy drinks green tea.
All at once crows emerge from the gardener's belly,
the man (*what* man?) arrives on the train (*which* train?)
and begins to place wood shavings from his newspaper
into the bottom of the cup. Dandelions blossom
in the yard, in the field, among the gardener
and the crow. All the bellies (*what* bellies?)
of the world (*which* vowel?) begin to calm soybean
vibrations of the thorax acting like a crow
searching its wing for air. Searching the train
(*what* train?) for news (*which* food?), the man (*what* calm?)
drinks a cup of dandelion (tea?). All at once
a boy emerges from his belly, in the train, in the field,
among the tracks and snow (*what* snow?). It's cold,
and wind flowers down flakes of burnt white skin.
All the crows (*what* train?) of the belly (*which* shavings?)
ease up through the thorax like the slip of a tempered
voice. The bottom of the cup. Dandelions. Crow shout.
Search the cup for a tea leaf, souchong, and news
of the porcelain grip, the laying by Chinamen
(*which* thorax?) of the track.

A Bit of Music from the Lower Spheres of Enrique Lihn

George Kalamaras

> *Pain has nothing to do with pain.*
> —Lihn

Nada

To lie on your death bed—naked but for a feather covering your groin with blue peacock fire—proofing your final book of poems, remembering Kafka doing the same?

—❖—

tiene

To say *Te recuerdo* and not just mean *I remember you*, but *I recall how the world is doing absolutely nothing by dying to the inconvenience of one of Joseph Cornell's little boxes?*

—❖—

que

To wake at four in the morning with a sudden missing toe nail, not exactly sure which one, yet wincing for sleep into a cup of boiled milk like the transfigured Christ peering into the curls of either his mother Mary or his cousin Mary or the former prostitute Mary or a family friend named *Mary* or a country named *Chile*?

—❖—

ver

To be precisely nine words in Spanish and merely seven in English, said Enrique Lihn searching a mirror for the eighth and ninth pieces of chin stubble?

—❖—

el

    Those who are going to die, Enrique Lihn mused, *are going to die?*

—◆—◆—

dolor

    To say *como un cubo de aqua sucia* and not just mean *like a pail of dirty water,* but —more precisely —*we recommend lethal manuscripts that play the role of landscapes?*

—◆—◆—

con

    Come on, amigo. Let me out of this fucking poem so I can die in piece by bloody piece?

—◆—◆—

el

    Nicanor Parra wept at Lihn's bedside, inserting aniseed seeds into the nostrils of his fellow anti-poet, sobbing, *Now he is at rest, now we too can eat broiled monkfish and sunbathe in the sea-salt welling up from inside the cells of our poems imitating poems?*

—◆—◆—

dolor

    Enrique, while still ambulatory, confided one morning to the corner butcher that he wanted no elegy, only precisely nine lines as temporary footholds in a garden of sinking stones —*don't you mean ribs, Señor Lihn?,* the butcher asked, *a fardel of stinking baby back ribs?*

—◆—◆—

Nada tiene que ver el dolor con el dolor

    A bit of music from my lower spheres is all I ask, pleaded Lihn into the sound of swelling in the pleura of his left lung, *merely seven tones in English —one each for the letters of my first name, yet two shy of pain, in Spanish, having nothing to do with pain.*

The Only Thing

George Kalamaras

I believed they held the secret water
that would help me feed my father's blood.
My mother and new dad who loved me.
Bone gnawings in the sink. Hair clipped short.
Those *"We Were There..."* history books
at the French and Indian War, or with the Algonquin
swelling the banks and splitting the Wabash
hatchet-red. I tried and tried like a ranting rain.
I even slid slantwise on the lawn when I scuffed to school.
But when you're Greek you tend to smell grass
as conspiratorial basil
ready to flake off into the first truckload
of Albanian- or Turkish-bound hay that passes.

Blood is thicker than water, my Nono
from Zakynthos would say. He'd stand,
serape-wrapped, with shepherd staff
near the old pump house in Cedar Lake.
Indiana was how my mother, brother, and I lived
in the early years with grandparents.
He had no sheep. He had
built wooden arbors to support grapes
and hold wars he told
of how the Greeks could always tough it out.
Midnight invasions in Crete. Turkish knives in socks.
How savvy it was to sleep in the horse's belly.
Alexander razing all the way
to India through Afghanistan.
How in 1913, as a boy like me, he'd fish
by tossing dynamite over a cliff
into the Ionian, then dive
in, gathering basketfuls "when their white

bellies rose to the surface."
Water-logged lava. Infant skin.
Like anemic blood cells, the grapes
stung the wood. Year after year they tasted
good and stung the wood. Two days before *Christos
Anesti*. Good Friday—that's what it felt like

all week while waiting for Sunday
visitation, counting my life backwards
after nine when my father stopped calling.
There's no way to describe it. I won't try
to say it was all bad to lose your father
to another wife and kids. To your mother's
sudden husband. The kicking in his gut
was probably what did it—twelve Sundays,
Thanksgiving, Greek Easter, and two
weeks in August—like a prolonged tax
season, sluggish clock hands
perpetually trying to catch up.
Like bees in your bed. You know it's good luck,
yet you hear the buzzing below
as a swollen throat. There's really no way
to talk sense to them—any of them—
since they have their own paths to take:
great migrations from Kabul
to Isfahan, Isfahan to Oubangi,
Oubangi to Reunion, even
from Zakynthos and Salonika
to the court order between Indiana
and Illinois. They move by sound,
some secret noise charted by blood,
a migratory flinch moistened by the lung-
like larvae. You can try lying there
perfectly still each night, a cropped brown lawn
singed with rain, but the buzzing won't stop.
Like olive pit spin in a saucer,

several bites taken out
when they all went for the meat.

Born gnawings in the sink. Hives in red metal
awnings. Hair clipped to the length of rain.
Shepherd crook without sheep. Grapes on the damp.
The old pump house still drawing
up too much iron. None of it
makes sense if you stop searching the sheets
for entrails of bees. If you go down on
your luck and assume the rain
will sail into your harbor
one night by cloud-covered moon
and slit your throat. If you don't abandon
the buzzing at your feet and instead imagine
the entire weather from Kabul to Reunion,
desert parch back from the fertile Indus to Alexandria,
the settling of Indiana and Illinois
into horse blanket and beaver posts, into
Algonquin debt. Border skirmishes near the river
that make the washing of the Wabash—
though containing many years of hatchet hang
and rain, though still thinner, say,
than blood—the only thing that cleans.

Borrachitarme Voy

Paula Gunn Allen

It isn't as though anyone
listened much in those days—
in movies slinky post-War women wore
tight-woven soft black straw hats
lightly brimmed, alluring veiled,
and post-War girls wore shiny black patent leather shoes.
Inside their soles Buster boys and magic frogs
plucked promises that only Let's Pretend could keep.
Halcyon days of Ralston and Cream of Wheat
were not at all like those where everything up
for grabs goes tediously unresolved. Still
alfalfa fields nod quiet in the blaze of July sun,
and arroyos flood sudden violence down down
and never reach the wine-drunk sea.
Every season someone's brother drowns.

Infestation

Molly Hansen

There was a crack in the foundation of the house, and that's how they'd gotten in. That's what Jack said anyway. He'd read in a book from the library that a mouse could squeeze itself down to the thinness of a pencil. He bought some spackling compound and patched the crack, but that didn't help any with the mice that were already inside. Beth was the first to notice the droppings. She found them one morning on the kitchen counter, small, dark, and pointed at both ends. After a few days, there were gnaw marks, too—tears in the corners of cereal boxes, flour sacks, anything paper or cardboard. So they put all their food in Tupperware and made sure to wipe away their crumbs.

These were the only signs of the mice at first. But after a week or so, Jack and Beth started to see them. One would zip along one of the baseboards before disappearing behind a cupboard or inside a closet. They'd find them under the sink in the kitchen trash, too, rummaging for food. It didn't matter that they kept the trash sealed—they'd eat right through the plastic.

Once when Beth was up late reading, she heard a noise and looked down to see one staring up at her—like it was a dog or a cat that belonged there on the rug next to her bed. She wasn't frightened, only startled. It was tiny, not much bigger than her thumb, and grey with pink eyes, feet, and tail. It was there only for a few seconds, but long enough for her to make eye contact. She didn't tell Jack.

She was the one who insisted on buying "live" traps.

"We ought to at least give them a chance," she said.

"But they're leaving shit all over the house and ruining our food," Jack said. "And they make me jumpy. Just the thought of them creeping around. I want them dead."

"But you haven't even seen one."

"That makes it worse."

"Please get the live traps," she said. "For me."

"Fine," he said after a long breath. "For you."

Beth was watching the rain turn to sleet outside the living room window when she heard a shattering of glass in the other room.

"Goddammit," Jack said from the kitchen.

"What is it?" she said.

He was standing there, his hands covering his face, when she came through the doorway. It was just getting dark and she switched on the light. The coffee pot lay broken at his feet.

"Another one," he said, lowering his arms. "It just ran across the counter and down through one of the stove burners. I was making coffee, and Jesus, it scared the hell out of me."

"I'll take care of this," she said, taking the wastebasket out from under the sink.

"I don't know how much more of this I can take," he said as he left the room. "This can't go on."

Beth picked up the large pieces of glass and the plastic coffee pot handle and threw them in the trash. She wiped up the water that had spilled when the pot broke, then swept up the shards of glass. When she finished, she went into the living room, where she found Jack lying on the couch with his arms folded over his eyes.

"Everywhere I look, I think I see mice," he said. "I thought I just saw another one. And the sound of them, scurrying behind the walls and in between the floorboards. I can't take it."

"I know," she said. "I hear them, too."

"Those damn traps aren't working."

They'd bought the live traps as Beth had insisted and baited them nightly with cheese, peanut butter, and cotton (Jack said they liked this for nesting). Somehow, though, the mice were able to take the bait without triggering the trap door.

"I just wonder how many there are by now," he said.

He'd told Beth that a single female mouse could produce up to forty babies per year—and the babies started mating when they were not much older than a month.

"It's only been a couple weeks," she said.

He just lay there without saying anything. His arms were crossed over his chest now, but his eyes were shut.

"Do you still want coffee?" she said. "I could boil water on the stove, then pour it through a filter."

"How can you be so calm about this?"

"They're only mice. They're not going to hurt us."

He opened his eyes and looked directly at her. "You can stand it," he said, "because you're not on my end. You don't know what it's like."

"What are you talking about?"

"Why are you so late some nights?" he asked.

"I told you," she said. "I go to the library."

Beth had been taking night classes. That summer she told Jack she didn't want to wait tables forever. She wanted to graduate before she was thirty.

"You met someone in one of your classes," he said.

"Please, Jack. You know I can't study here. I either fall asleep or end up on the couch watching TV with you. I thought we were past all this."

Once, two years ago, she'd had an affair. The guy was someone she worked with down at the cafe. He was gone now, somewhere out east. She and Jack had gone to counseling. She thought they had worked things out.

Beth took a step closer to the couch. "Jack," she said. "You know it's hurt me, too."

"Not like me," he said. "You haven't lost your self-respect."

"Please," she said.

Jack rolled over to face the wall. "I don't want any coffee," he said. "I'm going to sleep."

The next night, Beth could feel Jack staring at her. It was three or four in the morning, and she had been asleep until Jack switched the lamp on next to his side of the bed. She saw him grab the glass and pack of cigarettes that were on the nightstand. When he turned off the light, she shut her eyes and listened to the wooden floorboards creak under his feet. As he neared the door, he stopped, and after several seconds, Beth opened her eyes. Jack was standing in the doorway, the light from the hall casting him in shadows. When he saw she was awake, he turned and left the room. She got up to go to the bathroom. She had just flushed the toilet when she heard a loud whack from downstairs. There was another, then one more, before the sound of crashing glass, cupboard doors slamming shut, things falling. She heard Jack yell something, but couldn't tell what. She grabbed her robe from a hook in the bathroom and slipped her arms through the sleeves as she headed down the hallway.

By the time she rounded the corner at the bottom of the stairs, the house was quiet. She found Jack at the kitchen table, lighting a cigarette. The kitchen was a mess. The trash had been ripped open and its contents spread everywhere. The dishrack was on the floor, surrounded by the plates, glasses, and silverware that had been set in it to dry. Canisters of sugar and flour had been knocked over on the counter and so had the dishsoap next to the sink. A broom was lying flat on the floor next to Jack.

"Jesus," she said. "What happened?"

"I came down to get a drink," he said, "and they were everywhere. Six or seven of them. A couple on the counter and one on the floor next to the dishwasher. Then I opened the cupboard and three or four more jumped out of the trash." He shrugged his shoulders. "I tried to smash them with the broom."

She took a carton of orange juice from the refrigerator and sat down in the chair across from him. She drank right out of the carton.

He put out his cigarette and stared down at the table.

"My mother gave me those dishes," she said. "What's gotten in to you?"

"They were everywhere," he said. "The mice."

"I think you've done more damage than they have." She nodded toward the floor, then took another sip of juice.

"I'm going to poison them," he said. "Tomorrow, I'm buying a box of rat poison."

"You can't," she said. "I already told you. What if one finds its way back outside to die, then a neighbor's dog or cat eats it? It might die, too. Secondary poisoning."

"There doesn't seem to be a problem with them leaving the house."

"Okay. So they die in here. Behind the walls, under the floors. The stench of their rotting bodies. I don't want that."

He stood from his chair and kicked an empty cereal box that lay next to some egg shells and a crumpled cellophane wrapper. "Why are you always telling me what to do?"

"I'm not," she said. "I'm just telling you what I think is best."

"Well, I don't trust your judgment."

"Don't start," she said.

Jack walked across the room, stepping on pieces of trash.

"Why don't you clean up this mess?" she said.

"No," he said. "Not now. I'm going out."

"Where? It's past four in the morning."

"That all-night drug store on 6th and Maple. I'm getting some more traps. And poison if they have it."

"We have to be up for work in less than three hours."

"I don't care," he said. He grabbed his cigarettes from the table and left the kitchen. Beth followed him into the living room, where he took his coat from the front closet and pulled it on over his pajamas.

"You're crazy," she said

He looked at her, then shoved his feet into the pair of shoes on the rug. He opened the door and slammed it shut behind him.

Beth lay down on the couch and switched on the TV with the remote. It was mid-November and there was a program on about the first Thanksgiving. A bald man with a grey beard and glasses was saying that on the first Thanksgiving the Pilgrims didn't even eat turkey or pumpkin pie. "That's an American myth," he told the interviewer. He went on to explain how the tradition got started, but Beth didn't listen because she thought she heard something in the kitchen. She turned down the volume on the TV and sat still for a moment. She didn't hear anything, though, and she was tired, so she lay back down.

She dozed until Jack got home. He came through the door carrying a plastic sack and went straight through the living room and into the kitchen. Beth got up and followed him. She watched him dump the contents of the sack out onto the counter. There were several yellow boxes—small and cardboard, about six inches long, a couple inches wide, and an inch tall.

"Look," he said, pointing at a label on one of the boxes. "Non-poisonous: Can't harm children or pets."

"What are those?" she said.

"Glue traps."

Jack picked one up. There was a perforated seam outlining a door on each of the short ends of the box. He pressed the doors open with his thumb, turning the box into a tiny cardboard tunnel. He held it up for Beth to see. Inside was a thick strip of glue that looked like melted caramel.

"One tries to run through here," he said, "and it's not coming back out."

Beth took one of the traps from the counter. She read the top of the box. "Ready to use. Just place and dispose."

"Dispose?" she said. "You mean the mouse gets stuck and you just throw it away?"

"I guess."

"We can't do that. It'll starve to death."

"Never mind," he said. "I'll take care of this."

"Jack," she said.

"There's nothing to discuss."

He started setting up some of the traps around the kitchen. He put a couple on the counter next to the wall, a couple along the baseboards, and one in the cupboard with the trash. He scanned the room. There was a narrow space in between the refrigerator and the wall and he put one there, too.

"The box says we don't even need bait," he said, taking a seat at the table.

"Why don't you help me clean up?" she said. "We might still be able to get a couple hours more sleep."

She went into the other room to put on some shoes so that she would not cut her feet on the broken glass. Jack was still sitting at the table when she came back.

"Come on," she said. "This is your mess."

Jack got up and helped. When they finished, they went upstairs to bed. The branches from one of the trees in the yard scraped against the window. The furnace hummed and a car sped down the hill out front.

Beth had not been asleep long when she heard the first squeal. It was high-pitched and it came from downstairs.

Jack sat up and threw off the covers. "I think one of them's stuck," he said.

He ran downstairs and Beth went, too.

Jack turned on the light in the kitchen, and they could see the tail end of a mouse sticking out of one of the traps on the counter. The whole box shook as it struggled to free itself. It wouldn't stop squealing and Beth put her hands over her ears.

"Oh god, Jack. Oh god. Listen to it. It's making me cringe."

She turned her head away.

"Our first catch," he said. "It's about goddamn time." He walked closer to the counter and watched the mouse thrash back and forth.

"Jack," she said. "You can't throw it away. We can't just leave it like this."

"Yeah," he said, taking his eyes off the trap. "I suppose you're right."

He stood for a moment, staring at the floor. "I've got some two-by-fours out in the garage. I'll smash it with one of those."

He grabbed the trap, the mouse still thrashing and squealing, and went out the side door. Beth watched from the window. He turned an empty trashcan upside down, and set the trap on top. He went into the garage and came out with a two-by-four. He held it tight with both hands and raised his arms high above his head. Beth turned away so that she only heard the smack of the wood as it struck the trap.

She went outside and stood a few feet from Jack, who was still holding the block of wood.

"Is it dead?" she asked.

"Yeah," he said, staring at the flattened piece of cardboard. He jerked his head toward the house.

"Listen," he said, "I think there's another one."

He tossed the two-by-four to the ground and they both ran inside. This one was wriggling and squealing just as frantically as the last.

"Hurry, please hurry," she said. "I can't stand them like that."

He took it outside and killed it like the one before. He came back in and set new traps in place of the two he had just thrown away. Beth watched him walk to the sink for a drink of water, his eyes wide and his face flushed. He had just filled the glass when another one started squealing.

"Jesus," she said. "What's happening?"

Jack clasped his hands together and laughed. "My god!" he said, "I think I read something about this. When a mouse hears another one in trouble, it comes to see what's wrong. Like it might be able to help. They're not like rats, who run away." He looked at Beth. "That must be what's happening! They're all coming out to see what's going on."

He bent down, snatched up the trap, and ran back outside. Beth watched him kill it this time, and she kept watching the time after that and the time after that because more and more kept coming. He was raving, grabbing the traps and crushing them, running back and forth between the house and the yard—like he couldn't wait to get his hands on the next one. Then something happened. On the ninth or tenth mouse, Jack's aim was off, and he hit the trap on the edge, sending it flying through the air and onto the ground. He picked it up and set it back on the trashcan and he started hitting it again and again and he didn't stop.

Inside, another mouse was stuck and it was squealing just like the others had. Jack was still outside smashing the trap and Beth could hear the sounds, one whack after another. She looked down at the mouse in the kitchen, violently trying to tear itself loose, and she was afraid that it might rip the skin off its feet. She picked up the trap. It shook and trembled in her hand and she felt like she might be sick. She went outside to the car and set it down behind one of the back wheels. Jack looked over at her from beside the garage.

"I'll kill this one," she said.

She started the engine and backed over the mouse. There was no way it was not dead. In the light from the headlights, she could see Jack continuing to smash the same box with the two-by-four. She pulled out of the driveway and started up the hill. She didn't know where she was going, but she knew she couldn't go back. Inside the car it was cold, and she wished she had been wearing her coat when she left the house.

Mangos

Jeffrey S. Chapman

Thelma cuts up mangos for fruit salad and hands me a large flat pit. I sit out on the veranda and watch the storm pound over the ocean, like it does every day at noon. The storm comes fast, the storm goes fast. There is not a lot of flesh on the mango pit but it's enough and the juice drips into my beer and onto my shirt. Fibers stick in my teeth. "You look like a kid with a popsicle," she says. Then she laughs heavily so the skin hanging loose on her arms jiggles.

"We're hardly kids anymore," I say.

"Speak for yourself, big boy," she says and laughs again. Thank God she goes inside and I can listen to the rain hit the roof of the veranda with large heavy drops.

On schedule, the rain slows and leaves the beach steaming and muggy in the sun. The German in the next cabin carries her towel back to the sand and resumes her tanning. Today her bikini is fluorescent green trimmed with blue and again I contemplate talking to her, maybe about her collection of bikinis, or to ask her why she and her kind don't shave. I don't have much to say to Germans.

Thelma reappears and pulls a chair next to mine.

"Lunch is ready," she says.

"I'm not hungry," I say.

She looks at me, tilting her head back to see out from under the large, drooping sun hat she wears. There's still a moist wind blowing the palm trees.

"I guess we can eat later," she says eventually. "Or maybe you want to..." she trails off suggestively.

"I might snorkel," I say.

"Should we go to Suva tomorrow?" she says, heading inside to eat lunch.

"Sure." People speak of the market in Suva—bananas the size of your finger that taste better than sugar and pile after pile of colorful spice—and the old colonial hotels. I want to see Suva before I leave and I want to leave soon. Fiji is nice enough when you live in a hut on the beach and eat mangos bought from street vendors and cook lentils in coconut milk from coconuts fallen from the tree in front of the house — my first day here I learned to husk and split a coconut on the edge of a metal chair — but enjoyment will only go so far.

So I start writing a letter:

> Dear Floyd,
> I'm very sorry. Please take your wife back.
>
> Your friend,
> George

I fold it and put it in my pocket when I hear footsteps coming out of the hut. Thelma wraps her arms around my shoulders and kisses my ear. "Did I ever tell you," she says, "that the most common name for cats in New Zealand is 'Cat?'"

Blue Mesa Review Interviews Arthur Sze

Poetry editors Larry Goeckel, Charles Linsmeier, and Tani Arness met with Arthur Sze over lunch at the Old Mexico Grill in Santa Fe in late October 2000. During the course of the meal Arthur discussed his approach to teaching at the Academy of American Indian Arts, and his life in Santa Fe. Relocating to a large corner booth after the meal, with the weather outside headed towards winter and Cuban music playing in the background, the interview moved comfortably through the afternoon.

BMR: You mentioned that you write in the morning. Do you use notebooks or a typewriter? Do you tend to write on a computer? Do you have any set practices?

SZE: Every writer has his or her eccentricities or rituals in terms of writing. I like to write first thing in the morning, and in the late afternoon when the light is changing is a really good time for me. If I'm writing well I'll write in a rhythm where I'll work in the early morning, then I'll take a break and come back in the late afternoon. Then I'll work the following morning and then the following afternoon until it all coalesces.

In terms of my actual writing practice, I write on an electric typewriter. I know a lot of poets like to write hand drafts of their poems. I just find that I go through so many drafts, my hand gets tired and it's hard to keep up with the pace I'm associating or moving the poem forward at...The electric typewriter has been really good in the sense that I'm able to work for hours at a time and not get fatigued. I also like to be able to see the length of the line or visually sense the line as I type. Sometimes I'll have four or five drafts in motion on pieces of paper that I am looking at as I'm typing.

BMR: I'd like to get a little background on you, like where you grew up, where you've lived, when did you start writing, and who your early influences were.

SZE: I was born in New York City in 1950. I went to a public elementary school in Garden City on Long Island and I went to a private high school, Lawrenceville, in New Jersey. As I mentioned over lunch, my father was born in China and was a chemical engineer for many years and his big hope was that I would follow in his footsteps. I was very good in high school at math and science. In many ways I came to poetry late. I disliked poetry. It was taught so poorly in public school in New York. I remember having to memorize "The Rhyme of the Ancient Mariner" and having to look for symbolism and I just felt very uptight about that whole kind of approach. I enrolled in M.I.T. in 1968 and I was in a math class, totally bored, so I took out a pen and started to write. A few days later I wrote again and pretty soon I was writing all the time and suddenly I realized it was poetry that was happening. In many ways, even though I was really good in public school at math and science, it was something imposed on me. I knew I was writing very badly and poorly at poetry but I had a very deep sort of excitement. It was as if I had suddenly discovered something that was powerful and exciting, and I knew that I wanted to pursue it. I knew that I wanted to transfer somewhere and study poetry.

In 1969, Denise Levertov came to M.I.T. and taught a combined workshop with M.I.T. and Harvard students. You had to submit a portfolio of poems to be accepted in her class. I had been writing on my own for about a year and submitted the work, and she accepted me. She had just come east from Berkeley and made the west coast sound so exciting and interesting.

I decided that that was it. I dropped out of M.I.T. and applied to Berkeley and I hitchhiked 3,000 miles west. When I told my family that I was leaving M.I.T. they were of course shocked, bewildered, stunned. But anyhow, I went out to the west coast and worked that summer. My parents kind of changed their minds and thought, 'Maybe Arthur will change his mind in a few years and we'll go ahead and support him.' I had the very good fortune of studying with a poet there named Josephine Miles. I wasn't a formal English major. She approved whatever I wanted to take. I created an individual major in poetry. I took classes in philosophy. I really wanted to be able to read classical Chinese poems in the original so I took Chinese language every day for the two years that I was at Berkeley. I also took conversational Mandarin. I took Chinese literature classes. It was neat because I got to take whatever I wanted and have someone who believed in me. For my B.A. in 1972, I assembled a manuscript that became my first book of poetry, *The Willow Wind*. I came to Santa Fe from the west coast and I've been here every since.

BMR: What writers were you reading at that time? Who were the early people that made you want to write?

SZE: I was very fortunate in that when Denise taught at M.I.T., she was an example of what it means to be a poet and of someone committing their life to poetry. Every few weeks she would bring in a visiting poet. So in 1969 I got to hear, in addition to Denise: Bob Creeley, Robert Duncan, Gary Snyder, and Galway Kinnell. I think Merwin read. It was an amazing group of poets that she brought in during the course of the year. So I was really energized and excited by that. When I moved to Berkeley, the bay area scene was very active. You could hear pretty much anyone, and everyone came through at some point.

BMR: How would you say some of your autobiographical experiences have shaped your work? Can you cite things that have influenced you such as science or, as we were talking about earlier, your travels?

SZE: I think in terms of science imagery and vocabulary. When I first started out writing my own poems I tried to stay away from that. If you look at the early poems in *The Willow Winds* or *The Two Ravens*, they're very much oriented toward nature and in many ways I was looking at ancient Chinese poets as my models or sources of inspiration. I thought of science as something I had left behind. But after a number of years passed, I got to the point where I evolved as a poet, and began to feel like, if you're a really good poet there's no inherent poetic vocabulary. Such a vocabulary can be very restrictive and constricting...I call it the blood and moon school of poetry. It can also be very powerful; poets like Lorca use it very well. I thought, if you can use *fork* or *dishwasher* or very mundane things in a poem then you're a good poet because you transform and incorporate them. Then I got to the stage where I thought, why not use *electron* or *quark* or *magnetic field*? These are all things that I knew or learned in high school. I thought, why not turn them to my advantage because I had that training and certainly not all writers have it. I got to the point where, as a writer, it was important to use everything in my experience.

BMR: The sense of place, how do you work that in?

SZE: Sense of place is really important, and I think of it as a grounding to the poem, just as in drama there's unity of place. To compress and intensify things in drama you bring together all the characters and you make things happen in one place and you also telescope the time. I like the idea of somehow situating the poem physically, giving it a particular physicality. It doesn't have to be New Mexico, but certainly many of my poems are oriented that way or towards Asia. A sense of place provides a way for you to have a lot of free association and imaginative leaps but it keeps your feet on the ground, too, and I feel like that's really important.

BMR: You mentioned that in your poetry you use a lot of your academic training both from poetry and other fields. Language poets who have been staunchly anti-academic are beginning to receive tenure at a number of universities. What are your feelings on the role of poetry in the academy, and does teaching promote a certain conformity, or does it open up possibilities for poets by enabling them to work in a career close to their craft?

SZE: I think you're raising a number of issues—if I understand it right. One might be the influence of language poetry on the American contemporary scene in poetry, but also how a movement in poetry can start on the outside and then sort of move into positions of establishment. Also, maybe whether there is a particular stance or location that's good for a poet in terms of whether one teaches at a college or university. I'm not sure where to start. I would say in terms of society, to choose to be a poet is to be in a position of resistance. We live in such a consumer-oriented society. To be a poet means you obviously have to care about language, about creating something that is alive with words. I think it's such a struggle to make a living as a poet that I don't want to settle for an easy kind of *Beat* stance where you just say, 'Oh you can write wherever, on the road...' and things are fine. It's possible to write in an Ivy League college and write well. But it's difficult to do that. I've turned down offers to teach at prestigious colleges and I really prefer the Institute of American Indian Arts where I teach because the students have a kind of rawness. They come there with a lot of amazing life experience. Their English skills aren't necessarily polished. But I don't ever have to worry about being lost in academia. I never feel like people take themselves too seriously.

I think the scene *can* become too closely defined or too narrow. In terms of the language poets they have certainly been an influence on my work, but it's also an interesting paradox that they were initially sort of anti-establishment or anti-academy, and now many of them are in important academic positions.

BMR: Earlier, we briefly spoke about structure. I'm curious, what structural devices interest you? I noticed an affinity for poems that wrap back on themselves, that redefine their beginnings at the end, and I've got an example maybe you could comment on. There's also the concept of the "parallax view." That's a term you use quite a bit in your writing. In a review of your book that I read, the reviewer was talking about the rock gardens in Kyoto and how all the views reveal something different. So let me hit that quote and we'll go from there.

In the poem "Piranhas," you start out with "Piranhas in a wine dark river," and by the time the poem goes through its paces the piranhas have moved into a more abstract, spatial area, into a bottomless lake full of piranhas. "Piranhas luminous, opalescent in the black water." It seems a real transformation of the concept you started out with in the beginning. So is this sort of reentering the poem something you do or you think about before you start? How do you get there?

SZE: That's a wonderful question. I think in terms of structures, certainly one classical approach is to make a circle, to set something in motion and to move out in a way where you might not know quite where it's taking you, and that's part of the pleasure and excitement of discovery, but, ultimately to circle back is a way of snatching or coming back to that beginning moment. As a poet early on, I tended to circle back more and I now prefer poems that are more open-ended, that start somewhere open and pause and then, instead of circling back and closing down, they keep opening and they keep bringing more and more of the world into the poem. On one very elementary level, you think of the idea of poetic closure. Certainly Yeats talked about it when he presented the concept of how the well made poem had an end that was like putting a lid on a tobacco box. It made this sound when you sealed it and created this wonderful container. In many ways, I think my own feeling about structure, or aesthetic preference, is to move away from that. My experience of the world is much more open-ended, much more simultaneous. I like structures that might be open to synchronicity, to a kind of world view where one thing that appears to happen in one place might not appear to be connected or related to something else. But in fact as you look at it or experience it more closely, you find they are intimately and profoundly connected.

To come back to the issue of space and place, the Zen garden that you mentioned in terms of a structure has been really important to me. The Zen garden Ryoanji in Kyoto has 15 stones in a sea of raked gravel, but one of the things about that space is that you can only walk back and forth along one of the four sides, and as you do so you can never see all 15 stones. They are situated at certain depths and at certain angles so that when you enter you can see 12 at the center, and when you look out you can only see 11, and when you get to the far edge and look back you can see 14, but you can never see all 15. I discovered that one of the meanings of that space, which I think of as a wonderful metaphor for poetry, is that you can constantly be discovering and rediscovering, but you don't necessarily see it all at once. You have to walk back and forth, go through the process of the poem. It's there, but you can't linearly see it all at once.

BMR: Continuing with the idea of process, looking at a poem like "Six Persimmons," can you talk about where the inspiration might have come at the beginning, and where it ends as far as your editing? I know that the I Ching has been important to you.

SZE: The poem that's based on the I Ching is actually "Before Completion" and if you want we can come back and talk about it. Let me say for "Six Persimmons" there's a famous Zen painting by a Chinese painter named Mu Ch'i. He was a Sung Dynasty painter. I don't know if you know that painting. It is very famous with six persimmons and a lot of white space, and the persimmons are at different stages of ripening. One of them, for instance, is very big and heavy, darkly painted, and others are almost transparent. The persimmon is a really important fruit, and there's a whole aesthetic of it in China and Japan. If you pick a persimmon early, it's incredibly tart and bitter. But if you let it ripen and ripen on the tree, if you resist that early picking until the leaves have all dropped in late autumn, they're incredibly sweet. I have this image of just resisting the easy picking of a poem, better to let it ripen and ripen. In terms of the structure of that piece, I had the idea that the shape of every section would be the same—they're each 18 lines long. I also thought that the opening should be dramatic and kind of harsh. There's an opening scene of walking down death row and I let it gradually ripen and ripen, until there's a love story. By the end, it becomes very sweet. I had that open-ended structure to play with, and when I write sequences I never am able to write them in order, meaning I had this sort of larger structure in place starting with something kind of bitter and letting it sweeten, and that the size would be the same. I wrote section three or four first, and I worked my way outward. Eventually, I choreographed them into the sequence that they're currently in.

BMR: Do you want to talk about the I Ching now?

SZE: Sure. I Ching literally means book of changes. For me it goes back to Heraclitus, a philosopher whom I really like: *You cannot step twice into the same river.* Every moment in time is unique, special. You can ask the oracle the same question but ten minutes later your place in the world is different because the time, the place, and the river have changed. The I Ching always fascinated me. It's revered as a classic in China. The origin of "Before Completion" is that I visited China in 1985, and I became good friends with a younger generation Misty School poet named Gu Cheng. After Tienamen, he was expelled from China. It's a tragic story. He ended up in New Zealand, and he actually axed his wife and hanged himself there. She was about to leave him. He didn't speak any English. He had been reduced to making Chinese food and trying to sell it in the streets of Auckland. He basically disintegrated. A friend of mine called me one morning very early and woke me up and she said, 'Have you heard Gu Cheng just killed his wife and hanged himself?' I was really shocked and stunned and thought, 'God, what am I going to do with this?' You know, sometimes you get those shocks in life, and I thought, 'I'll try throwing the coins to the I Ching and see what the book says.' So, I took three coins and I threw them six times to create the pattern of solid and broken lines, which is what the I Ching is based on. I threw the very last hexagram which is called "Before Completion" and that's how I got the title to the poem. When I looked up the commentary, I thought, 'Oh, isn't it interesting that I threw the very last chapter of this book and it wasn't called "After Completion."' It was called "Before Completion" and I had this idea of somebody who dies before they complete their work. When I looked at the six lines, I thought, 'Isn't this interesting that there can be solid lines and broken fragmented lines?' It just leaped into my mind that maybe I could write Gu Cheng an elegy in six sections where some of the sections would be equivalents of solid lines; they would create a block-like form. They would have a lot of body to them. Other sections would be very fragmented; that would be the equivalent of the broken lines. I didn't hold myself strictly to that pattern in the sense that if you look at hexagram 64, it's a broken-solid, broken-solid, broken-solid pattern. What I did was look at that pattern and decide that I didn't want to have my hands tied. I wanted to experiment artistically and see what might work. I wrote one of the fragmented sections first, and then I wrote one of the solid ones and built the poem from the inside out.

BMR: I'd like to ask you a question about color. You get away with using a lot of color and sometimes the effect is just stunning. I'd like to just read a couple of lines from "The String Diamond" into the interview: "There's the violet haze when a teen drinks a pint of paint thinner" and then, "There's the yellow when you hear they have dug up a 4,000 year old corpse in the Taklamaklan Desert." You specify a series of fantastic shades of spectrum and carefully delineate them. Where do you think this interest came from in you?

SZE: I think every writer has his or her obsessions. One of mine has to do with color and physicality in the world, and even though I'm not painting now, I did paint when I was a teenager. My mother was a painter. She painted a lot in the Abstract Expressionist style in New York City. She used to go to the Art Students' League. I grew up exposed to a lot of painting and visual color. It's there in my background, but I do have an obsession with seeing the hues and shades and trying to give color more definition that just green or blue. The shades of color are to me like shades of emotion, and that's what that section of "The String Diamond" was trying to do.

BMR: Your writing seems to dwell in quietude. There's a silence behind your poetry that I sense when I read it. Would you care to comment on that? Is that part of your process?

SZE: It's become part of my process. I think on one level, as an aesthetic position, I strongly believe that the poem asks the reader to slow down. We're in so much of a hurry in the day-to-day world of the materialistic culture that we live in, that poetry asks the reader to go slow and experience the multiplicity of the meanings of words and how they can be used in combination with silence. Silence is really crucial to determining rhythm, the language, where the pauses are, where the shifts are. But I also like the idea of breathing space, that if a poem is dense, and I think my poems are dense at present, that a reader needs time to just let an image or an incident sit and be there in the mind like the way the Zen garden has a lot of white gravel around the stones. The garden isn't just the stones, but the sense of the white space that expands is really crucial to energizing the stones that are there. So I have almost a yin-yang dialectical view of silence where the yin is the blank or empty space that can somehow charge or leverage the words that are there. For instance, in the fragmented sections in my sequences, that's deliberate. I want the reader to have that pause, it's part of the music—that sense of silence and measure to steep the language that's there. It's really important.

BMR: Then are you conscious of your readers' perceptions or their views in writing and also, when you consider publishing, does that enter into your mind as you're writing the poem? Obviously much of your poetry is very personal. Does the reader's perception come into context at all?

SZE: Do you mean, am I trying to make it more accessible for a reader or for publication?

BMR: More so for the reader.

SZE: Wallace Stevens once said the poem is 'resisting intelligence almost successfully,' and I love the idea that it doesn't reveal itself all at once, that if you read it once and got all of it, so to speak, there wouldn't be a need to go back and reread it. I like poems that have a mystery that's like, 'Oh, where did that come from?' or 'Wow, I wonder what that is?' It communicates with you before you can intellectually articulate what's going on. That's part of the physicality or sensuousness that I'm committed to, and I feel like it's important for a reader to have that so that the reader will feel the impulse to come back and reread and the pleasure to say, 'Oh, I didn't know that the ripening in the persimmons was the structure.' Maybe that was just the structure I used to create the poem, but there's enough sensuality and physicality in the poem so that a reader is going to go back and say, 'Wow this really changed from the beginning. I want to reread it and see how that happened and re-experience it.' On the one hand, I feel the reader's presence in the sense of wanting to make an experience that's pleasurable and slightly challenging. I don't want to make it so difficult that the stone is below the surface of the garden, so to speak. That it's invisible. I want enough of it there so that it resonates with the reader. I also want the reader to stretch a little bit and be open to new ways of experiencing.

Just as a final thought, I would say that after the poem is done I might then think: Where aesthetically is there a good match for this poem with a certain magazine? I think it would be a disaster to say, 'Okay, I want to publish a poem in the Paris Review. What kind of poems do they like? I think I'll write that kind of poem.' That would be horrible. The important thing is to pursue your own aesthetic obsessions on your deepest level, to write the best poem you can, to take chances and risks and in many ways let the poem write itself. Trust that process, and when the poem is done, then it makes sense to say, 'Okay, is there a fit here with a magazine?'

BMR: Back to discussing some of the pressures of being a teacher in a time when writing workshops are everywhere across the nation. There's the debate that goes on with some people saying that creative writing can't be taught. Do you have any thoughts about that?

SZE: I guess my feeling is at the most fundamental level, you can't teach someone to be a writer. But on the other hand, it's extremely important to be well educated as a writer. There are different ways of going about doing that. Ultimately, I think the models that one has, that I have as a writer, are first through the great poets, and then also of having peers, other poets of my generation, who can challenge me or who can say, 'Arthur, this section is clearly bad, get rid of it,' and who aren't just going to say, 'It all looks wonderful.'

I think in terms of M.F.A. programs, there's a huge proliferation. Yes, there are mixed results, basically. That's where you get the connection with peers, with other people your age who can stimulate and challenge you. I think that's fabulous. It's such hard work to be a writer and I think some writers go through these programs and do extremely well. I know other writers feel like they go through those M.F.A. programs almost in opposition to them. That for instance, there's a prevailing aesthetic or whatever and their work may or may not fit into that. That's part of the struggle they have. So it's a mixed blessing. In terms of craft, you can learn a certain amount. If you have good teachers, you can learn a lot, but it's not absolutely necessary. Some writers it's good for, and other writers have found their own way.

BMR: Do you have a sense of any pressure you might have felt in opposition to, or in accordance with, a prevailing aesthetic?

SZE: Different writing programs do have different aesthetics depending on who's teaching there. For instance, I think of Buffalo as having a very definite aesthetic that's strongly influenced by language poetics and language theory and that can be its strength. It can also be a weakness. It's really important, I think, if someone is considering what M.F.A. program to go on to, that it be a good match.

BMR: In the poem called "The Negative," you refer to an Asian sense of fatalism. You write, "A Chinese poet argues that the fundamental difference between East and West/is that in the East, an individual does not believe himself/in control of his fate but yields to it." A similar outlook on fate occurs in Middle Eastern, African, and South American writing. Yet in America we regard ourselves as the center of positivity. Our cultural outlook is centered on the belief that we are in control. When people fail, we scorn them. Would you say something about what you see as the cultural differences between these two points of view?

SZE: You can think of it even in something as simple or fundamental as Asian painting. For instance, the place of man in the cosmos of the world is much smaller. In Chinese landscape painting, the human figure is the person who tends to dissolve into the landscape. In America, we like to think of ourselves as the sort who take charge and control our fates. This is what we choose to do. It's interesting that you chose that passage because the unnamed poet there is Gu Cheng, the very poet who ended up killing himself in New Zealand. I met him in 1985 in Beijing, and we didn't argue. We talked all night, basically about East and West, and it was interesting because I told him about how I had come to poetry. I thought writing my first poem at M.I.T. was by accident really, but in a wonderful sort of way. Gu Cheng felt like he was fated to be a poet—that it was his burden and his destiny. There was even then a kind of heaviness, that he in many ways had not wanted to be a poet, but it was his fate to do that. I think in China it approaches the native viewpoint of the smallness of self, of trying to live in harmony with the world and the cosmos at large, but also the sense that it would seem presumptuous or egotistical to say, 'Oh, I've chosen to be a poet.'

I've seen that in other things as well. For instance, take calligraphy. I don't mean to knock Santa Fe easily, but when I first came here I met someone who was teaching calligraphy and he said, 'I'm really good at it. You should come and take my class,' and I said, 'How long have you been studying it?' And he said, 'Oh, nine months—I studied in New York. I've got it down.' It just seemed so presumptuous to me. I think of Chinese artists that I know who are master calligraphers, and when I asked them how good they were they would say, 'I'm really a beginner,' and I would look at their calligraphy and it was unbelievable. I mean there were just amazing amounts of work. There's a kind of humility there and so I think oftentimes, the stance, the way that one looks at how one chooses what one does and how things happen in life, can be so fundamentally different. That, I think, is one case. Here you choose to be a poet; you choose to be an engineer. In Asia it's seen as if it was fated that way.

BMR: A lot of your work gathers its energy from juxtaposition and of course that's understood in Asian poetry. That's how haiku works, but I'd like to look at it a little differently. Is this a deliberate reflection of your perception of the quotidian mind, the day-to-day way we think, which rapidly jumps from one thing to the next, or do you think it's more of the general trend to form the poem as a collage.

SZE: That's a wonderful question that you're raising, and I have a long answer to it. I think when most people look at my work and think of juxtaposition, they do think of collage. They think of Dada, or surrealism, or movements in western painting. But I want to call the reader's attention to the fact that the Chinese language itself is based on juxtaposition—that if you look at a classical Chinese poem there's juxtaposition between the lines of the poem. There's juxtaposition between two sides of a caesura. There's a juxtaposition between nature and man that occurs in a classical line of Chinese poetry, and if you look at the structure of Chinese characters, if you put the character sun and the character moon together, it makes the character bright. The Chinese language is actually built character by character out of juxtaposition. All the elements of the juxtaposition aren't concrete, and that's where Ezra Pound was wrong in thinking that every element to the Chinese character could be broken down into something concrete. There are elements that are phonetic that contribute phonetic elements so it's more complicated, but the structure to the ideogram itself is based on juxtaposition. On the one hand, there's the lineage or tradition in classical Chinese poetry that I learned by reading and translating classical Chinese poetry, and then also, this sort of juxtaposition of how one thing happens here and then our attention jumps to something else. I guess I'm not interested or I'm opposed to the kind of easy or superficial juxtaposition where it's just the consciousness jumping from one thing to the other to the other. If in my poems I'm laying out juxtapositions, I'm trying to create some kind of tension, or sense, below the surface of the poem. Things are interconnected in a way so that it might appear to be an accident, but not quite. There's a reason these things are being brought into the configuration they are—into a tension for the reader. In many ways I'm trying to take very different elements and bring them into focus and to create an energy or focus of attention. That also goes back to the idea of parallels that you raised earlier, with the idea in astronomy where you look at something far away and then you move somewhere and you look at it again and it seems to have changed place. It hasn't changed place; you've changed place without maybe even realizing it. I like to play with this idea that since we can't step outside of ourselves sometimes our ways of looking at the world or experiencing the world are deceiving. It might appear to be different than it is. It might appear to have changed locations, but we might have changed positions.

BMR: I'm curious about the work that you're currently working on. What influences are most relevant to you presently, and how have those influences affected the projects that you're doing now?

SZE: I just wrote a poem in nine sections called Quipu. It turns out that's an Inca recording device. I have obsessions with cultures and the idea that ancient cultures are obviously much more sophisticated than we oftentimes give them credit for. One of the things that I happened to come across was an exhibit of artifacts from Peru, and as I pursued this, I discovered I have this obsession with strings which you can tell. It's in the "String Diamond." It's in a lot of the poems. When I saw that the Incas used strings, I decided to find out how did they this. It turns out they had no written language, and what they did was they had corded strings they would pull out, a bunch of string, and when they opened them up, there would be one main cord and hanging off of it would be cords of different colors: blue, red, yellow, orange. Here are the hues again, the shades and the obsessions...And they would tie certain knots, in different kinds of knots, at certain locations. It turns out, for instance, Quipu could tell them how many bushels of potatoes were in Cuzco because they would all be on this one line, and how many bushels of potatoes were somewhere else. Or, it might tell them how many people lived in Cuzco. The knots could even be shorthand for words in the oral language. Poems could be recorded and Quipu's histories were recorded on these strings. I wrote this poem called "Quipu" that has to do with, instead of a simple memoir of nine months that records certain key incidents, using this idea of string in sections of the poem could be like the strings with the different cords. They would have different sort of shapes to them. Some would be fragments but have long stretches, long lines. I used that cultural principal as the structure for the poem.

BMR: As you work are you aware of specific challenges? People talk about the challenge of keeping the energy level up or of exploring different voices. Is this a challenge for you as you work?

SZE: As a writer there are certain obsessions I have that, rather than try and run away from, I want to take and twist in new ways. For the "Quipu" poem, I wanted to have an attention to language, to the very simplest words of the language. For instance, I took the word "as" and I looked it up. It has 14 different definitions, and I used it differently each time in the poem. There are times the reader doesn't need to know that, but there are challenges to myself as a writer to do things that I haven't done before. I want to formally use this word "as," which seems so innocuous, each time in a different way. I've never done that or tried that before and to me that was like the knotting in the poem.

I like to vary the levels of diction in a poem. I like to incorporate cursing or conversational language. I like to weave in different textures. For me, that's one of the challenges you mentioned for those times when a poem goes slack. Sometimes I might have a hundred sections that are fragmented: they're going to shrink down into the ones that somehow maintain attention. That takes a lot of time and it's a matter of trying what works and what doesn't seem to work. It takes a lot of time to choreograph but I firmly believe the poem needs to escalate in tension. You don't want it to slacken. You want it to have a crescendo or some kind of growth or largeness of power and spirit.

BMR: I'm going to ask you a question you probably haven't been asked. There are a lot of references to organic drugs in here.

SZE: Which ones?

BMR: Psilocybin, I see that a lot. What value do you think the hallucinogenic experience has? Does it provide an insight into the wholeness of existence or is it merely a delusional state of mind?

SZE: In terms of psilocybin mushrooms, I had the experience of taking them in southern Mexico in the State of Veracruz up in the mountains with some friends, and I had maybe a mild hallucinogenic experience. I don't think of it as, 'Oh, one needs to do that...' Again in a way, being open to life and being willing to see what might be there, but I didn't feel it was life changing at all. In fact, in that particular poem "Shooting Star," it is a way of avoiding reality. These guys are basically zoned out on peyote or mushrooms and it's a way of not dealing with the world. So clearly, drugs can be misused. But in some ways I feel like a poem can be a kind of hallucination. "Piranhas" is that, a kind of heightened state of experiencing the world, so that after one reads the poem they can look back at the world with refreshed eyes or renewed eyes. I think there's something valuable a poem can do. I guess I'm being very cautious about psilocybin, meaning, I think if it's used sparingly or used with the idea that it might open up the possibility of how one looks at the world or experiences the world, I think that's fine. But certainly if one uses it too much, and there have been plenty of cases of that, then it's a way of not dealing with the world, and that certainly isn't helpful. The idea that using it will be life changing is erroneous, too. I think in many ways the most miraculous and powerful things are right in front of us, if we only know how to tap into them or make use of them.

BMR: You actually write about various cultures and various experiences you've had. Do you experience a compatibility problem when you use techniques and forms from various cultures? Do you find it at all difficult to successfully integrate these elements?

SZE: I think it depends on if there's a genuine sympathy between the cultures. In many ways, for instance, the Inca or the Mayan are cultures which have influenced my work, and I've come to think of them as somewhat Asian. For instance, the Mayan obsession with jade or the Quipu. I was really shocked and excited about two weeks ago to talk on the phone with Michelle Yeh, a scholar of Chinese poetry. I told her about the Quipu poem I was working on and she said, 'Isn't that interesting. I have a friend who's a scholar at the National University in Taiwan, and he's writing a book on strings as the first form of Chinese writing that pre-dates Chinese characters, and I'd never heard of it before.' I'm dying to know what that connection is. I think when there is that sympathy between the cultures, it works.

Six Persimmons

Arthur Sze

1   *"Cabron,"* rings in his ears as he walks down
the corridor to death row. Where is the epicenter
of a Los Angeles earthquake? Hypocenter of "Fat Man"?
He watches a woman pour honey into a jar crammed
with psilocybin mushrooms. A few cells down,
a priest intones and oozes black truffles in olive oil.
He is about to look at the poems of a murderer,
sees a sliced five-thousand-year-old silkworm cocoon.
x: pinhole, eclipse; the, a; shadow of mosquito,
fern frond uncoiling in mist. "Dot," says a Japanese
calligrapher who draws a dot beginning on the floor
off the page. He looks at the page, shrugs,
there is nothing there, and pictures budding chamisa
in a courtyard, yellow yarrow hanging over a bed.
In Waime Canyon, 'apanane, 'i'iwi.x: it's
the shapes of ice in an ice floe, a light-green
glazed lotus-shaped hot-water bowl. He open his eyes
and recalls staring into her eyes as she comes.

2   A visual anthropologist dies in a head-on collision
and leaves behind an Okinawan bow, whisk,
Bizen bowl, hammock, New Guinea coffee beans,
calligraphic scroll, "In motion there is stillness."
Walking along the shifting course of the Pojaque River,
I ponder the formation of sunspots, how they appear
to be floating islands, gigantic magnetic storms
on the surface of the sun, and forming cooler regions,
become darker to the human eye. I ponder how
he slowed the very sharpening of a pencil
but sped up La Bajada behind a semi in the dark,
and, when the semi shifted in the right lane,
was sandwiched and smashed into an out-of-state
pickup driving down the wrong side of the highway.
I hold the blued seconds when—Einstein Cross—
he cursed, slammed on the brakes—the car crunched
and flew apart in a noise he could not hear into
a pungent white saguaro blossom opening for a single night.

Arthur Sze

3   Green dragonflies hover over water. In the mind,
     the axis of absence and presence resembles
     a lunar eclipse. Hiking a ridge trail in the Barrancas
     we notice the translucent wing feathers of
     a red-tailed hawk circling overhead. Once,
     inadvertently, I glanced out the bathroom window
     and noticed yellow yarrow blooming in sunshine.
     A man does not have to gamble his car away
     and hitchhike out of Las Vegas for the mind to ripen.
     Bill Issacs slices an agaricus lengthwise, points
     to the yellow base of stripe, says, "Xanthodermus."
     Although he has walked up a trail into spruce
     and fir, mycelium in his hands has spread out.
     Although asthma may be passed from one to another
     one mind may be a sieve, while the other may be
     crystals growing up a string. Is sun to earth to moon
     as mind to shitake to knife? When one mind
     passes to another, green dragonflies hover over water.

4   Is the recollecting mind an aviary? Once he pushed
through hermetically sealed revolving doors
into a humid forest where he sighted a toucan,
but where is the o'o a'a? A pin fits in a pocket,
but how do you put a world inside a world?
Two twins, ex-marines, stretch okinawan bows
and aim their hips and eyes at the target;
the arrows are not yet not yet released.
As death burns a hole into a piece of paper,
a fern frond in the Alaka'i Swamp uncoils in mist.
He glows when she puts her hand on his chest;
the sun spins faster at the equator than at the poles.
He lays six blossoming orchid branches on the floor,
stares at the shapes of flower vases on shelves
in the storeroom. It is as if all the possible shapes
of the world were waiting to come into being,
as if a new shape was about to come into being,
when, x, a calico cat scratches at the door.

5   When you stoop to examine a lichen but find
alongside, barely exposed, several gold chanterelles,
I bend to earth in my mind: observe striations
along a white cap, absence of annulus, dig,
unearth a volva. We go on in the woods
and stumble into a cluster of teeth fungi
with dark upturned scales on their caps.
Who notices in the early morning Saturn slip
behind a waning gibbous moon? This year,
a creation spiral slowly incandesces in my hand.
I slip a white elastic band off and loosen
your hair, rub my hand in your palm. I love
when wet sunlight splashes in your face, recall
grilling shrimp near a corner of the screened porch
while rain slants across the field. In the
few weeks of a year when blood-red amanitas push
out of the earth, we push into a splendor of
yellow plumeria, orange hibiscus, bird of paradise.

6 Pears ripen in a lacquer bowl on the butcher-
block table. A red shimmer arcs across
the northwest sky as a galaxy bends the light
of a quasar. Yellow ranunculi unfold in a glass vase
while fireflies blink in a corner of the yard.
A physicist employs lasers and slows atoms
down to approach absolute zero; a calligrapher
draws the silk radical twice, then *mountain*,
to form "the most shady recesses in the hills,"
As the ink dries, she lights two red candles
in the bedroom, notices near the curtains
taro in the huge tin tub, and spots a curling leaf.
He hears the gasp when he first unzipped
her jeans, knows the small o is a lotus seed
slowly germinating in his mind, but the
brevity of equation makes him quiver and ache.
When they turn to each other in a wet kiss,
their fingertips glow in the skin of their days.

The Blue Kimono

Lucinda Lucero

1943

It isn't just any day or time of year. The country is at war and has been so for two years. At the north end of Santa Fe, a Japanese internment camp sits atop a mesa. Not so far away from the camp, Anna wears a blue-red wool sweater. It pills at the elbows. She chops wood under a distant sky. The December air is crisp and polar. As if in meditation, she sighs and closes her eyes. Anna believes in goodness, but tells no one lest they judge her failings harshly.

Her husband, Marcos, does not fight. The Selective Service declared him 4F. Now, Anna thanks God and sleeps at night. Marcos works as a guard at the Japanese camp. And Anna gives thanks. She worries that internees spy for Japan. Japanese soldiers captured her brother, Ramon, and many other New Mexicans with the National Guard on Bataan in the Philippines. She grieves with those who have lost husbands, sons, and brothers, like the Perea family, neighbors whose two sons were killed, but she wants to believe with absolute certainty that President Roosevelt will stop Hitler and his allies and their evil. She gives her loyalty to those fighting and their families. She doesn't understand how Marcos can sympathize with the Japanese internees. She says to herself, "Marcos wants to be friends with the Japanese. I know my husband, but this I do not understand. How can this be goodwill?"

The Agua Fria neighborhood of Santa Fe gives Anna respect and affection. She attends mass almost daily, works for the Democratic Party at the local precinct level, and transcribes letters for those who do not know how to write and want to send news to loved ones in uniform. When Anna and Marcos' ranchito in Peña Blanca failed during the Depression, they and their children moved to Santa Fe and lived for a while with Marcos' mother. Anna found it difficult to share a kitchen, the children, and her husband. If it had been the other way around — if they had moved in with her mother — Anna knows Marcos would have been fine. To her, he is a person whose inner core never seems to waver.

As they often do, Anna and Marcos sit at the kitchen table to talk. The biggest window in the house is in the kitchen. It looks out on a few trees and the peaks of the Sangre de Cristo Mountains. Today, before supper, surrounded by their two older children and the one-year old, Anna and Marcos voice their different views of the Japanese, and especially the Morimotos. Here, before the War, the Morimotos owned a large farm in California's Santa Clara Valley. Their eldest son, the one in uniform, studied to be a doctor at Berkeley and the two younger boys attended high school.

"Anna, I'm grateful for my job. It pays well for Santa Fe."

"And so am I, but should you be friends with them? They could be the enemy."

"The Morimotos are good people. They are the same as us. Yes, they are in their fifties, and we are at least twenty years younger, but all of us believe in this country. Since May, their son has fought in Italy." Anna tucks her arms into the folds of her red sweater. Abruptly she untangles them and points a finger at Marcos. "You want me to trust people who might be spies. I don't care what you say; they're not American."

"They are as American as anyone else. If Mexico went to war with the United States, the government could put us in camps."

"Don't be ridiculous. We have been in New Mexico for three hundred and fifty years. Besides, Mexico isn't stupid enough to go to war against the United States. However you look at it, they have a place to stay; they are warm. I don't understand why you worry about them."

Marcos tells Anna that the Japanese wives have complained to their husbands, and they, in turn, have complained to the authorities that the women want privacy, but there are no individual shower stalls for them, and they must bathe in a group. He speaks often of their formal manners and their respect for each other and their traditions. She knows that he wants her to sympathize with them, but the Japanese captured her brother along with many others, and the Red Cross has documented that the Japanese give prisoners only rice to eat.

"Civility is important to them," says Marcos.

"I have seen the news clips at the movie theater. I do not agree that they are good people. The Japanese want to kill my brother.

Friendship with these people cannot be."

"You are wrong about this," Marcos says. "But I understand how you feel."

"You can't be right."

Anna understands that Marcos is at ease with himself and with others. She, however, worries about her soul, about whether she has loved her husband and children enough, and about carrying out her duties as a citizen. Most of all, Anna wants to do what is right. She knows that Marcos loves her, and she loves him, but unlike her, he makes peace instinctively.

Anna lowers her head when Marcos picks up both of her hands and brings them to his lips. Her love for him is abiding. All afternoon she bakes, and he smells a delicious mixture of sweet flour, yeast, pumpkin used for *empanadas*, and stewed apricots on her hands. He picks at dried flakes of flour close to Anna's thumb. Against her protestations, he puts each finger in his mouth to lick off the dried pastry flour.

"It is true that I have many friends, but I have only one love. *Hay querida*, you are romance and soul," Marcos says. "And pastry."

Like so many times before, he makes her laugh.

"Marcos with the beautiful freckles," as Anna sometimes calls him, built their house. Anna and neighbors, in the custom of northern New Mexico women, plastered. Under Anna's directions, Marcos brought the rose dirt from la Bajada for the mud stuccoing. Marcos painted the trim blue.

"I envy and depend on his strength," Anna often says to herself.

She observes the dark smoothness of the back of his neck as Marcos turns to look out the window. His neck is neither thin nor grotesquely fleshy, and she never tires of looking at it. She wishes for night, and for the children to be asleep.

Not often, Anna endures days when she does not want to be a mother or wife. Today is such a day. Even though tired after a second day of baking, Anna kneads *masa* for tortillas and cooks a big meal of beans and fideos.

"Brighita, stop lying about. There are other things to do besides reading a book. And stop winding your hair around your finger."

Brighita's lustrous hair bobs. Her many mischievous freckles around her nose are noticeable. She often says that she will become a teacher.

"This is homework. You. You always say school comes first. Don't you?"

"Not one more word from you. Get up. You are ten years old; I need you to help serve the food."

Manuel, the oldest at twelve, comes into the house with a blast of cold air.

"Manuel, you walk in with only a smile," says Anna.

Manuel, tall, dark, and self-possessed, shrugs—a man about his own business. David, a one-year-old with chubby cheeks and a thick cowlick, moves about from chair to chair. He finds a piece of a cookie on the floor and makes himself comfortable behind a chair, as if he knows he shouldn't be eating food found on the floor.

"David, *mi hijito*, give Mama the cookie."

"EEEEEEEEEE," David screams, and cries inconsolably.

Anna turns and shrieks at Manuel. "Bringing in chopped wood is your job. Now, do it. *Flojo, hijo mio.*"

With a few words from his mother, who reminds him that he has chores, Manuel metamorphoses from independent man to dutiful son.

Anna irons and washes uniforms for the guards at the camp and saves most of the money, but she sets aside a little for treats. On Sundays, they sit down to eat. In the air is the fragrance of cooking beef and the rising and baking of bread.

But today is not a Sunday, and Anna binds the beans. The roux she makes leaves a delicious nutty aroma. They eat beans every day. Marcos and the children do not complain. Anna looks at them. Friends tell Anna that they, too, experience frustration as mothers and wives. She, nevertheless, wants to be better. Shame and regret wash over her. This is her little family. She reaches for Marcos' hand and says, "Our life is a good one."

Family grace said, Anna expects a peaceful meal. Marcos compliments Brighita for helping her mother with the Christmas baking. Manuel's eyes look to the side as if he does not need to listen to this talk about his sister.

"What I do is more important than what Brighita does," says Manuel. In bold words, using his hands, Manuel tells how he helped the priest prepare *farolitos* by filling brown paper sacks a third full with sand and setting votive candles in the middle.

"I will go back the day before Christmas Eve to line the path to the church and the edges of the roof with *farolitos*," he says.

"No, you're only twelve. The priest won't let you get on the roof," says Brighita.

"The *farolitos* will light the way for the Christ mass at midnight," Manuel says.

"You're nothing but a *flaco* church boy. You go to church to help the priest, blessing yourself, genuflecting, blessing yourself, genu..." says Brighita.

"*Basta*," says Marcos. He ends their words, but not their anger.

At the end of the meal, Brighita pulls back her chair from the table in time to miss Manuel's kick. Brighita stands and then does a half turn toward Manuel and smiles, guileless as an angel, only her monkey eyes belying malice. Anna turns to look at her oldest son, Manuel, intent on getting a taste of the newly baked goods.

After the children are put to bed, Anna and Marcos sit at the kitchen table to talk intimately as husband and wife.

Marcos pats her hand. "We are fortunate," says Anna.

"In a different way the Morimotos feel blessed," says Marcos.

"Do we have to talk about them?"

"Anna, yes. Life is also better for the Morimotos. They received today two letters from their son who serves in the 442 Regimental Combat Team."

Anna doesn't want to understand their joy and pride, but she does. She, like most in the community, worries about loved ones fighting in the War. And like most, she cannot separate the Morimotos from the country of Japan.

"Do the Morimotos know that my brother, like so many others, eats rice balls in a Japanese camp in the Philippines?" asks Anna.

"Anna, they too are in a camp," says Marcos. "And there is no justice to it."

"They have enough food, and no one beats them." She cannot admit to Marcos or to herself that the Morimoto son is a loyal American.

"Nothing has clear boundaries, Anna. I know you, and however difficult the path, your heart will find the way. They feel so honored.

They want to share their joy with us. They will send us a gift."

Anna trembles. "Right now, I live with fear. When does this war end?"

Marcos stands behind Anna and places his arms around her. He eases her out of her chair and turns out the lights as they walk to their bedroom.

This year Christmas preparations will require more than usual from Anna and Marcos. David will be the infant Jesus. The priest has honored them by asking them to portray Joseph and Mary. They will perform in Las Posadas, the nine days before Christmas. Each night of the religious pageant will repeat the exact drama of the first night. Mary and Joseph will go to eight homes where they are denied a place to stay. Symbolic of either the nine months of pregnancy or the nine days of a Catholic novena, the ninth home will be the inn that gives Mary and Joseph shelter. On the final night of Las Posadas, Mary and Joseph will go only to the Church, which will serve as the Inn.

They must undertake a new status. The respect and deference troubles Anna. Neighbors and friends are gracious, yet they anticipate a spirituality from them that Anna fears she does not possess. People pray that Anna and Marcos' new image as Mary and Joseph will please God and that He will protect them from their enemies. She and Marcos will reenact the plight of the Holy family seeking sanctuary — sanctuary the community craves for its country and loved ones. Their status symbolizes the wish to show God their sincerity and reverence for peace.

Mrs. Rael, a woman in her fifties, comes to visit Anna. She is a widow with two married daughters and a son, who, with Anna's brother Ramon, was captured by the Japanese. Like most, but especially now in this wartime, she wishes to do good works, fervently hoping that God's good graces will protect her son.

"Anna, you have much to do; I will watch David for you. I have brought some musk oil. You may want to dab some behind your ears. I mean nothing bad; I just want to show my respect to you."

Anna's tongue moves impatiently in her mouth. She wants to shout, "I'm Anna. I'm not the mother of God." But, of course, she doesn't. She is ambivalent. She wants the spiritual blessings, but dreads the public role and her own hypocrisy.

Jorge Silva comes over and brings them half a cord of piñon wood.

"Let me pay you," says Marcos.

"This is the wood that you like, *que no*? You and Anna will play the Holy Family; I must show my appreciation. Please do not give me money; this is my Advent offering."

And so, people show respect and much kindness, as if Anna and Marcos were older and long-time residents of Santa Fe. These friends and neighbors act in such fashion to improve their spiritual being. Anna's parents plan to come from the village of Peña Blanca. They will sacrifice to make a small donation to the church in thanksgiving.

Every night Marcos and Anna say the rosary. They petition the Virgin Mary to ask God to guide them to properly represent the Holy Family. Tonight, they kneel by the side of the bed and meditate on the statue of the Blessed Virgin Mary. As they say the rosary, David toddles about, tripping over their legs, asking them to hold him. Brighita quits her prayers, sits back, and cradles him in her arms. After a while, he runs about, chirping happily in his own toddler language. He comes to Manuel, who picks him up, but he continues to kneel and pray. Of late, Manuel talks about his call to the priesthood, but he is one who changes his mind about careers yearly. Marcos and Anna take turns leading prayers for each decade. Concentrating on the spiritual mysteries of the rosary, Anna closes her eyes and feels at peace. Her family is one.

Anna continues to question the difficulty of her role in Las Posadas. She does her Advent baking and packs pastries to give as Christmas gifts. Nevertheless, the stirring, the rolling of dough, the sweet full smell of baking keeps her busy. She instructs Brighita and Manuel to look out for David. They complain and tell her that this is their day off from school, and they want to see friends. This time of the year it is too cold to stay outside. Most of the afternoon, Brighita and Manuel run from one end of the house to the other, sliding into their final destination, "home base." Each time they reach the end, they call out, "Ollie, Ollie, oxen free." David stumbles about, trying to keep up with them, shrieking, "Eeeeeee."

"Brighita, stop throwing pieces of tortilla at Manuel."

Anna scolds, spanks, and puts them to bed. David, without playmates, wails as he hangs on to Anna's leg. Anna sits down on the kitchen floor and stacks his alphabet blocks, so he can knock them down. They play and Anna continues to put trays of cookies in the oven. Content and happy, David impresses Anna with his simple goodness. In all this fun, she forgets a tray of cookies. Swirls of smoke escape from the oven door. Anna jumps to her feet and pulls the cookies out of the oven. She picks David up and rushes from window to window, cranking them open. She opens the front and back doors as well. When Anna stops, she feels David's warmth. She looks at his face, and he's happy, thinking that they are playing a game. "I have been a bad mother," she says. David gurgles and with fat dirty little hands pats her face.

"What would Mary do? Certainly not yell or spank." Anna knows that she lacks patience sometimes, as most mothers do. But now, she is Mary. "Acting the part of Mary is announcing to everyone that I am holy or at least that I am spiritually wise," she says aloud to the house. Anna wants to have fine clothes, to own a big house, and to go places. Mary would feel compassion for the Japanese internees. She understands in her own certainty that Mary would not be thinking about material yearnings. Marcos is untroubled about being Joseph, but then he is, as always, a different person from Anna. She knows that Marcos is at ease with himself and deserves to be Joseph. When they first moved from Peña Blanca to Santa Fe, Marcos needed to work and took a job at the La Fonda cleaning the lobby restrooms and mopping and washing dishes for the evening meals at the hotel restaurant. Anna had begged him to wait for another job. Marcos said, "You do not need to worry about what people will think or say."

It is the second anniversary of Pearl Harbor, and events are recounted in print and over airwaves. To Anna, the Morimotos should not matter. But Marcos tells her that he likes talking with Mr. Morimoto about his two tractors and learns from him the importance of fertilizer and contour planting. They mostly talk about farming and growing things. Marcos tells Anna that the Morimotos, born in the United States, speak with an accent and are kind.

Anna and Marcos sit at the kitchen table drinking coffee after the children have gone to bed. Her light blue chenille robe wrapped firmly around her waist delineates her trim form. Anna's dark hair and pinkish skin tones are striking. And when Marcos tells her she is beautiful, she understands that he loves her. She stares at the strong hands firmly placed on the table. She reaches for his hand to feel its warmth.

"Then why do you work as a guard?" Anna asks.

"Because it is my job, and it feels good to feed my family. But I am sad because I know that the men, women, and children have committed no crime," Marcos says.

"I know better. The Japanese would not be imprisoned if this were really true. The government considers them enemies. So do I." Anna makes excuses to cover her doubts; she is Mary, but she is also the sister of a prisoner of war.

"All I know is that he is a farmer like I am one," Marcos says.

Mr. Morimoto has told Marcos that after the war he will stay in New Mexico because land should cost less than in California. Marcos tells Mr. Morimoto that Alameda, north of Albuquerque, is wonderful farming land, and he should go there.

"He is a good man. We like farming. The Morimoto's son in uniform never liked the farm. The Morimotos feel the honor of their son who wears the American Army uniform."

"But the American government doesn't trust them. They keep the Japanese in separate fighting units. They will not send them to the Pacific like they sent my brother," says Anna. Marcos reaches over and cups the right side of Anna's face.

Marcos tries to explain the Japanese heart. "Japanese parents honor their children."

"So do we, " says Anna.

"But they like rice. Not me, I stick to *frijoles*," says Marcos. Marcos always knows how to make Anna laugh. He turns up the volume on the radio, and they jitterbug to a Benny Goodman song. He twirls Anna around the kitchen floor. They keep a quick step to the rhythm, a dance in perfect harmony.

Two nights later, Anna and Marcos sit again at the kitchen table. Out of friendship, Marcos has learned how to bow as Mr. Morimoto does, and sometimes, he drinks tea with him. Anna doesn't think Marcos should be bowing or drinking tea, even if the Morimotos are farmers.

"Is this not foolish?" asks Anna.

Marcos has told the Morimotos that they will play Mary and Joseph. "They see it as an honor for us."

"We save money; we still have our land. Mr. Morimoto will have to buy a new farm. The government forced him to leave the one in California. This to me is proof that they are the enemy."

"I don't understand how Mr. Roosevelt can make a farmer do this? The Morimotos plowed their field. They did not carry guns. They were born Americans."

"We were born Americans; so were our parents and their parents, and even before that we have always lived here. And yet, easterners arrive in New Mexico and tell us we are not American. Even after this treatment, we are not in camps. The government, who has never cared about us, now calls my brother an American and sends him to die, if necessary, for this country."

"Anna, it is true that many times we have not been treated in our land as Americans. But this is also happening to the Japanese. They are not part of the country of Japan. Few people in the United States want to accept this, including the government."

Anna normally takes sugar in her coffee, but she adds none and takes a tentative sip, finding it bitter to swallow. Marcos moves her hair behind her ears, and they both smile.

"It is the Christmas season, and we must give gifts to the Morimotos," says Marcos.

"I fear them."

"*Querida, linda*, it is what we should do," says Marcos.

Because Anna does not want to refuse love's request, the next morning she sends a box of *bizcochitos* and *empanadas*, the fruit and meat kind. She packs wooden statues of Mary, Joseph, and Jesus, carved by Manuel. She guesses they are Catholic. Anna doesn't know. Does anyone give cookies to her brother? Is she not being disloyal? The questions do not end, but the ever-present love for her husband remains steady and firm, like his hands.

"I try to do what Mary would do," Anna says.

"You are the heart of the family," Marcos says.

This makes her happy.

In the evening Marcos arrives with a bottle of Japanese wine and a large box. Anna churns. She does not want the Morimoto gifts.

"Open the box. Open it," Brighita and Manuel beg.

Anna lifts the lid of the pearl grey box. Folded in delicate white tissue with embossed butterflies lies a light blue dress. A "kimono" Marcos calls it.

"Mama, it is beautiful," says Brighita.

Anna changes and walks into the living room over to the chiffarobe to see herself in the full-length mirror. The blue kimono fits perfectly and drapes against her bare skin like nothing she has ever worn.

"*Querida*, you look heavenly," Marcos says.

"Oh, Mama, you look like a queen," Brighita says.

Manuel bows. "We should drink tea."

Anna moves back to the mirror and runs the tips of her fingers over the buttery smooth silk and fingers the delicate slender pleats of the royal blue sash. She can see that it fits her.

"Mrs. Morimoto thought you would want to wear it as Mary. She regrets that she did not have a headscarf for you, but I said that you have a while *mantilla*. Mrs. Morimoto said, 'I wish I could meet Anna. Tell your wife, I humbly appreciate all the gifts.'"

Anna smiles uneasily. She does not want Manuel asking for tea.

"With your long hair parted in the middle, you look like Mary. I will tell everyone," says Brighita.

"I cannot wear it."

Anna retrieves the butterfly tissue from David who is off in the corner happily playing with one of the tissue sheets, his idea of a gift. She pries open his little fists and takes the tissue from him. He screams and Marcos picks him up. David's legs straddling his neck, he holds onto the tiny hands and gallops about. David's tears turn to laughter. In the bedroom, Anna, determined not to shed a tear, wraps the butterfly tissue around the kimono and places the sky blue silk in a drawer.

"This is impossible," she says to no one, but maybe to God.

Neither her parents nor anyone else would accept the idea of her wearing a Japanese dress to play Mary. Sons, husbands, and boyfriends fight in the War. Only one letter from her brother! Softly, almost inaudibly, Anna says again with eyes closed and a slow shake of her head, "This is impossible."

"You are not from here; you look different from us. We have no room for you," says the innkeeper of the first house.

On a clear cold night, Anna and Marcos stand as Mary and Joseph. "Please, my wife is with child and we need a place to stay," says Joseph. The procession sings religious songs of the season and carries candles to light the way. At the second, third, fourth, and fifth homes, the responses are much the same. At the sixth home, Joseph says, "We are travelers; we need hospitality, a place to stay and your understanding." The door is slammed in the faces of Mary and Joseph.

At the ninth and final house, the innkeeper responds. "I have only humble accommodations for you, but there is room. I welcome you." At this point Mary and Joseph enter and so do the rest in the procession. The hosts give them hot chocolate, *posole*, and *bizcochitos*. Marcos talks with everyone, and Anna is moved by this pageant, not sure exactly how, except that it feels right to play Mary and to be Anna.

On the second night of Las Posadas, Marcos brings news from the camp. The Morimotos receive notification from the government: Their son is missing in action in Italy.

The day before Christmas Eve, Anna cleans the house. No sooner does she finish washing the floors, than she hears a sharp knocking at the front door. She pulls the door open and there stands Padre Le Rue, his face red, his breathing rapid.

"*Buenos dias le de Dios,*" Anna says. In New Mexico it is customary to use this very formal sixteenth-century phrasing of "God's good day to you." Indeed, this is the greeting that Marcos gives Anna, first thing, every morning, as their parents and their parents before had done.

In his resonant French accent, Padre Le Rue says, "No, no. Manuel fell from the roof of the church."

"How is he?"

Anna does not wait for an answer, but throws on her coat and calls on Brighita to take care of David. Father La Rue, a fat, bald-headed man, always so calm, even staid, trails Anna, the unbuttoned bottom-half of his soutane catching the wind. He periodically shouts, "The doctor is on his way."

Out of breath, she rushes to Manuel, who lies on the ground covered with blankets, a few parishioners surrounding him. He struggles to fight back tears as she strokes his pallid face. To Anna, it has been a long time since Manuel has looked so young and helpless.

The doctor kneels before Manuel. Dr. Rice, a wiry man in his sixties and imperious, delivered David and all of Anna's children at home. He pays no attention to her. He is the only doctor in Santa Fe.

"He broke both his arms and two fingers." He shouts this as if Anna is to blame.

His manner angers her. But he is the doctor, and Manuel needs him. "What about his legs, his head, and insides?" Anna asks.

"Anna, his legs are fine. We'll x-ray at my office to be sure. I don't think there is any internal bleeding. As for his head, there is no concussion now."

Marcos arrives, and they place Manuel in the flatbed of a neighbor's truck to transport him to Dr. Rice's office, a small adobe with thick walls. Rice, a very capable doctor, puts casts on Manuel and fits him with a splint on his two middle right fingers. As always, Dr. Rice dictates orders. Because everyone knows his concern for the patient is paramount, no one argues with him.

"For the next three to five days, I will come to check on Manuel. We should watch him closely for headaches, nausea, dizziness. If he shows signs of any of these or any other problems, come to my house day or night. Manuel appears to have a hairline fracture over his right hip; he will need to lie flat in bed so it will heal. This may take several weeks. You are in charge."

Anna spends the rest of the day hovering over Manuel, unable to avoid thoughts about Mrs. Morimoto's probable loss of her son. In the evening, Marcos' mother stays with Manuel. This is the next to the last night of the Las Posadas.

"I don't want to leave, but we are expected," says Anna.

At their return, they say a rosary at Manuel's bed. Anna is scared and thankful all at once, scared that Manuel may not recover, thankful that he is not dead. Unwillingly, she thinks again of Mrs. Morimoto's tears and her gift of the blue kimono.

On Christmas Eve, Anna awakens early. She lies still, bricks seemingly heaped upon her chest. The heavy burden of sadness that Mrs.

Morimoto carries troubles Anna profoundly. She thinks of the goodness and generosity of the woman who gave her the blue kimono, spiritual in use and material in beauty. With effort, she rises and makes a fire in the stove and adds cinnamon to the ground coffee. It perks, and she sits at the kitchen table to drink a cup. She savors its taste and heat. She looks out her big window. Just to the side, a robust cottonwood tree stands large and sheltering, and on the other end, a piñon tree with hundreds of pine needles remains green. Marcos buys piñon wood by the cord, and they use it all winter long. It is a bit more expensive than other woods, but he buys it for Anna because she prefers its aroma. "It is like being in the fresh air of the mountains, woody and very fragrant," Anna likes to say. The morning sky, a dark gray, hangs low, threatening.

"I am sure it will snow. I know my sin, what threatens my soul." Anna understands her troubles better when she speaks them aloud. Indeed, she hears herself and moves to take action. The Morimoto's son is missing and my son has broken bones and maybe more, she thinks. And I reject a woman and a gift because I lack courage. There should be a room at the Inn for them, she thinks.

In the bedroom, she takes the box out of the drawer. Marcos is not yet awake. Anna dresses, puts on her make-up, and pulls her hair into a chignon. At the chiffarobe she checks her appearance. She looks well, but somber. Back at the kitchen window, Anna squints to see beyond her little forest.

Around seven, Marcos comes into the kitchen, ready for work.

"I thought you would not wear the kimono."

"I am going with you," Anna says.

"It's not allowed," Marcos says.

"You will take me. There are ironed uniforms to deliver."

"Once there, I cannot leave my duty. You will have to walk, maybe in the snow."

They drive north about a mile and a half in their black 1938 Ford-60. On top of a hill sits the camp, a tall barbed wire fence surrounding it and guards at the gate. To these guards, Marcos has to do a lot of explaining, but they let Anna in.

About a hundred and fifty yards in, dozens of wooden barracks neatly align. They emerge as old and ugly, no doubt carryovers from World War I. In comparison to Anna's solid, pink adobe, they look rickety and drafty. Every which way Anna looks, she sees sharp metal points of the barbed wire there to wound and limit movement. There is not one tree, not one cottonwood to offer a gentle protection from an unforgiving sun. The government cleared the land to make room for the structures and to give guards a better view of the internees. She wants to escape.

In the center of the grounds, on a pole about thirty feet tall flies the American flag. While some of the boys in scout uniforms beat out a drum rhythm, the Japanese in clear voices pledge allegiance to the flag, most with their right hands over their hearts, but a few with their right hands extended upward to the flag. Anna did not expect this overt loyalty. She and Marcos wait for the end of this daily observance.

"I have come to thank you for my dress, the kimono," Anna says.

Mrs. Morimoto bows in a very dignified manner. Anna also bows, but she is clumsy. Mrs. Morimoto does not seem to notice. They go into one of the barracks where Mrs. Morimoto serves tea in small flowered porcelain cups without handles.

Large pearl earrings call attention to Mrs. Morimoto's dark hair and finely chiseled features. She wears the latest style of dress, a surplice cut navy gabardine with shell buttons that are thin and lustrous. Anna did not expect her to be so beautiful or to look so prosperous. They sit on a floor mat at a very low, polished wood table. Anna does not like the taste of tea, but says that it is good. Mrs. Morimoto offers Anna one of the *bizcochitos* that she sent to her. Anna looks at Marcos. He nods in assent; so she takes one, and the tea tastes better. On a waist-high mahogany table, two rich looking wood boxes rest, the larger one supporting the other. To Anna it looks like an altar. Mrs. Morimoto points to the table. "We are Buddhists." Anna does not know what this is. Mrs. Morimoto seems to understand.

"You are Catholic."

"Yes."

Anna pulls out her rosary. "I want to pray for your missing son."

Mrs. Morimoto's look is quiet and sad, and she nods yes after a long moment. Anna kneels in front of the altar; she guesses it is okay with God. Marcos has gone outside. Anna asks Mrs. Morimoto if she would like to kneel. She doesn't know her first name, and somehow thinks that today it would be wrong to ask. Mrs. Morimoto kneels, and then sits back on her heels. Anna prays aloud the five sorrowful mysteries of the rosary.

When Anna is done, she stands. "I should not have sent the statues of Mary and Joseph."

"You have faith and believe."

Anna does not know what else to say, so she bows deeply, and this time it feels true.

On her way home, Anna lifts her face to the sky. She tastes the cool snow. Gently, the snow removes her make-up. It is the Advent season of peace. It is a time of war. Anna must make sense of it.

After Anna gets home from the detention camp, she prepares for Midnight Mass. Marcos, Anna, and David will be on the altar with the priest for the finish of Las Posadas. She wonders if she should wear the blue kimono.

It is not certain if Manuel has sustained any further damage. Anna does not hide her anger; Manuel should have been more careful. Father La Rue comes by to see Manuel and brings candy for the children and a bottle of wine for Anna and Marcos. She asks the priest to stay for lunch. She gives him beans and hot red chile, which he likes. She knows he worries, but he leaves in a better humor.

Marcos' mother comes to stay with Manuel while they go to Midnight Mass on Christmas Eve night. Brighita feels very grown up because she will sit with friends. Anna dresses in the kimono. Marcos holds her hand and smiles. His mother's eyes open wide, and she begins to shake her head.

"They are American. The Morimotos gave this to Anna. Their son is missing in action," Marcos says to his mother.

"Oh!" she says.

Anna changes out of the kimono. Friends and neighbors will only understand that their husbands and sons fight the Japanese. She does not want to disturb their need for peace on this night.

Wrapped in their warmest clothes, they walk to church with neighbors. They sing Christmas songs, "*Vamonos todos a Belen*," "Silent Night," "Come All Ye Faithful," and Anna, whose voice is very poor, sings—something she never does. Tonight she does not care. A light snow, a white lace on trees and beneath, stands out against the night. Marcos carries David, and Anna holds Brighita's hand.

Anna, David, and Marcos take their places in a crèche made especially for this event. In the mass, Father La Rue honors this season of peace and follows with a prayer for the protection of those in uniform and victory in this time of war. There is no ambivalence toward the enemy.

"Hark, the Herald Angel Sing," they joyfully intone at the end of mass. They have prayed for peace and goodwill toward men.

"Anna, you have done well in playing Mary," says a neighbor.

But Anna has learned that there can be no perfection in playing the role, nor can it be about a specific religion or season.

"Oh no, I did not play Mary as she really is."

In the still dark, Anna hears bells.

Thanksgiving 1999

Peggy Tahir

My mind is full of menus.
I read your poems, longing for the un-exotic.
The soup Babette prepared was clear,

A consomme to begin, nothing to clutter the palate.
Birds light on the clothes line.
Wind chimes of shell clatter in the afternoon.

I eat corn chips and think of spicy pumpkin soup.
In the next poem, a radio is playing.
There are at least nine versions of spring.

I could make the lime crème fraiche ahead.
Pepitas are easy enough to find.
A bird eats a snail on the walk.

I'll soak wood-chips in wine to flavor the turkey,
Smoke it slowly on the barbeque.
Next a series of dreams:

Drunken dreams, driving dreams,
Running-to-the-sea-shirtless dreams.
A maple glaze for the ham.

There are many birds being named.
Detailed flight patterns.
Numerous clouds.

I'm hoping it won't rain, not that it matters.
The fire is *in* the kettle.
Carmelized onion tart a sweet side dish.

You turn toward the ocean, looking for insight
On the low road. Maybe kindness.
And for dessert, clafouti.

From Here to Playa Luna

Emmy Perez

Partying after midnight, techno ecstasy speeding through her veins. She's not even dazed as the frenzy of hearts contained in skin grains pulse around her. Bodies like long wheat feathers blowing seaward before El Niño rain. Rapture. Industry. Colored lights and flashing lights, corolla of lights, she closes her eyes and sees sparks igniting the universe of her brain.

Next thing she knows she's carried off and dumped in the trunk of a Caddie, Thunk! Cool metal on her skin, she's lumped over lug nuts and hub caps, funnels like glass beakers, oil rags, burning rubber stench, funk in the trunk, while bass vibrates from quivering speakers.

Javier, the bastard, smuggled her from the warehouse on a leash. He roped her while she was grooving, techno rhythm gliding like bells on a reign underneath her crimped mane.

Venice Beach that morning, incense floating, golden braids down her back. She remembered blading, in a two-piece, spray-painted on her feast.

Her headphones loud and rapping:

> Oh my honeys
> like what you see?
> Got some Pow!
> on my Wow!
> One, two, three —
> numer-olo-gy
> equals six sorority hoes
> you can do them
> but you can't have me.

Her father was a boxer, muscle-bulging, kick-ass genes. Her mother quite petite, but lots of Pow! where it counts.

Gold's Gym after skating, hardness-building in her arms, thighs, calves and waist. But the cake super moist, baking quickly, rising higher in the heat.

Later, at the warehouse, she was in ecstasy. Her sequined tube top, her spangle, her banner, her blue sparkle shadow, glittering all over Mr. A, B, C, and D. Stamen pollen, pistil stardust, ticker tape parade—she was a botanist gathering synthetic rhythms to rearrange the sand dunes of her brain. Belly flat and gorgeous, inhale at the waist cinch sack, then Boom! Boom! bootie, shorts tugging, snug-snugging.

Javier came charging, with a collar and some techno treats. He said, "Girl, if that's how you're gonna tease, I'm taking you on a leash, taking you to the ocean's edge on my Husky's leash."

When the Caddie stopped at three a.m. near Zuma Beach, he opened the trunk and fumbled for the rope. She jumped out, delivered three kicks to his kidneys and a round of punches to his mope. She said, "Boy, if that's how you're gonna be, treating me like a sucker, I'll beat you from here to Playa Luna. My father was a boxer and he taught me how to watch my back. You're too scared to have a gun, so if you know what's best, your wimpy ass better pick me up a six pack and drive me on back, motherfucker, drive me on back."

Bare Feet on the Streets

Emmy Perez

How many feet are bare on the streets? Echinacea is known to prevent and cure colds. Echinacea dreams can cure bare feet on the streets. A makeshift pharmacy in downtown Santa Ana gives fake echinacea shots to children in bare feet.

Oh — don't worry — the fake doctor says. It's only echinacea. Besides her fever is 103° and a doctor in the hospital up the street would ask for next month's rent. Echinacea is a natural shot. Nectar from coneflowers. Butterflies never get sick.

So the child takes a shot in the thigh of the fake doctor's flowers and walks out the shop into the summer heat with bare feet and a fever of 103°.

Will the shot cure my bare feet? — she asks her mother, also walking down the street in almost-bare feet. The mother wears worn down chanclas — balder than the tires they were made from. She was saving the money from the shot for a pair of Payless sandals for her daughter's hot feet.

Don't worry about your feet — I'm worried about your head being so hot and your delirious dreams crying out for things I can't give you. This echinacea shot is going to fill you with flowers and cure your heat with the strength of butterfly wings.

They cross Main Street, pass all the banks, wedding boutiques, and butcher shops. How will butterflies and flowers cure my bare feet? — she asks her mother, hopping down that street burning her bare feet. Dark circles under the child's eyes force the mother to look up into the sky. She wonders if her daughter remembers being in her belly as they crossed north into Arizona with sky, sky everywhere and not a drop to drink.

When we get home you're going to bed with a cool towel on your head. You're going to dream you are a bee sleeping in a yellow flower. Like the bees in Chihuahua sleeping in buffalo gourd flowers — a pretty squash flower — in the mid-day heat. The flower's blossom is soft as lips and will protect you from the sun's making your fever 103°. When you wake up you'll have wings like bees and fly to Michoacán to thank all of the butterflies that loved the purple coneflower running through your blood. In Michoacán, there will be bushes full of flowers for you to nuzzle, eat, and sleep. Monarch butterflies are born knowing the way to Mexico.

Mami—when will I get to Michoacán?

Sleep, my bee, sleep.

SASE

U.N. Atana

When I first met him, he was the Indian Prince I had been holding out for. I was punching the returned book *The Palm Wine Drinkard and My Life in the Bush of Ghosts* through the check-in beeper at the World Bank Library, touching the orange-green cover of the first contemporary African novel ever published, and wondering how far away it all seemed from the heavy traffic outside streaming by that hot July afternoon on Pennsylvania Avenue. The library was quiet, the crowd simmering down, except for a homeless man wandering the shelves and a group waiting in line debating a recent famine relief loan to Mozambique that was garnering massive support from conscientious rock stars. The Nigerian man in the group waved his head back as his blue batik gown swayed under him and laughed, "That rock star is going to return and show off a picture of himself with a poor Mozambique farmer as if he had visited with the Queen."

Kaythar joined in the laughter. He was wearing a deep pink shirt which set off his dark skin. His thick lips and black skin made him seem a brother to the Nigerian. His eyes had twinkled when he passed me coming in, his face brimming with a warmth that was reserved specially for fellow Indians, to show that he noticed me and that we were all unified; I returned his smile, but did not feel any gratitude towards him for noticing me because I knew he bestowed that same smile to the Indian taxi driver and the Indian janitor.

The homeless man came up to the counter and began waving around a pamphlet, "Statistics on the North-South Divide." His disheveled army jacket hung over him like a wool blanket, swinging over his wide, white belly, and making his legs look small.

"I'm reading this book outside," he said.

"You can't check that book out," I replied. "You're not a bank employee or a library member."

"I live in the city."

"It's not for the general public. It's for the bank economists."

"I'm taking the book."

I wanted to appear modern and resourceful in front of Kaythar, so I stepped around the desk and walked up to the homeless man.

His eyes were bloodshot. I snatched the book from his hand, like it was one of my job qualifications, swung around and began walking back to the haven behind the library counter, eyeing the stack of books waiting to be checked in. The homeless man suddenly lunged in front of me. He pulled out from his pocket a thin rusting knife. I stepped back, tripping over Kaythar's slightly extended foot, and glided down to the floor against his strong and gentle arms. I was fine and could have opened my eyes and returned to my professional duties.

But I didn't. There was commotion above, and loud voices, and I lay there and willed my eyelids to stay immobile. His pink shirt smelled like roses and his arms were a warm home.

"I think she's fainted," he shouted. "Can someone bring water?"

I heard voices above, felt his arms move, and then tasted water at my lips.

"What happened to the homeless man?" I opened my eyes after a few seconds.

"I gave him $20 for a taxi ride to the shelter," Kaythar replied.

"He'll come back tomorrow looking for you." I started getting up.

"He needs it more than I did," he said, letting go of my shoulders.

"I'm embarrassed that I'm a damsel in distress," I added.

"I guess I'm your hero."

"Sounds like a Hindi film in the making." I stood up and wiped the dust off my pants.

"Boy falls in love with girl as she's passing by in a bus." He straightened his pink shirt.

"Followed by a song and dance number with ten scenes and dress changes."

"And the parents are forcing them into arranged marriages with other people."

He picked up his book that had dropped to the floor, *The Distribution Network in a Starving World*, one of the library's bestsellers. I prided myself on assessing a person's mind from books read, the way a grocery clerk assesses a body's health from food purchased.

"Reading these kinds of books was how we got our kicks growing up in the censorship era," he said. "That, and Eagles songs."

"I didn't have it much better." I replied. "My parents would put their hands over our eyes whenever there was a kissing scene. Of course, they would continue watching."

"I thought growing up in America you would be liberal."

"My parents are 1950's India. On top of that, they were librarians. I rebelled, but only behind their back, and only in college."

"Are your parents trying to force you into an arranged marriage?"

"The threshold age is 28, a year from now."

"My mother sends me pictures of girls every day. They think it'll bring me back to India. I told them after this project. But I don't know if I'm making as much of a difference as I thought. It's hard to represent 300 million people starving to death. Even talking with you makes me feel like a traitor. You're a Brahmin and an American. I would have been stoned by both my caste and yours if I had even talked with you in India fifty years ago."

"I didn't even know I was a Brahmin until I was seventeen and my parents only told me then because I was writing a report on it for school. Anyways, I'm a new world phenomenon."

For the next few weeks, every time the library doors swung open, I would look up, hoping to see his pink shirt against his black skin. I wanted to faint, or at least pretend to, and awaken again in his arms. When I had almost given up, when I had beaten up myself for being so anachronistically dependent on a man, his photograph appeared before me on the profile page of the bank newsletter. He was presenting a slide show and lecture about a desalination project in Madras that would provide drinking water to several slums. He was going to talk about his travels back to decide which Madras neighborhoods would be washed away. When I got off work, I paced back and forth past the auditorium entrance until I forced myself home, convinced that there was no use getting my hopes crushed.

His academic success both awed and scared me. My parents had come in the mid-60's to do graduate study in the bay area in library science, not because they had yearned to, but because that was the program they could most easily get accepted into. It was a few years after Independence, the Brahmins had inherited control from the British government of major government and educational institutions to the dismay of the D.M.K. party, which represented most of the non-Brahmins. They won power and instituted a mandate that 85% of all state-sponsored educational seats would be reserved for the lower castes, or scheduled castes, and that the state language would be returned to its Dravidian roots, cleansed of all Sanskritized, or Brahmin, influences. Some stayed and changed their names, and others, including my parents, left either to the North or out of the country, sensing their power slipping, knowing it would be impossible for them to make a comfortable living with a caste war coming that they would lose hands down. Years later, when I considered my career options, it again seemed practical and easy because the track was well laid-out, although I was not under the same constraints.

The next day, at the end of my shift, he walked through the library front doors. He wasn't wearing a pink shirt, but a short-sleeve, light blue cotton shirt with stiff pressed collars that brought out the boyish edges of his shoulders.

"I was in India for three weeks but all I thought about was you," he said, leaning forward on the counter. I could see the wet pink insides of his lips. "I really feel like I'm in a Hindi movie. It's sad that that's the only model I know of on how to seduce a woman."

I thought his words were a dream, like the song of a bird chirping to me alone but it wasn't a dream and he wasn't a bird but a man making his landing in front of me.

"I'm not that much more experienced," I replied. We walked out together, crossed K Street, past the homeless encampments at Dupont Circle and all the way down Connecticut Avenue. The air was clean and sparkling from the abrasive thrashing winds of a just completed afternoon thunderstorm: the wetness lasts only a few hours, but its restive beauty marks the daily boundaries of temperature and light.

His studio apartment, a block past the zoo entrance on a side street off Connecticut Avenue, was sparse, a wooden table with two chairs next to a mini kitchen, and a sleeper sofa up against a window overlooking the zoo. There were several shelves of books and a few scattered framed pictures of Indian landscapes.

Kaythar strolled to the stove and began making tea. I picked up one of his photo albums from a shelf and sat down at the table. The album was filled with black and white photos of Indian women in cotton saris carrying pots of cement on their heads to construction sites and of child vendors banging knives the size of their arms to smash coconuts for men sitting in shaded cars wearing sunglasses.

"This is the neighborhood I grew up in." He leaned over my

shoulders, holding the cups of tea. "This is where the bank wants to build the desalination plant. It's going to displace 5,000 people from their neighborhoods, but it's going to bring 20,000 other people drinking water."

"What are you going to do?"

"The bank isn't as popular as it used to be, but it's still the best place for someone like me to get some good experience. I don't know what I'm going to do though."

There was a photo of his parents alongside his seven brothers and sisters, surrounded by numerous cousins, in front of a small thatch hut. His mother had the same coal-black skin and large warm eyes, strong shoulders and a determined wave to her lips. Even through the dust in the photo, I could see her thick eyebrows that joined and matched her thick kinky hair. His father had a sad, resigned smile, and leaned toward his wife almost protectively. They looked as if they were about to walk out of the picture and join us for tea.

"When I told my father I was going to take a trip to America and it would be more than 10,000 miles, he said, 'Oh, that won't be far, I've traveled 24 hours to Bombay.'" He finished in Tamil. "Except for a few trips to Banglore, they've never left their Dalit village outside of Madras."

He pulled his chair closer to me as he sipped his tea. I sipped my hot tea and pulled out from my wallet a picture of my family. We were feasting around a table on some Thanksgiving Day years earlier, surrounded by biscuits, apple pies, and stacks of *masala thosais*. My mother was wearing a fuschia silk sari with shiny new white sneakers and my father was standing beside her strightening his *dhoti*. I was wearing a new silk *pavada* and aggressively opening presents my parents gave to me to celebrate *Deebavali*, which they scheduled over Thanksgiving weekend for convenience sake. My parents and Kaythar would probably never meet each other, both because I would never bring him home until there was a wedding date, and because I was afraid of his dismissal of their escape to American suburbia.

"How long has it been since you've been back?" he asked, staring at the picture.

"Fifteen years," I said, embarrassed.

"That long? Do you remember anything?"

"Small things, like the smell of corn roasting on the street, the crowds. Mostly people, relatives, family, my grandmother's hug when I was leaving. Not much more."

Over the next several weeks, we walked home together almost every night. We would stop to take pictures of ourselves together along the way in front of bridges and historic houses, and then pick up vegetables from a vegetable stand in front of the zoo. We would sip tea, and chomp down rice and *sambar* he scraped together as I poured over more pictures.

"Is this here?" I asked, leaning back on the sofa and pointing to photos of sewage plants floating across the Chesapeake Bay and tenement houses lined along the Anacostia River. He handed me my hot tea and peered over my shoulders.

"When I was growing up, I thought this was the greatest country in the world. All I wanted to do was come here. But once I got here, ironically, all I did was miss home. I started taking pictures of what it was really like here, the underbelly of modernity." He pronounced "modernity" as if it rhymed with maternity. He put his hand on my shoulder and leaned over. He kept his hand there and sat down next to me and put his hands around my shoulder. I stiffened slightly because we had not made any physical contact up until that time, but then I relaxed as his warm hands held me very lightly. I was reminded of falling to the ground, and his arms catching my fall. He leaned over and kissed me. I felt as if I were fainting again, held in the cup of his arms, and then water touching my dry lips.

Easily, we slid against each other and joined, like a fist to a palm. His warm body was close, and I again smelled roses and felt his hips heavy on mine, our arms entangled, our feet entwined, without clothes, amidst the sounds of roaring lions and singing elephants and the warm tropical breezes of an August night coming through the window. My American accent and archetypal South Indian looks must have both repulsed him as a mutant and attracted him as a hybrid flower. I didn't tell him I had never gone this far before; after all, I was giving myself away to an Indian prince. Maybe I should have confided to him that he was the first, technically speaking, but I didn't want him to hold on to me for tradition's sake. And I didn't think he would believe me. I wasn't sure if he had done this before either, knowing how the Indian code of celibacy applied equally to men. Funny, how

I had always expected it to matter, but in the end, it didn't.

"It's amazing you grew up here, you seem so Indian."

"I'm a new world phenomenon, I'm a chameleon," I said, not quite sure whether or not to take his comment as a compliment.

"Do you ever want to go back?" he asked, his hands caressing my shoulder blades, sitting up on the sofa.

"I grew up thinking I would, but the older I got, the less I felt the desire to. Anyway, my family is here."

"My family is there. And my work is there. There's so much I want to do. I really want to make a difference."

"Everyone says they'll go back but they don't."

"I know. But I hope I'm different. It's something about the land, something about the sea breeze, something in the air, that when I step off the airplane, I know I belong there, and nowhere else."

I thought of lying to him and telling him that I had once been a child begging in the slums and then adopted by a childless couple and brought to the U.S., but I didn't want to hold on to him with that kind of lie, and I didn't want that kind of sympathy.

"I'm sorry, I don't know if I can promise you anything. After a year, you'd hate me for taking you there."

"I figured that."

Night after night, roar after roar, I began practicing my broken Tamil with him, and remembering my India from his albums, hoping when the time came he would carry me with him over the threshold back home, his vision becoming mine. He was gentle with his lessons. But I always drifted to sleep and in the early morning woke alone, knowing he'd already dressed and gone to the refuge of his work. I clung to my cocoon; the sensations streaming through my body lulled me again to sleep. The elephants would continue singing, but the lions were always asleep as the tropical nights turned into unbearably humid days. I had once been certain that the love I had for him would precede marriage, that Indians should experience sexual attraction divorced from social bonds because we rarely exited marriage for such a seemingly slight reason as the loss of desire. But I knew he felt that this love making in an apartment with an Indian woman, even one marginally Indian, lay outside the boundaries of probity. He placed me last in his long line of American women, at most a bridge to a real Indian wife. Rising from our conjugal bed in the late morning moonlight to taxi across town to his work, he saw home as absolute, and I saw it as relative.

In late October, when he returned from yet another trip to India, he wore a *kurta*. His hair had grown longer and fell on the back of his neck in black waves. He had finished his report while in India: he proposed destruction of the slums. In celebration, or at least as closure, I ordered take-in of an elaborate meal from an expensive Indian restaurant.

"I don't know what I've done," he said, leaning back on the sofa.

"You have a chance to make a difference," I said hollowly. But I wasn't so sure what the difference was and so let him brood and wrestle with his demons of complicity.

I stared down at the set of new pictures he had just developed. Mostly desalination plants, sewer lines, cows mingling, but a few of him unexpectedly happy, smiling in front of the airport, one against a rickshaw, and another against a bright blue ocean. He seemed as if he were in a different country, one that I didn't know, and one that he didn't bring back with him.

"This food doesn't taste Indian and it's overpriced," Kaythar said, looking down at the table lined with Styrofoam bowls filled with sautéed eggplant, turmeric lentils, and buttered white rice.

"We're paying for the rent and the décor," I said. The restaurant was three blocks from the White House, and was reputedly the President's favorite Indian restaurant.

"Look at your plate," he said. "It's still full and you're not going to finish everything on it."

"Why do you care if I finish it? It's already accounted for."

"You seem proud of missing the point."

"It's just a piece of bread."

He pushed back the open sleeves of his *kurta*, looked down, and wiped the plate with his *nan*, leaving only streaks of bright yellow turmeric.

One *nan* was left in the basket between us, wrapped in plastic wrap, its burnt edges still warm. I couldn't resist—I scooped up the *nan* and wiped my hands on it as if it were a napkin, holding it in one hand and cupping it over the other, rubbing the dried curries left in the hollows between my fingers, the *nan* soaking up the eggplant sauce on my fingertips. When the film of sauce had been absorbed, I flicked the *nan* over the full plate, as I would discard a used napkin.

"I saw so many starving children on this last trip. Do you think the joy of irritating me was worth depriving a starving child of that *nan*?" he asked.

"Please. Let's not try to be saints," I said, leaning back and looking out the window at a passerby walking home on this late October night, a few days before Halloween, carrying bags full of masks and costumes.

"Americans are less than 5% of the world's population, yet they consume more than 30% of the world's resources. Don't you care?" The whites of his eyes widened against his dark face.

"It's not my fault." I swallowed and turned over a clump of cold eggplant on my plate and moved the *nan* over to the opposite end. Kaythar turned away in disgust. I avoided his eyes and thought about the restaurant walls decorated with rosewood-framed pictures of British Raj, ex-pats hunting Bengal tigers and sipping tea at exclusive clubs. I understood the irony of eating food from a restaurant where at one time we wouldn't have been allowed to enter unless we were servants or slaves.

He reached over and picked up the *nan* on my plate and mopped it over his plate to absorb the streaks of turmeric. He slowly chewed the *nan* and stared at me, his dark eyes not flinching. I couldn't avoid his eyes; I leaned over and ripped a piece off the other end of the *nan* and pushed it down my throat without tasting it. We finished the remaining bowls of food on the table, stone silent, even though we were both beyond full.

"Who are you getting married to?" I asked. I hadn't really known, or even suspected, but it became clear to me as I was saying it.

He didn't seem suprised at my question. "I'm sorry, but I don't see how it can work out with us. You've known it all along, too."

"Do you really think a woman from India is going to have a better chance of understanding you?"

"A woman who's grown up there will want to return."

"Just because someone was brought up in India doesn't mean they have a monopoly on what it means to be Indian. There's no such thing. And you'll find out in a few years when you're trapped in a marriage you hate."

"Everyone in the world has a patch of land that they're responsible for, that no matter where they go, they'll ultimately need to face. And I want to face mine."

It was a full moon and I could see outside the window that my location was the problem — the passing traffic orbiting around its center at 19th and Pennsylvania — the galaxy bordered by K street, Pennsylvania Avenue, 17th, and 23rd. Nearby sat a group of homeless beggars next to a hot dog kiosk run by an Ethiopian woman and passed by rulers pedigreed from Polonious. All I did in life was keep track of books about places no one relished reading about except the educated like him, who wielded it all into theories about wealth transfers between the north and south. My world didn't connect to anything of that world, considering that I wasn't even as close to that world as he claimed to be; it served only as my watering hole, a job which I had taken to supposedly return something to the India I had left behind. Only when I licked the stamp before I sealed an envelope addressed to these places did I really give anything back.

I defended my profession to myself, like a hag against younger whores. I worked only two blocks away from the locus of power, neighbor to the rulers of the most powerful empire in the world, and it didn't matter one iota. I'm irrelevant, not even a passing beggar, but Kaythar wouldn't deign to admit that he was probably only a little less so. I was nothing, I would contribute nothing to better the world because we had abandoned India for economic opportunities to forge our own cocoon. No grand departure. No arrival in a refugee boat. And, therefore, no room for return.

I conjured up this Indian woman, long black silky hair with pearly white skin living in a palace embodying the purity and wonder that was once India. I had no choice. The next day, I called my parents' contacts in the Indian community to track down the other woman's identity and address, and caught the next flight to Madras.

———————

"NRIs over there." The customs officer shouted in Tamil, pointing to the opposite end of the airport terminal. I mouthed the words out silently, NRIs, or Non-Resident Indians, curling my tongue up against the roof of my mouth and then flicking it out as a retroflexive R, the curliest of the three distinct Rs in Tamil, the oldest language still spoken in the world. As I rolled my tongue out, however, I couldn't taste a smooth familiar oldness; rather, my tongue waved up against the sour roof of my mouth and rumbled over parched lips as dry as gravel. I understood the language like I understood the taste of breastmilk. I had always heard it at home when my parents named Indian food or recited Tamil poetry. But I was illiterate in the language and had never heard it spoken as a public language before. The rhythm was the same but the syntax and conjugations were different, and it hit upon my ears after fifteen years like the voice of an unknown dead twin.

When I arrived in front of the customs officer, I pulled out my American passport, which was sandwiched in between my address book, my wallet, and a collection of pictures of Kaythar and me. The officer peered at my passport, his forefinger caressing its American label. He had traced thousands of people like me. For him, this was only a job, not a lighthouse beacon to sight traveling ships and guide them around uncharted shores. He didn't command those kinds of solitary eyes signaling that he dreamed about traveling the world seas. Locating, located, to be located, I refused to displace myself once again. Under your feet, that's your location.

I exited the airport into nowhere, an outer vein of Madras, and I quivered at the thought of the trip to the city, looming in the distance and ready to devour the incoming traveler. In spite of a slight chill in the late afternoon air, I could taste the smog corked in the bottled atmosphere. The zoom of planes taking off and landing amplified the unending horizon. The taxi drivers leaned on their taxis and assaulted me with their million eyes, assessing my every movement, daring me to run back and take cover in the shade of the terminal. I clutched my purse close and pulled my one duffel bag towards me, at the same time taking stock of my disoriented self and the contours of my body standing exposed in slacks and shirt. Is that how everyone responds when they first encounter this country where generations are born and die under ancient skies and once-sea-covered land? I caught myself, straining not to take on the attitude of a mutant breed of colonialism, to exoticize the place of my own birth and childhood.

When I told the taxi driver in Tamil the destination, he pegged me, "Second generation *iyer* from Tanjavur brought up in the American south. Your parents left during the Anti-Brahmin days?"

"How did you know?" I asked.

He shrugged as if it were obvious from the way I spoke and looked. "You want to go there?" he asked when I gave him the address.

"Yes," I replied. He slipped into a reticence, as if I were just the dice in a taxi driver's game of teasing out origination accents and destination addresses of passengers. Here I was returning, like a Scarlett O'Hara attempting to reclaim a burnt Atlanta, a generation after the Civil War had been lost.

I stared out the window at the cross-section of the street, as if at a holographic museum. Strolling cows, rolling rickshaws. Scooters swayed in front of us and motorcycles zoomed past us while buses roared by. Brown and black-skinned people darted and weaved through the traffic. Coconut milk trucks fenced in by strewn green shells and limca vendors opened up their stalls, the city awakening after the afternoon hibernation from the heat. Corn roasted over small fire pits lining the sidewalks.

"Protests for days here," the taxi driver said. "These neighborhoods are going under water." He traversed wide highways, then maneuvered down medium-sized streets that led finally into a narrow alley, which seemed like a marketplace: families heating tea on makeshift sidewalk fires juxtaposed against well-dressed women carted around on bicycle rickshaws driven by rail-thin dark leather-skinned men who were around thirty but looked like they were in their eighties.

The driver said the charge slowly in Tamil, as if I were a foreigner, and I paid the overcharged amount he demanded because it wasn't worth arguing over the equivalent of ten cents.

Then he disappeared behind me and backed out of the alley into the wide street again, zigzagging quickly out through the dusty roads, leaving me alone.

As if my twelve-year-old self were leading the way, I followed an alleyway filled with boarded-up homes. I tried to match the address on my sheet of paper with the address on the doorways. The street was crowded with children playing and people coming home from work. An old, thin man with stumps where his arms and legs should have been was sitting on one side of the alley street. I handed him a $5 rupee without thinking twice. A young girl came out from behind him and scanned me up and down with her right eye. Her left eye was an open infected wound, the whites of the eye along with a bandage coming off. She was a skeleton, except for the bulging belly from lifelong hunger. She smiled with her one eye when I placed a $10 rupee in her hand. She followed me for about half a block before she joined other children playing on the alley street.

I hadn't thought much about this place, but now the dim memory became a place, a junction where I could connect family to identity. Odd that I hadn't yearned to return to India in fifteen years, never anxious that I lacked some core in my personality that could be replenished only by the shock of an India trip. No, I never craved that experience, even when all the other Indian kids growing up in the U.S. were making their way back every two years to recharge their Indian identities. The longer I stayed away, the less reason I had to return, and the more the money I could put to buying a car or paying for a college education. Anyway, I thought I carried India around in my mind, that the memory was sufficient—I had lived here in a small house, and then spent years afterwards reading about India, from Amir Chitra Kathais as a child to history tomes as a teenager—the grainy memory of India lodged in my mind next to Disneyland visits. This had deceived Kaythar, I know now on reflection, made him judge me initially as Indian, whatever that word means; only later did he distinguish himself as a *pure* Indian.

I arrived in front of the house. I could tell from the way the street widened and then narrowed at a sewer line that it was the one I had spent my first twelve years in, even though it was now abandoned and run-down. The inside of the house had bare green cement floors, the same matching green cement walls and ceiling, and a square opening cut out high on two walls for two small windows with bars. The house was dark like a garage and had a musty smell. Very little breeze flowed through. The sour taste in my mouth from the flight and the damp musty air commingled.

I remembered how I waited for my parents to return from America with their educational degrees and take me back with them. I had just finished dinner, and, not seeing any paper towels, I had walked over to the cupboard and taken a kleenex from the decorated box sitting in the cabinet. My grandmother rushed over, "No, no, don't take that. Your parents sent it over from America. It's very expensive here. Don't waste it." She grabbed the piece of kleenex from me, folded the two sides over again, and then put it neatly back into the box like it was her most prized necklace. The other kleenex in the box had only slightly yellowed edges despite being stored in the cabinet for years. Then, as if thinking about it again, she said, "No, it's all right. Use just one piece. I probably won't see you again."

The enormity of my decision to visit India without my parents dawned on me: my grandmother should have greeted me here and guided me around this ancestral home, not left me alone and single to find someone and some place I didn't know. I wanted to call the taxi driver back to haul me to my apartment near 16th Street in Mount Pleasant, a street with large art deco buildings, each a familiar face and time. My parents left here, dreaming of what wonders they'd have for their children, their parents, the luxuries, the nuggets of wisdom, but in the middle years, all that initial hope had been sucked away by the immeasurable hours spent sparring with their children, trying to mold them into the life that they wanted for them and for themselves. It's only years later when the children return willingly that the work is done, the seeds harvested, the life over.

I opened my duffel bag and unwrapped the bright blue cotton sari that Kaythar had brought me back from his last trip. I took off my jeans and wound the sari around me inelegantly, knowing that the current wrapping style was lost on me. I took out a picture of Kaythar hugging me in front of the zoo entrance. I had labored solely to arrive at this departure point. I looked down at the picture. He ridiculed a tame profession of scribes: librarians are not social catalysts, just gentle caretakers of human achievements. I turned from the house and walked past street lamps just beginning to light up and children playing outside.

More comfortable melding into the crowd in a sari, I boarded the bus to Besant Nagar, which was packed with people returning home from work. I inched my way towards one of the empty handles on the left side of the packed bus. A group of young men hung out of the doorway and swayed like a billowing bedsheet as the bus roared around a corner. It defied engineering laws to pack this many people into one bus—yet it ran. The scent of coconut hair oil, fresh jasmine, and face powder wafted through. I was squeezed out of the bus at the ocean stop amidst large colonial houses that lined the boulevard like

Massachusetts Avenue.

I slipped my hand into my purse to retrieve my wallet and address book. It was not there. I unzipped the compartment and peered down, seeing the outline of my passport, but no wallet or address book. I scanned the faces on the disappearing bus who might have slipped their hand into my purse, but could point to no one in particular as the thief. A shade of gray frame confined me, simmering black oil gushed over and cracked my placidity. I didn't belong here, or anywhere, and everyone knew it. Why did I think otherwise? For a moment, I considered reporting the theft to the police, but reconsidered when I pictured the hassle of finding my way to the police station only to be told they would not be able to retrieve the items, let alone find the culprit. Anyway, I rationalized, the thief probably needed the money.

I ventured in the direction of the ocean. The streets were clean, the roads not as congested, and the ocean breeze caressed the neighborhood. Discarded coconut shells encircled trucks packed with green coconuts. I stopped by one and drank the milk from a coconut. I threw the empty shell to the floor, like the other people did, and then asked the vendor which house had the young lady engaged to an Indian in America. He pointed me to a beautiful two-storied house at the end of the street before the drop to the ocean. Signs along the road read in English, "Down with Hindi."

An old woman, who, dressed in a simple white cotton sari, appeared to be a servant, opened the door to the house at the end of the street. I told her in Tamil my name, my connection to the household, and my desire to congratulate the bride to be while I was in the neighborhood. The old woman invited me in and then told me that the daughter had already left for the airport.

The living room had a mauve sofa, two printed chairs of a Kashmir design, and walls decorated for *Deebavali*. Behind the sofa was a large bay window, above which fishermen boated across the horizon in the evening light. There was a photo of a young woman in a sari against an ocean. I recognized the background as the same that was behind Kaythar in the pictures of his last trip to India.

"That is the new bride. You know how it is, Indian men go to America and they want that kind of wife." The future bride was dressed in a yellow sari with her hair pulled back and braided.

The old woman grabbed her bag and shouted at an autorickshaw driver loitering at the corner to take us to the airport. We whizzed through the streets, the noise of the motor drowning out any possibility for a conversation. The airport looked familiar. Even though I was dressed like a foreigner going native, with the old woman leading the way, I invoked few stares.

The old woman maneuvered us quickly to the visa line. Ahead of us was a young woman with almost-white skin and short black hair cropped like a boy. She floated in the visa line like a bubble. She was wearing jean shorts and a tight T-shirt that said "Sexy." Her long legs were smooth and glazed with a golden sheen, as if she were a Miami beach lifeguard. She was a gazelle—beautiful, elegant, but not the type of subtle princess beauty I had pictured. I still had the picture in my purse and thought about slipping it into her hand. She turned her head towards me as if she were assessing me, staring quizzically at my bright blue sari falling inelegantly. I had been naive to imagine that the reason for my appearance would not be obvious. As long as there had been arranged marriages, there had been other women, other relationships hastily unarranged beforehand.

She showed her passport to the official, the same man who had peered at my U.S. passport a few hours earlier. A young girl who looked like her sister hugged her close, and then the rest of her family standing close rushed her from all sides. I stared out at the terminal. I wanted to speak, say the words that would keep her here, and prevent Kaythar from returning, but I decided against it. As the planes revved their engines for takeoff, I walked back and forth near the customs official's desk until I forced myself to leave, convincing myself there was no use in crushing her hopes.

Out West

Stefi Weisburd

The sky is relentlessly blue and empty
of gossip. Never mind the cherry blossoms
at your old house or the tulips that missile
through your lawn as if they were old love
letters. In this kind of desert, birds do not take
lovers. They wait for Spanish broom pods
to burst in the last light, scattering seeds
like roulette balls into cinder block and dirt.
Going out the door I notice my chard
has emigrated to strangers' yards.
How the marigolds you planted
backed out of their roots, gave up the earth.
Yesterday I saw a woman ahead
of me pushing a baby carriage uphill
with your purposeful gait, your long
curled hair. I could have passed
her and seen her face, but with your real
body in Boston these three years,
I stayed back for the purity of the
deception. First she, then I walked
under the honey locust. One
of its branches stripped of leaves.
That's where the lone crow perched,
cawing as it faced East.

Four Stories

Pedro Ponce

Garden

Every spring, my father planted tomatoes. He cleared the weeds from a patch of dirt behind my room. He worked the dirt with a shovel and mixed in steer manure and compost. The sharp smell rose to my window. Then he set the young plants into holes dug with a hand shovel, mounding the soil around the base of each plant.

I was responsible for watering. I gave the plants small drinks from a cracked plastic jug. When the plants were firmly rooted, my father dug small channels in the soil for water to run through. Now, I didn't have to stoop over each plant with the cumbersome jug. Instead, I could just put the end of the hose into the nearest channel and turn on the faucet. Water filled the space between plants, turning what was once a patch of dirt into an archipelago seeded with miniature forests. By early summer, tomato blossoms fell from the ripening fruit; yellow petals littered the channels like tiny boats.

One year, I asked my father why he only planted tomatoes. We were standing in front of the seed display at the local hardware store. The seed packets were arranged on shallow open shelves and sorted alphabetically by name of fruit or vegetable. Under the name printed at the top of each packet, you could see pictures of the promised results: radishes as round and red as Christmas bulbs; green beans splayed like elegant fingers over neatly trained vines; melons that seemed to emerge from the ground clean and quartered for dessert plates.

My father answered my question with a slight shrug. He said he didn't know. I begged for my own piece of ground where I could plant anything I wanted. My father hesitated. There was a bare stretch facing the neighborhood laundromat, but this had not been planted for years. The soil was so hard, it would have to be broken up with a pick and then sifted for rocks. I promised to do all the work in exchange for fertilizer and my choice of seeds.

I set to work that day. I broke up the dirt and ran it through the sifter, an open box made of four plywood sides and wire mesh at the bottom. The mesh caught rocks, spare change, and rusted metal scraps. Soil the consistency of sand drained through. Fertilizer gave it the rich brown color I had admired in the pictures on the seed packets.

I planted two rows each of radishes, carrots, green beans, and corn. I watered diligently, digging the irrigation channels myself when the plants were big enough.

But my garden looked nothing like what I'd seen in pictures. The radishes came out of the ground looking like flattened grapes. The carrots were little more than orange toothpicks. Worms burrowed into the bean pods and the corn was kernelled in uneven rows like diseased teeth.

I never gardened again. But occasionally, I find myself trolling the aisles of hardware stores, especially when I arrive in a new place. There is nothing more beautiful than the sight of seed packets perched in neat, orderly rows. What can a garden give you that isn't found in the crisp paper smell of unplanted seeds?

Secrets of the Stars

This was during better times. We talked at least once a week and could say even the most excruciating lines with absolute conviction.

I love you, she said.

I love you, too, I answered.

I miss you, I said.

I miss you, too, she answered.

What are you doing? she asked.

Watching TV, I said. On the dusty screen, a woman was offering me the secrets of the stars for only $2.99 a minute.

How was your day? she asked. Tell me everything.

And so things proceeded, like an obscene phone call rated for a general audience. I described my day and she described hers. I tried to imagine the smell of her hair after a shower, the coffee that burned her tongue, the geometry of her office in a city thousands of miles away. But my attention always drifted back to the flickering screen in front of me.

Hello, she said. Are you still there?

They're going through the most compatible signs, I said. Mine's next.

There was a long pause. Well? she asked.

I go pretty well with Scorpio. With Pisces, even better.

What about me?

Her sign appeared at the bottom of the screen highlighted in red. It says you're restless and you'll end up cheating on me.

If she said anything, it was drowned out by a burst of traffic from her end of the line. When things were quiet again, she spoke up. There's no one else, she said.

I know, I said, and promptly changed the subject.

One of Everything

I decided to celebrate my freedom. It was nowhere near the Fourth of July. I made a table out of a splintery plank and stacked milk crates. Over this, I draped a paint-splattered tarp.

I went through my kitchen and took out plates, cups, forks, knives, and spoons. I took the saltshaker, left the peppershaker. I came upon two saucepans humping lovelessly in the dish rack. Simplify, I said, separating them. I kept one of everything. The rest I took outside.

My selection was limited and customers were few. A neighbor from next door turned the full saltshaker suspiciously in one hand. A quarter, I said. No charge for the salt. She passed on my offer and left for a sale down the street.

By afternoon, I had still sold nothing. Two women approached to inspect my table. The prettier of the two wore a wedding band and smelled like sunscreen and the ocean. She ran a bronzed finger along the flowered rim of a bowl.

Are you moving? she asked.

I told her no, I was simplifying. I was there to stay.

She considered some silverware and a stack of plates but a loud honk drew her away. A rental truck pulled up to the rowhouse across from mine. She leaned into the driver-side window. A light breeze rippled the back of her skirt.

It was close to dark when I went back inside. I taped a sign to my table that said FREE in big block letters.

That night, I dreamed of a wall of cabinets as high as a skyscraper. The ones I could open were all empty and each closed with a loud crash.

In the morning, broken plates and shards of glass littered the front lawn.

Submitted for Your Approval

Do you know what your problem is? she said.

What? I asked.

You're a cynical fucking bastard.

No I'm not, I said. Cynics don't exist. You're either a fulfilled romantic or an unfulfilled romantic.

And you're an unfulfilled romantic?

Absolutely, I said.

We decided to sleep together, not because of my keen insight into the human heart, but because it was late and because no one else seemed interested and because all the alcohol we had consumed promised us pleasure.

Later, I got out of bed for a drink of water. I returned with my glass, sat at the window, and watched leaves spiral down to the street.

Hey, she said.

I turned around.

If you're not going to drink that, don't let it go to waste.

She reached for the glass, which she finished in five loud gulps. She handed it back smudged with lipstick. I inspected the watery blot in the light from the window.

Hey, Mr. Unfulfilled Romantic. Are you coming to bed?

When I'm ready.

She slumped down again. Well *that* figures, she said.

harry took

Todd Moore

a 45 slug
thru
the right
lung
the im
pact
turned
him a
round &
he had
the il
lusion
that he
was running
but he
was fall
ing some
body was
yelling
fuck you
the blood
in his
mouth was
almost
a word

Mapped Water

A. Papatya Bucak

At the canyon's bottom, twenty feet from the creek, Claire, David and Jasper, who is off his leash and has to be called back, find a clearing with a fire ring. A place where others have camped. Claire takes this as reassurance that they are far enough from the water in case it rains. It has been off and on cloudy, though hot, all morning. They hiked four hours to this spot, first through the woods, then down the steep canyon trail.

While David pours water for Jasper, Claire unbuckles her pack, and slides it off her shoulders. She is short, thin, and pale. Blonde. Her t-shirt is wet in patches where the pack touched her body. She pulls her hair out of its ponytail, shakes it, then pulls it back again, feeling the soreness in her shoulders when she reaches behind her. The only sounds in the canyon are the creek water rushing and Jasper lapping filtered water from his dish.

Claire pulls her damp t-shirt over her head, again feeling the strain in her shoulders. In her sports bra, she shakes the shirt out and hangs it from a tree branch. David looks up from his pack and yanks out the tent.

David is strong and tall in ways, after a year, Claire still does not expect. He has muscles on the backs of his arms, the wingspan of a swimmer, and is handsome like the boyfriends of other women. Claire thought when she fell in love it would be with someone who was picked on as a boy. Someone who, like her, spent his childhood on a couch, reading.

From her pack, Claire pulls the tent poles, and David tosses her the tent. Together they find a flat spot and test it as they would a bed, lying down and stretching their arms and legs into sleeping positions. Jasper licks at first Claire's face and then David's. They laugh and Claire thinks, we are moving like waves, coming in and going out. She chokes and sits up. As she coughs, she puts her hand on Jasper's snout to push him away, and David pounds her on the back.

"I love you," Claire says in a strangled voice.

Taking his hand away, David says, as if it is the right thing, the normal thing, "I know you do."

Then, as is their routine, David leaves her to put up the tent while he filters water. He walks away with Jasper, who has black fur too hot for Arizona and one ear that won't come down, following.

As Claire hooks the rain fly into place, David returns with an armful of sticks, one, which he hands to her, longer than the others.

"Walking stick," he says. "Let's walk along the creek."

Claire puts on a dry t-shirt and the old sneakers David suggested she bring. She tests the walking stick on the ground; it is a good height for her. Then she follows David into the creek. The water is a shock, so cold that Claire steps back and for the first time considers sending David on without her. But she reminds herself she will get used to it and steps back into the water, letting it soak through her sneakers. Jasper scrambles past her, carelessly, chasing David, who already five yards ahead, steps from stone to stone. Following David's damp prints on each rock, Claire tries to match his strides, but they are too wide. Even with her walking stick, she has to follow different, slower routes and falls further back.

David is earning a graduate degree in water. All his life he has been fascinated by water and Claire loves this about him, the idea of a miniature David drawn to riverbanks and creek beds and their mysterious behaviors. Once she flew with him on a research trip to see the Willamette flood. The night before he was so excited he was unable to sleep. Claire's fascination is with fascination itself, with the things other people fall in love with.

The canyon walls come closer until finally there are no stepping stones, and she and David, who waited for her where the water deepened, wade, and then swim between red rock walls. With each stroke Claire pushes her walking stick ahead of her on top of the water. Sometimes Jasper swims for it, but he cannot get his mouth around it. When they swim David slows and checks on her, then pushes ahead. Never before has Claire swum in clothes, shorts and a t-shirt, old sneakers. Their weight surprises her. The creek scares her though she knows it ought to be a comfort.

When David first took her backpacking almost a year before, they ran out of water on their second day and Claire, though she doesn't mention it, has never forgotten. There were dry rocks where David expected waterfalls. Water that was mapped had moved on.

They had cooked with rain and the next day, embarrassed, David had scooped water for them to drink from a still, dark puddle trapped between rocks. Claire had stared at that water, hesitated on the edge of its possibilities, but when she drank, it tasted of nothing but the chemicals David had added to make it safe. He took her camping six or seven times after, each time teaching her more to keep her safe: how to hang a bear bag, how to light the stove, build the best fire, things she never thought she would know. She could, now, camp alone.

At one bend where the creek is only four or five feet wide and the banks gone, with David and Jasper again ahead out of sight, Claire pauses and stands with water almost to her waist and forces herself to see the red canyon walls. They are mammoth. It is impossible that this creek has carved these walls.

All day Claire has been too much inside her mind, only remembering her body because it is tired. David is planning a summer trip to Wyoming and he has not invited her. When they met, he was in his first year of his master's degree, but now he has only a few weeks to decide between schools for his Ph.D. He can stay or move a thousand miles away. He, she knows, is confused. He is not good with decisions.

Further on, the creek widens and the water becomes shallow. Claire tries again to walk only on rocks. Usually when she and David hike she searches for something to count, red-winged blackbirds, fire-marked trees, footsteps; today, as she steps rock to rock, she counts the men she has slept with. She ought to be reviewing goals for work, preparing for a Monday meeting, but without meaning to she is thinking of men. The first four guys come easily to mind, clumped together in her memory: Jason, Justin, Marty, Rob, all in college. It had taken only four to set a pattern, to say, "Who am I to say no?" Even alone she is embarrassed.

Tired from walking and swimming, Claire's legs shake as she presses down on each step. Her sneakers are soaked and she slides more than once, until finally, stepping too far without planting her stick, she falls. She makes no sound, no attempt to catch herself, lands hard on one hip, her feet and hands, walking stick, in the air. There will be a bruise—the kind so dark she will want to show it to people as if it were a Girl Scout's merit badge. Claire is proud of her scars; each mark saying you have been here and here and here. When a scar on her knee from a fight when she was twelve faded to nothing by adulthood, she felt cheated. The scar seemed like evidence she might one day need to prove she was strong.

If David were with her she would laugh to show she is all right, but instead she sits in the water letting it swirl around her as a trickle of blood runs down her shin. When she stands it is even harder to walk.

A year and a half ago, after a year of living alone, working all the time, a year of living in shock at the person she had become in college, Claire moved to Arizona because she had a friend there, Ruby. Live with me, Ruby said. You'll find a job. What Claire found was David. In their first conversation, he admired her for starting over, moving somewhere new, all alone. She found a job, too—at a pharmaceutical company where she wears a suit and pretends she feels like an adult every day. On Monday, the boss wants to know her plans for the company's future.

When Claire told Ruby she didn't think David loved her anymore, or worse never did, Ruby said, "Too bad you don't believe in God."

"So I could pray?" Claire said.

"So you could be a nun," Ruby said.

Claire never fell in love with any of the men she slept with in college. And none of them fell in love with her.

"You've got to see this," she hears David call back to her and then a splash. Forward through another bend, she sees him, his pale arms flashing in the sun and his black hair slicked back, swimming around a large slab of red rock. She swims to the rock and climbs on. It feels like a floating raft though it is secured to the creek bed. David climbs up beside her. He has taken his shirt off and she remembers the moment her bare skin first pressed against his. Three months after they started dating. Ruby said it was some kind of miracle, a guy who would wait that long.

"Don't you want to swim?" he asks. "It's deep here."

From the water, Jasper barks.

"Cold," Claire says.

David touches the back of his wet hand to her cheek as if checking for fever, as if he has misunderstood her, then jumps back in the creek. He goes all the way underwater and when he pops back up, Jasper butts at him with his head, as if he is trying to save David from drowning.

Claire wipes the water from her face and moves further down the rock into a patch of sun. It bothers Claire, the way David touched her as if nothing is wrong between them. His shirt is balled up next to her, and she shakes it out, and lays it against the rock. "I fell," she says.

He glances up from the water. "You okay?"

She nods and he, after looking at her, as if giving her a chance to say more, turns back to Jasper who wants to play.

"Who was it," she asks, "that you came here with? You know, the people you said didn't want to hike the creek when you came here before."

David tilts his head back into the water as if cooling it. "Gwen," he says. "It was just me and Gwen."

He says Gwen's name as if it is a question, as if he is unsure of whether or not he has mentioned her before. Claire crosses her arms over her stomach. David had told her Gwen, his ex-girlfriend, hated to camp. When David brought camping to Claire like a gift, one she had not known she wanted, she thought it was a sign. That this was something they would share forever. She knows that Gwen still affects him, that when she calls, it affects him. With every step, he has probably been mourning her. David looks at Claire from the water. He looks wounded, as if on the verge of asking for help. Gwen broke his heart.

What Claire loves about David is this: he has a heart that can be broken.

She decides to swim. She jumps in feet first and is surprised at how much colder she is when her head goes under. When she rises to the surface she swims towards David, who is splashing water at Jasper. With one hand, she reaches for David's arm, as if he were the edge of a swimming pool. She does not really want to swim, only to hold onto him in deep water.

He turns and swims away from her, then splashes her as if they are playing. When she does not respond, he splashes her again.

For the first time, Claire is angry. She swims back to the rock and climbs on, lies in the sun with her eyes closed.

By nightfall the clouds are back so that there are no stars and no moonlight. Claire hangs a flashlight around her neck and aims it at the sky, a talisman against rain. Just in case, David uses the groundsheet to build a shelter, a makeshift extension of their rain fly, for Jasper who won't fit in the tent. Far away there is thunder.

"David?" Claire says, turning towards him. She wants him to say they are far enough from the creek, that he has considered the possibility of a storm, and they are not in danger of being struck by water so deep and forceful it will bury them, rather than sweep them away.

"It's not going to happen," he says and curses as Jasper's shelter collapses on one side.

Afterward David sets up his lantern and sits with Jasper beside him while Claire looks around, sees his tent, his stove, his light. She is in a world of him. He gestures for her to sit next to him, but instead she goes to brush her teeth somewhere far from camp where bears can come later and sniff at her spat-out toothpaste. She is afraid of bears. Secretly though, she hopes to see one. Secretly she believes if a bear saw her she would be able to soothe it, to befriend it until it opened its arms to her and held her to its enormous chest, and let her sleep warm against its fur.

When she returns Claire climbs into the tent claiming a headache, and to her surprise, as if she really is sick, falls immediately to sleep.

When she wakes again hours later, David is beside her, though she has no memory of his coming in. It is hard to enter a tent without disrupting things, but it is the kind of thing he does regularly — an act of magic — the gentle filling of space.

The first time they made love, Claire's body worked its way up the bed so that she was in danger of rocking her head against the headboard, and to rescue her David took her head in his hands. Claire wonders now who that woman was. The one he had been in love with. The one he had thought she was. That woman gave him a rock and he kept it in his pocket for weeks. He brought that woman a fallen bird's nest he found in Washington, carrying it in his lap on the plane. When she wasn't paying attention, he took that woman's photograph. He held that woman's head in his hands, and then somehow, somewhere discovered she didn't exist, and here instead was a different woman, and he couldn't seem to imagine how she got there or who had invited her.

Claire presses her legs together inside her sleeping bag and huddles her feet. She is wearing her long underwear, but it feels loose and not warm enough. She has removed her socks inside the bag, and she moves her feet trying to find them. She can feel the bruise on her hip and is tempted to dip the flashlight into her bag to look at it. There is a rush of wind and the tent rattles as if a giant paw is swatting it. It sounds as if there will be a storm. Claire moves closer to the middle, closer to David, wrapped tightly inside his own bag. Outside she can hear Jasper rustling, his fur brushing against the tent flap.

Claire pulls one hand out of her sleeping bag and lays it on David's back. He does not stir. Moving still closer to him, Claire takes stock of her emergency knowledge. "Don't panic," is all she can think of. Don't panic, she repeats to herself. Don't panic.

Her father once, in line at the grocery store, had turned to her and said, "You're not good in emergencies." She had been too disturbed to answer, not because she disagreed, but because as far as she knew she had never been in an emergency.

The wind hits the tent again and Claire considers opening the flap to let Jasper in, but there is no space for him, something would tear. "David?" she says again, this time shaking him gently. When he still does not move, she sits up, her head bowed so as not to hit the tent's netted loft, and looks down on him. His fleece has drifted away from under his head and only his hands are tucked there. This man is such a stranger to Claire she cannot tell if he is sleeping or faking sleeping. She shakes him again.

"What?" he says without opening his eyes.

"I...maybe we should let Jasper in," she says.

David rolls over so that he is looking at her. "He's fine."

"Why did you want to come here?" she asks.

He closes his eyes, then opens them again. "To show it to you," he says.

Claire lies back down in her bag, facing David, their eyes, mouths, bodies, inches apart. "Why don't you want to show me Wyoming?" she says.

David touches his hand to her cheek, just as he had on the rock, then says, "Do you want to see it?"

The first time he invited her camping, he had begged her to come and told her everything she might see and everything she might feel. He had said, if you hate it, I won't mind. If you hate it, we'll never go again.

Claire does not want to go to Wyoming; all she wants is to be invited. "I don't know," she murmurs and when David doesn't say anything she reaches for him, kisses him, tries to get closer.

"Claire," he says pulling his head back. "I...I'm tired."

"Okay," she says and rolls over so that she faces the tent wall. The last time they made love, two weeks before, he had not wanted to. Claire had kissed him and he had pulled away and she had kissed him again. For a second they had remained paused there, lips together, nobody moving, and then his body had relaxed into hers, and he had kissed her back.

She draws her bag closer around her. Soon she hears David roll over so that he, too, is facing out, closer to the tent wall than to her.

When Claire thinks David is sleeping, she slides out of her bag and unzips the tent flap. Her boots are tucked under the rain fly and she pulls them on with only her feet outside. Sliding out of the tent, her jacket in her hands, Claire muddies the knees of her long underwear, and a soaked Jasper comes forward to see what is happening. She realizes she was wrong. There is no storm coming; it has already gone. The ground around her is soft with soaked up rain. Jasper licks at her face, then tries to sneak around her into the tent. She pets his head, then tugs him away from the entrance. Her hip aches and she rubs at it. The flashlight is still around her neck and trailing its feeble light she walks, with Jasper, to the creek's edge.

Shivering, Claire pulls her rain jacket on over her long underwear. The creek is moving faster than before and the rock where she and David sat and washed their dishes is under water. While she slept, it had rained and perhaps then David had lain awake making sure they were safe. It is windy and dark, but Claire can see, in shapes of darker and darkest, the trees and air and rocks. There will not be any need to wake David or to move to higher ground. They will talk tomorrow or the next day or the next.

Dropping down, not caring if she is on rock or in mud or on sand, Claire pulls Jasper in close to her. Both of them are shaking, and Jasper is damp, but Claire wants to feel the bulk of another body against hers. It is impossible to imagine going to work on Monday in this state—wanting to grab every person by the waist, by the hair, by the arm—wanting to hold tight to everybody. She drapes one arm around Jasper's middle and he tucks his head into her chest. She hugs him closer and whispers into his ear, "I am good in emergencies." He shifts against her and Claire lets go.

Thirty feet behind her is a canyon wall, across the creek another. She can hear the water shaping its path between them. From David, Claire has learned to measure water not by the space needed to contain it, but by how much force it holds. One day this knowledge will be of use to her, but if a stranger came upon her now, Claire would grab him to her, pull off his clothes, pull him inside, make fists on his back as she pressed herself as close as possible to his warm, damp, wet, dry, cold skin. She would do anything to seduce him, to feel twice her size.

Lemons

Sandra Yannone

Sometimes in the state of grating
the lemon peel, Delaware

disappears, the light propagates
through the kitchen window, and the unfair

city squints back to my side of the glass. I scribble
recipes onto the backs of paper napkins. I have quit

setting my clocks to resemble the principles
of others who believe that I commit

sins with women. What they can catalog
won't cover the head of a straight pin.

I am grating the lemon, casting out their smog
as best I can. The zest of kitchen Zen

blows through the sturdy canvas
of my lungs, sustaining air, not deviance.

At the Kiva

Seth Biderman

"You know, I used to live here," said the man.

The bartender nodded. He was looking down the bar at the brunette, whom he had decided was fairly attractive.

"I used to live here long before you were born, *muchacho*."

The bartender did not like being called *muchacho*, but he nodded again. "Is that right?"

"Yes," said the man.

The brunette was from Detroit, in Santa Fe only for the weekend to visit her aunt. This she had told the bartender while he mixed her a Long Island. Dropping in the straw, he had replied that he hoped her visit was eventful, which he had considered a fairly clever thing to say. He wanted to talk to her again now, but it was too late to pick up the old conversation and too soon to start in with something new, so he passed a bit of time by listing, in his head, the names of the states. He began with "Alabama," and ran through them to an alphabetical tune from elementary school, which he was secretly proud to still know.

At "New Jersey," a waiter came in and slapped a drink order on the counter. The bartender banished the tune from his head, blushing slightly.

"Slow night," the waiter said.

"We'll see," said the bartender. He jerked his head toward the brunette, but the waiter had turned toward the gas fireplace and did not notice. The bartender began mixing the drinks. As soon as the waiter left, he would check on her again. He liked his chances. She was not so attractive that she would be stuck-up, and she had not seemed stuck-up when she had talked to him. Still, the bartender had decided some time ago that women were very unpredictable, and he reminded himself now not to be surprised if this one turned out to be stuck-up in the end.

"Two four tops," the waiter was saying. "And I bet I don't turn a table."

"No?"

"No. I could use the money, too. They jacked up the season passes again."

"Terrible," said the bartender.

"Eight hundred bones for one season. It's like you gotta be some rich Texan to ski around here."

"It's terrible," said the bartender. "It should be half off for locals."

"You got that right," said the waiter. "They'd never do that here, though. Not with all the Texans."

The bartender finished filling the order and set the drinks neatly on the waiter's tray. "There's not much you can do with Texans," he agreed.

"I'll be waiting in ticket lines till Christmas if things don't pick up around here," the waiter said miserably. He turned to face the bartender. "Must be hell for you, a night like this."

"It's not so bad," said the bartender, and he jerked his head toward the brunette again. This time the waiter looked, and the bartender was proud to see him nod his approval as he picked up his tray and walked out.

There were two other customers in the bar that evening: the man who had called him *muchacho*, who was on his last whiskey, and an Indian-looking man who had a long braid of hair and wore nice clothes. Once he had sat at the bar, this man, and told the bartender that he managed one of the neighboring galleries, but the bartender had made it fairly clear that he had little interest in people who did not know if they were Indians or businessmen. Since then the man had always sat at the corner table and watched the gas fireplace as he drank. Tonight he was drinking slowly, and the bartender slid over to the brunette.

"Doing all right?"

"Fine," she said. She gave him a smile which showed too much of her upper gum, though her teeth were very white and straight. The bartender smiled back, though he could not help thinking that if he were to marry her, the upper gum would soon become annoying, and that after a while he would undoubtedly stop talking to her at the dinner table so she would not smile and expose it. For one or two nights, however, he could handle an upper gum.

"So how do you like Santa Fe?"

"It's all right, I guess. My aunt doesn't leave the house much."

"Is that right?"

"Yes," said the brunette. She looked down the bar. "I think that gentleman wants another drink."

This the bartender did not like. He considered himself a very good bartender who could take care of his customers without any help, but to humor the brunette he glanced over. To his surprise, he found that the old man was watching him, his empty glass held up in the air. The bartender moved over.

"Another whiskey, sir?"

The man set his glass down and pushed it forward with his fingertips. The bartender turned to the shelves on the wall behind him, and as he pulled down the bottle he spun it end over end, watching the brunette in the mirror. He filled the man's glass without spilling a drop and had the bottle back on the shelf in an instant. None of this seemed to impress her.

"It sure has changed a lot," the man said.

The bartender turned and faced the man irritably. He was an old man who had come in for the first time four nights ago, and every night since he had shown up at the same time, around six, always wearing the same blue jeans, the same faded plaid shirt. Every night he had ordered two Johnnie Walker Reds and left by seven-thirty, and until tonight he had not tried to make any small talk, which was fine by the bartender, who was not very interested in chatting with an old, one-shirted man. But tonight the old man had ordered a third whiskey, and turned chatty, and the bartender felt that he was doing it all deliberately, just to hurt his chances with the brunette.

"What?" he asked. "What's changed a lot?"

"The house," said the man. "I hardly even recognized it."

"Which house?"

"This," said the man. He lifted his arm slightly.

"The restaurant, you mean."

"It used to be a house, *muchacho*. When I lived here."

The bartender looked around the room. "This used to be an Italian bistro, before Mr. Greene took over."

"It was a house," the man said.

The brunette was watching with some interest now, and for her sake the bartender continued the conversation.

"When did you live here?"

"A long time ago," said the man. "Long before you were born."

"What—the sixties? Fifties?"

The old man tilted his head back and seemed about to laugh. "Long before that, *muchacho.*"

The bartender waited to make sure the old man had talked himself out, and then turned back to the brunette. He was surprised to find her still watching the old man very intently, her face tight, her mouth pulled down at the corners. The bartender looked and did not see anything more than an old man with a whiskey, but there was no telling with women, so he decided to let her watch for a while, until she saw for herself that there was nothing to see.

In the corner, the Indian businessman was, as usual, watching the gas fireplace. To pass the time the bartender followed his gaze. The fake logs were in their neat stack and the clean, blue flames licked over them gently. There was something else, however, something the bartender hadn't noticed in the entire eight months he had been tending bar at the Kiva Grill: a tiny orange flare, no larger than a fingernail, that would appear very suddenly at the tip of this flame or that, and then be gone in an instant. The bartender watched the flare with an inexplicable disgust, and then snapped the towel from his apron and began wiping down the drink counter, though it was already very dry.

Mr. Greene walked into the room, ledger book under his arm, and came behind the bar to pour himself a neat scotch.

"Mr. Greene," said the bartender. "This gentleman says he used to live here, back when it was a house. In the forties."

Mr. Greene didn't seem to be in a good mood. He set his ledger book on the bar, took a sip of his scotch, and held out a hand to the old man.

"Hank Greene," he said.

"Pablo Martinez," said the old man. They shook hands and the bartender saw that Martinez's hand was very rough and brown next to Mr. Greene's.

"Set him up," Mr. Greene said. He took up his ledger book.

"Sure," said the bartender, and as Mr. Greene left, he turned to the brunette with a smile.

She had not stopped her study of the old man.

"Excuse me," she asked, leaning toward him. "What did this room used to look like?"

This the bartender had not expected. He recalled being told once that some women were abnormally attracted to much older men, but he could not believe his brunette was one of them. He watched her carefully.

"The only thing that hasn't changed is the *vigas*," Martinez told her, pointing up. "And that fireplace over there. With real wood, *que no?*"

"Yes," said the brunette.

"This room used to be the *comedor*. There was a big round table that my father had made."

The brunette nodded and gave the old man a smile, only this time it was a pretty half-smile that did not show anything except the whiteness of her teeth.

"I had six brothers and one sister, and we were all of us born in this room," Martinez said.

"That's amazing."

"Right here, in this room. I was the youngest, and that was a long time ago."

"Just amazing," sighed the brunette. "Did you live here long?"

The old man looked up, as though seeking the answer on the ceiling. "Until I was twelve," he finally said.

"So why did you leave?" put in the bartender. He was annoyed that the brunette had given the old man her good smile, and though he could care less about Martinez, he felt he should say something so she would look at him again and realize that the bartender was easily the more handsome of the two, even if she did have a thing for old men. But she did not look at him at all. She looked into her drink as though embarrassed by his question, and it was Martinez who looked up at him, his eyes stern.

"We had to sell it."

The bartender nodded. Martinez kept looking at him, and he felt his face redden, though he could think of no reason to be embarrassed.

"And you, *muchacho*? Where are you from?"

"I was born here," said the bartender. "Right here in Santa Fe."

"*¿Y tu gente?* Your grandparents? Your great-grandparents?"

The question made the bartender feel like a little boy. He felt his face redden even more, and he did not dare look at the brunette.

"My grandparents are from Eastern Europe," he said.

"Eastern Europe's a big place, no?"

"Russia," said the bartender. "I think they're mostly from Russia. But I'm from here."

"No," said Martinez. "*I'm* from here. You're from Eastern Europe. Maybe Russia."

He tapped his glass. The brunette cleared her throat.

The bartender did not move.

Martinez tapped his glass again. "*Otra*," he ordered.

The bartender grabbed the whiskey bottle and filled the glass without speaking. He did not like Martinez one bit. He capped the bottle and watched the old man lift his glass. He saw how his face was pock-marked and worn, and how his nose showed signs of drink, and it occurred to him that Martinez was most likely jealous of the bartender's good looks and chances with the brunette. Struck by a pang of pity, he reminded him that his drink was on the house.

"I can pay for my own drinks," said Martinez.

The pity exploded and the bartender turned away, his hands trembling. He resolved not to speak to Martinez again, and began furiously arranging the bottles behind the bar.

"Do you think I can't pay for my own drinks?"

The bartender did not reply. He kept his hands moving so that no one would see they were shaking. A tiny burst of orange splashed the corner of the mirror and was gone. His annoyance grew, and he began silently rushing through the states again, the names flickering through his mind recklessly: "Alabama Alaska Arizona..."

"*Te hablo, muchacho*," said the old man.

The bartender's hands moved faster and faster; they flew over the bottles, shifting this one back an inch, moving that one forward, putting each in its place, and the names flicked by: "—Missouri Montana Nebraska Nevada—"

"*Oye*."

"—New Mexico New York North Carolina—"

"¡*Oye!*" shouted Martinez, and the bartender spun around in fury. The old man was leaning forward, his hands clenched like bird's feet to the edge of the bar. And then it hit him—Martinez was drunk. The song stopped at "Ohio"; his hands steadied. He felt himself returning to familiar territory. Drunks he could handle. He flashed a cool look at the brunette, and then he told Martinez:

"You're certainly welcome to pay for the drink, sir. It was only an offer."

Martinez glared, and then dropped his eyes to his glass. The bartender knew he had won. He moved over to the brunette. "We get all types in here," he shrugged.

"I think it's just amazing that he was born in this very room."

The bartender maintained his smile. "Yes," he said. "A lot of history in this town. Have you been to the oldest house yet?"

"No," she said, looking over at Martinez. "It must be hard to come back and everything's changed." She lowered her eyes to her drink.

The bartender waited for her eyes to come back up. They did not.

"Another Long Island?"

"No," said the brunette. "I should be going anyway." She looked at Martinez again. The bartender's stomach sunk; behind the brunette he saw the gas fireplace. The little orange flare seemed to be taunting him, and he moved away, defeated. He never would have guessed, not in a million years, that a woman like her would feel so sorry for a man like Martinez, who was not only old and ugly, but now drunk as well. He could not get over how truly unpredictable women could be, and felt, for an uncomfortable moment, that he might never figure them out. The moment passed quickly, however, because the bartender reminded himself that he was still relatively young, after all, and as he planned on tending bar for a long time, he would certainly come into contact with many more women, attractive women who would know for whom to save their good smiles. Slowly, his confidence began to return.

"*Oye.*"

The bartender looked up. He was a good bartender. He could handle an old drunk.

"Yes?"

Martinez tapped his glass. "You do your job, *muchacho.*"

"I think you've had enough."

"*No me importa* what you think. Give me another one."

The bartender shook his head.

"*Andale.*"

"I'm sorry, sir." The bartender reached for Martinez's empty glass. "State law prohibits—"

But Martinez had grabbed his hand, and now he held it very tightly.

He had a surprisingly strong grip and the bartender could not twist free, nor could he avoid being pulled close to the old man's face. His head began to pulse; he felt himself in grave danger of contracting a serious disease from the man's brown skin, or from the hot stink of his breath.

"Don't you ever, ever, talk to me about your *pinche* state laws."

"Let go of me," the bartender said. "Let go of me right now." Tears of fury, little boy tears, pushed up behind his eyes. He knew what he would do when Martinez let him go: he would jump over the bar and knock the old man out with a single punch. It did not matter that the bartender had never punched anyone before—he was certain he would do it now.

When Martinez released him, however, he only retreated against the wall of bottles, rubbing his hand. His fingers hurt very much and he quickly inspected them. Nothing seemed broken.

He looked up again to find Martinez clutching at his own chest, his mouth drawn into a furious frown. The old man's eyes locked onto his, and the bartender stared back, rubbing his hand. He stared into the eyes and saw that they were deepening, right at that moment, right as the bartender watched. It was as if he had suddenly become aware that the continent on which he stood was drifting, slowly, toward the West; the room began to swim and he broke from the old man's stare. Frantically, he searched the bar, trying to get his bearings, but the brunette did not look like anyone he had seen before, and the Indian businessman was a stranger, and even the beams that crossed the ceiling seemed foreign, imported. His eyes fell to the gas fireplace, seeking the familiar blueness of the flames, and there it was again— that little orange flare, dancing around like it had known everything all along.

"Get out," he said, turning back to the old man. "Get out of my bar."

The old man said nothing. His eyes had grown distant and his frown had relaxed. He looked strangely content.

"Get out of here!" the bartender shouted, terrified, but the old man simply began to tilt forward, toward the bar. His hand dropped from his chest to his lap and he continued to tilt, slowly, without gaining momentum, until his forehead came to a rest on the bar beside his unfilled whiskey glass.

Mr. Greene appeared in the doorway.

"What the hell's going on in here, Jake?"

The bartender shook his head, but the woman was looking up at him now, and the man in the corner who looked only at the gas fireplace looked up at him, and then the spaces in the doorway behind Mr. Greene filled with the curious eyes of waiters and bussers, and he could feel very distinctly every single eye that stared at him. They were like fingers prodding into his forehead, and though he was desperate to escape them, there was not a place in the world he could go.

Bottomless

Glenna Luschei

Throughout the fifty-two year
Mayan calendar,
they never
understood their love,
bottomless as the *cenote*,
vigilant as the jaguar
with his jade eye.

Her lament: loss, loss.
He complained
she burned the rice,
spilled the masa,
wept.

In that lake
she could recover
all she had lost.
If he let her go
for that new water sprite
she would dive
through the castles
and parapets
to discover
skeletons of lost love.

She could not hear
him purr, the jaguar
on the human-heart altar
of El Castillo.
She stitched loss
into her *huipil*.

They could not accept
the bottomless lake
they were offered.
They were not
Abelard and Heloise.
They were mortal.

Summer at a Farm in Nowhereville [Georgic No. 3]

John Surowiecki

A rabbit hangs like Mussolini's mistress
under the skirt of its own skin. They say
its red blood makes blackberries. They
say clouds harvest the breaths of babies

in whose cloudy new eyes you can see a
grandmother's last gasp. In gooseberries,
you can taste the cold sweet sweat of the
insane. Then: pears fall, liquefy, ferment;

by intoxicated bees we listen to European
orchestras and read about the underclass.
In their science, ordinary rain can drown
a sophisticated heart and summer seduces

with melon textures and jackets of minty
air: but nothing is said about the women
who come to bed on all fours, wobbly and
giddy and smelling of blackberry brandy.

People of Pull

Shawn Behlen

Every town needs someone to judge itself by in comparison, and so the residents of Pull watched for years as Lysette Nelson crossed streets against the light or carried an open umbrella with nothing to it but a frame. They watched her buy groceries, during which she sometimes wept, and fail eight times to get a driver's license and then drive anyway. They watched her cheer at her son's scholastic meets and his girlfriend's track meets, Lysette's yells of encouragement like something she scooped from inside herself and hurled.

They blamed such scenes on miss-taken medicine, on bad genes and the disfavor of God. They said, "Poor Henry Nelson," and vowed to patronize his laundry on the south side of town, out of their way as it was.

Two of them admitted to watching as well the afternoon she paced the Whitaker Street overpass. They watched her leap, thin and pale, watched her land on the median, where unknown weeds acted as brittle pillows. They said they had no idea that three ribs cracked, one puncturing a lung, or that a fibula broke, as did her collarbone. They were horrified to learn that a single jagged rock, hidden beneath the wildflowers, had dented the right front corner of her skull.

Three days later, Jay, Lysette's son, and Marcy, his girlfriend, sat in Jay's room, Marcy's house off limits to any of his family. Jay wore Marcy's throwing shoes on his hands while she brought up a website on Connie Price-Smith, a world-class shot putter like Marcy dreamed of being. At sixteen, she had thrown farther than all but four girls her age in the state.

"But you have to help me," Jay insisted. "For Mom. Remember what she always said about you."

He was referring to Marcy's future, to his mother's certainty that it billowed with greatness. A phrenological reader, Lysette Nelson had read this news on Marcy's cranium with the firm pressure of her fingers and palms.

"Jay, no," Marcy said. "Shut up." Marcy had grown up around Lysette, had loved her longer than she'd loved Jay. Marcy could never harm her.

"I just need you to come with me," Jay said. "It's not like I want you to do the actual deed. I'm her son." He tossed Marcy's shoes to the floor and dug in her gym bag until he came up with her sports bra. He looped it around his shoulders, clasping it over his shirt. Then he found her shorts, slid them over his jeans, and stuffed his feet into her shoes. "I wish I was you," he said. He put both hands to his face and rubbed hard.

"You look like an idiot," Marcy told him. Jay was almost forty pounds lighter and five inches shorter than Marcy. They were a favorite joke at school, in town.

Marcy wanted this day and this week over. She wanted to go back in time. Old Mr. Bolton down the street had left a month ago. Then Miss Alice, the biology teacher, had taken off amidst rumors that she'd been tutoring her subject too well to a certain student. And now, every day, Marcy read about house sales in the paper, about relocations and deaths.

"Come here," Jay said, and Marcy went to him.

She let him undress her and tug her to his sinking mattress. He fumbled with his own clothes, a condom, and positioned himself beneath her. "Cover me," he whispered.

Marcy lowered herself and rocked with an arched back that kept them face to face, her hair unpinned and curtaining their gazes. She studied Jay's skin, stretched so tautly over his bones that she sometimes thought it might snap.

When they finished and had lain awhile, cleaned up, Marcy gave Jay a kiss.

"I miss Miss Alice," she said. "She was like us, and that new guy, ugh." Marcy reached and cupped Jay's penis. She preferred it like this, less red and angry. Its beauty existed in what it could do, not in what it did. "And I heard that Priti Gatel's following that Ben guy to California," she continued. "And Suzie said at practice that Gindler's is closing next month. It's creepy, right?"

"Mom looks like a little bird," Jay said. "She doesn't trust the doctors. She wants Dad to stop. She wants all of them just to leave her alone and let it happen." He dropped his hand over Marcy's, stilling her inspection. "There's no one else to help her," he said. "There's just us."

At home, Marcy lay in the tub and sudsed between her legs. An exposed bulb flickered above her as she thought again of Jay inside her and of how she accepted him there. At times she thought of him as a blunt pin stabbing at an old balloon fully blown inside her.

When the front door slammed, she hurried from the tub to her room to dress and then downstairs to ready dinner. She boiled spaghetti in one pot, heated Prego sauce in another. By the time Marcy's mother had washed her hands, the back of her neck, and had changed from a skirt to jeans, Marcy had bowls and bread on the table.

Bell Peck, Marcy's mother, was a secretary at the First Baptist.

Marcy broke the silence. "Lysette might take visitors soon," she said. "I'd like to go."

Bell tore a hunk of bread and ate it. She was shorter than her daughter and trim at the age of forty-one. Bell was experienced in expressing regret that her daughter had taken physically after her ex-husband.

"That woman is troubled," Bell said. "Nobody at church is surprised at what she did."

Marcy nodded. She knew the ways of the town's caste system, of her mother's. Marcy's father had left seven years ago, and she had never been able to blame him.

"Lysette's a friend," Marcy said.

Bell waved her fork. "Needs more salt."

Marcy leaned to the counter and grabbed a small porcelain terrier, its eyes two tiny half-marbles glued on its face. Years ago, Marcy had dropped the dog's mate, used for pepper. It had barely cracked, but Bell had thrown it away.

Bell shook salt over her bowl. She chewed a mouthful of pasta and tilted her head. "Had some success today," she said. She spun more spaghetti on her fork and told Marcy about a couple she had counseled while Pastor Cook was busy. "The man cheated," Bell said, "so I told the wife how much I understood, that I had lived it. They listened to me. They're gonna work it out."

She just doesn't want to end up like you, Marcy thought. When she was careless, anger crept in like fatigue at the gym.

"Are you happy?" Marcy asked.

Bell peered over the edge of her plastic glass. "Getting mighty tired of that one," she said. She lowered her iced tea, squinting. "Those two today. I told them to go get pregnant, and one day I'll see that child in church. Do you have any idea what that means? That sort of thing keeps a small town going."

Biology was the one class Marcy and Jay shared. Mr. McKibbon, the substitute, stood at the front of the room like a man before a firing line. He coughed into his fist.

Instead of individual desks, the room contained taller tables, one for each group of four students, who perched on stools. Marcy and Jay sat with Jazmine Reese and Rashunda Whitehouse, two runners. They were beautiful, square-shouldered girls, horrified now that a fetal piglet curled before them.

Marcy wielded the knife, while Jazmine and Rashunda measured and took notes.

Jay read from the text: "…the skull will lift like a hinged door if cracked precisely."

"You one creepy little dude," Rashunda said. "Big girl, why you like him?"

Marcy was used to Rashunda from track. "Habit," she said, and then focused on the piglet. Its face stopped her, its little snout, its eyes flat behind thin, pale lids. Marcy glanced at Jay. People continued to ask about his mother, even though he told them, "You mean the crazy one?" or "She's about dead, but not quite, thanks."

"Maybe something else first," Marcy said. She arched to see a picture in their textbook, then pulled apart the piglet's chest before she could think about it. She exposed the heart and sliced it free as Jay instructed.

"Making me puke," Jazmine said.

Jay kept on reading: "The porcine heart exhibits many similarities to the human heart in anatomy, size, and function," he said. "Its tissues, with the help of glutaraldehyde, can be used for transplants between species. Unless of course the heart is broken in ways other than the physical. Then a heart should be allowed to stop."

"It doesn't say that," Marcy told him. "Quit it, Jay."

With one quick move, she sliced a transverse cut through the ventricles. The heart in her hand was smaller than she'd expected, its purpose and size together a marvel. When Marcy lifted weights or threw a shot, her pulse was often counted. She'd felt her own heart race and leap.

Marcy skipped practice that afternoon for the first time. She hurried through Safeway and then to the roadside park south of town. She claimed the picnic table without shade, wanting the sun like a blanket. Railroad ties and strung-together tires banked the hill behind her. To her left, three elementary-aged girls rode swings, their short legs pumping.

Their mothers sat on a nearby bench.

Marcy used to play at this park with her dad, used to be twirled against the sky, his hands the size of her chest. She dug in the Safeway sack, counting the months since she'd gorged. She pictured every nutritionist her mother had dragged her to over the years.

The chains on the girls' swings shrieked high, shrill notes.

"Well, I heard so," one of their mothers said. She was talking about Miss Alice, Marcy realized, about her and Tommy Technik. "That poor boy was just a sophomore," the woman added. "And if she thinks one county over is enough to teach again, she's got another thing coming. People in this town — people like us — we aren't the type to let such a thing happen."

Marcy studied the woman's tiny, strappy sandals and then began with the Twinkies, nipping both ends before licking the cream inside. She would be heavier after this, a big girl bigger. Swallowing, Marcy thought of times in the showers when she'd caught classmates inspecting her through wet hair, their glances like the quick flashes of a penlight bringing a dark room into shape. She was by far the tallest, easily weighed the most, and the other girls, at least the white ones, seemed to take her in with equal parts awe and revulsion.

Marcy grabbed the chocolate-covered pretzels next, the sweet and salty a perfect combination, the same term Lysette had always used for Marcy and Jay.

Marcy was nine when she'd met Jay's mother, when Pull's yearly watermelon festival filled the town square with rented rides and booths of prizes. Marcy stood behind the ring toss, discovering cotton candy, unwinding it, wrangling it into her mouth. It made her laugh, until Tammi Schauer walked up and told her, "Your daddy left you."

Tammi was a year ahead of Marcy at school, a girl who wore

culottes. Tammi balanced on the street curb, twisting a ring on her finger.

Marcy stared at Tammi, the cotton candy in her hand suddenly heavy. She stood and stared until Lysette, a woman Marcy had been warned away from for years, walked up and informed Tammi that her eyes weren't quite horizontally even. "That's pretty weird," Lysette said. "I'd hate that. I bet you hate that." Then Lysette smiled at Marcy while Tammi called them both crazy and ran away.

Lysette's eyes looked wet, almost teary.

Marcy walked away, too, and Lysette called, "That's okay. I understand."

In the years since, Lysette had been the first to support Marcy's earliest attempts at athletics, to discuss periods and sex, to imagine how proud Marcy's father must be of her. Lysette had deemed Marcy noble, had envisioned her future with touches to her head. And, when Lysette had become too scary, Marcy had walked away four times total, shame at her back like a propeller.

Mouth full, Marcy glanced up now to see one of the girls on the swings let loose and fly. While her mother screamed, the girl landed face forward, skidding across the dirt. The two other girls followed, eyes clamped shut as they headed for the ground.

Jay's dad sat in his old club chair, his eyes with as little visible energy in them as the buttons on either side of his head. Henry Nelson was tall, with prominently knuckled hands. Marcy turned from the doorway and stepped past, but Henry saw her and called.

The room was dark, two of its walls covered with family photos. Marcy settled on the ottoman beneath the window.

"I hate this room," Henry told her. "You seeing to my son?"

"Yes, sir."

"Good." Henry plucked at his shirt collar. "When I met Lysette, I was a young man," he said. "And now the world is small. Love works against you," he told Marcy. "That's what I've been explaining to them when they come in the shop, but they don't understand." He coughed, his mouth uncovered. Above his head, a mobile hung. He constructed them intermittently in the back yard, twisting wire hangers from his laundry.

Marcy watched the mobile and considered telling him her secret:

that it was the whole world she imagined throwing during track meets. The smaller she could imagine it, the farther she threw. Despite what Mr. Nelson had just said, it was becoming harder not to imagine the world enormous.

But she rarely talked to Mr. Nelson and didn't know how to start. "You saw Lysette today?" Marcy asked.

"I see her now." Mr. Nelson undid a button at his neck.

Marcy stood as the man's loneliness unfurled toward her. Everyone treated her in accordance with her size, instead of her age.

In the hallway she stood anchored by this afternoon's feast and watched Jay read on his bed. His floor was dotted with the latest round of used paperbacks, most marked and tattered. From these he learned the names of dead men he still deemed smarter than himself: Sumner and Lillebakken, Saccas and Trevithick. Marcy had come to think of the names as topsoil, sprinkled so that Jay's own name could grow high and others could hide behind it as he did these.

"Hey," Marcy said. When Jay looked up, she said that she would help him.

All Marcy wanted was to climb in bed and not think about tomorrow, but her mother called, "Dinner's a time for family, you know." Marcy turned into the kitchen and found Bell at the sink, scrubbing a limp mass of fabric.

"I finally called your father," Bell said. "Not like you'll listen to me about those Nelsons." She stretched the crotch of a pair of pantyhose beneath the water, fingers poking. "Couldn't get him," Bell said. "I had to talk to that woman of his." Bell rolled her shoulders. "Said she'd tell him, but she won't."

Marcy grabbed a dishtowel to press against the wet underwear already on the counter and soak up water. These were her underwear. She glanced sideways. "Mom?"

Bell's scalp showed through. She leaned to the water, knuckles grinding at a tiny stain. Watching her, Marcy knew that she herself might look like her father, might have his size, but it wasn't from him that she'd learned to push until a shot flew. "I'm worried," Marcy said, "about Mr. Nelson. Mom, this isn't his fault. You should talk to him, like you do to all those people who need you at church."

Bell glanced back over her shoulder, then forward. Beyond her, through the window, there was nothing to see but a wall.

"You're so good at it," Marcy said. "Like with that couple."

Bell stared through the window and sighed. With a wet wrist, she brushed hair from her temple. "That man needs to hear some hard truths," she added. "You understand that?"

When Marcy nodded, Bell hit the faucet knob with her elbow and took the towel from her daughter. She wiped her hands, opened the refrigerator, and pulled out a plate topped with foil. She plunked it on the table and told Marcy to sit. "You eat," Bell said. "You eat, and I'm going to tell you some things you need to hear again yourself."

Marcy and Jay made their way, the hallway hushed. Neither had spent much time in a hospital, and the place reined in their patter and gestures. At Lysette's room, they ducked inside. She looked nothing like the woman Marcy knew. Wraps covered half of her head, her eyes like loose marbles in two small cups. Even her smile looked crippled.

"Marcy," Lysette said. She uncurled the fingers of her left hand, but couldn't reach. Straps bound her wrists and ankles. At Marcy's touch, she whispered, "Honey, I'm so sorry."

Jay looked at Marcy straight on. "Right," he said.

Seeing Lysette like this, Marcy understood Jay's desire to complete his mother's flight. She also saw his mother's face in his, Lysette's features ready to sharpen as he aged.

A nurse entered before Marcy could speak. "Visitors," the nurse said to Lysette. "Bet you're glad." The nurse checked a monitor on the wall.

Marcy recognized her as Corine Reese, a soprano in the First Baptist Choir. From her mother, Marcy knew that Corine had conquered her addiction to alcohol and now raised a young son alone. Marcy's mother had helped this woman.

The nurse injected clear fluid into Lysette's IV line, then plumped her pillows. "She'll be under again real soon," Corine explained. "Just two or three more minutes, then it's time to leave." She closed the door behind her.

Jay yanked both hands from his pockets. "This is it," he said. He stepped forward and kissed his mother on the forehead, her nose, and then her mouth. "I love you," he whispered, tugging free a pillow. Jay stood, the pillow barely quivering. When the pillow touched his mother's face, Jay spun and thrust it at Marcy. He fell back with his hands in front of him, his face pinked and his eyes glassy.

"Do it," he said. "God, please. It's what she wants."

Lysette stared up at Marcy, her mouth twisting.

At least for now, Marcy set the pillow aside. She felt around the curve of Lysette's head, tugging tenderly until she found an end to the bandages and could begin unwrapping. She worked until Lysette's shaved skull was visible, the red-tinged square of gauze at the right front corner like a badge. Marcy eased both her hands beneath Lysette's neck and then higher, the woman's head resting in her palms.

Lysette's eyes closed, and her head weighed heavy in Marcy's hands. Her head felt huge.

Marcy pressed with her fingers, no one to turn to but herself. She leaned close, whispering, "You're a good woman, a good mother, a good friend," all things that should have already been said.

Eleven days later, most of the town's citizens turned out for Lysette Nelson's funeral. She was buried near Chenery Creek. The clay ground sat orange in a mound behind the tent. People fanned with anything available from handbags and pockets. "So sad," they all said before the preacher began, "to be sick enough to jump, to die alone in the middle of the night."

"A blood clot," they whispered. "You just never know."

Marcy and Jay stood in the front row with Mr. Nelson. He trembled, his head bowed. Behind them, Bell Peck reached to lay a hand on his back, and she was praised. As for Marcy and Jay, the rumors continued that they'd been barred from Lysette's hospital room after being caught there a week and a half ago, with that poor woman's wounds exposed and their arms around each other. "Like they were making out," everyone said, horrified. "Bet they feel guilty now."

But they didn't act guilty, didn't look sad. And the people of Pull were furious.

Their anger continued until the day after Marcy and Jay stepped from her mother's house in the dark, bags in hand, and then it warped with confusion. Two kids, gone, and no one knew where they might land.

It was, everyone agreed, a tragedy.

Frenchette

Lawrence C. Goeckel

*The unique and supreme pleasure of making love
lies in the certitude of doing evil.*
—Charles Baudelaire

The alleyway in front of her apartment
had a memory—
smelling of Spanish cigarettes,
a memory of the cobbled sound
of gloved hands applauding
gypsies with a balancing goat
"You must leave, I have grown allergic
to just 1/2 the bed"
She would tell her patrons
While her aged father slept
in front of a window
dreaming of the time the zeppelins
bombed Paris
Her exquisite flesh was perfumed
by cut flowers,
the first few drops of rain,
and the sun squeezed into an orange spot
over violet haystacks
Her legs were longing
in stockings
made from the nylon needed
for parachuting soldiers
Frenchette, descending
from the sky needed no parachute—
just a quick glance from
under the awning of the Cafe De Flore,
the negotiations of a small couch,
and the turned phrase, as in:

"Excuse me while I put on something
a little more difficult"
Loss of memory she regarded
as a man's greatest asset
For her—baffled sailors
ran their ships aground,
to wander drunk in the Quartier des Oubliettes;
Enormous foreigners
walking tiny dogs on long leashes,
asked questions no one understood;
The homosexuals
in the Rue de Bonaparte were swept
into a fever of imitating her;
And men with beautiful wives
longed for the wine fouled breath
of hags in rooms
by the last station of the Metro
Frenchette was the neon at alley's end
where factory girls rolled down their garters
She spoke the most precise of tongues,
that of the soul dedicated to pleasure
Bakers found their pause to see her pass,
then resumed polluting the air
with long loaves of bread
Frenchette abhorred open space,
preferring narrow streets
with lamp posts sheddding
handbills like leaves
Streets where the subterranean
claminess of the Metro was
relieved by the warm, polluted day—
where the boulevards whispered
to second story shadows
being bent over beds
While her father ate in lamplight,
without pleasure,
crumbs falling into his lap,

Lawrence C. Goeckel

the pigeons on her window ledge
cooed like she'd been good to them
Drunk on gin,
she placed black tape over
her nipples, and directed the postcard
photographer to caption her picture
"The tape of a wonderful death"
Admirers
took turns watching
through a key hole
as she combed
her beautiful thick pubic hair
in an enormous room
bearing one of the million
names of pleasure
She married,
dabbed champagne from her bodice,
and continued lying on the telephone
with the same slight smile as before
Her husband came home one night
and her hair was red, a wrong red
Frenchette gave him her hand
to be kissed, whispering
"Ah, my captor"
and put on her coat
A taxi waited outside the apartment,
its parking lights
staring up at her window
As her foot alit on the pavement
the city's searchlights,
long abandoned,
resumed carving tunnels into the night

A Wave Falling on the Beach

Lawrence C. Goeckel

The lighthouse beam briefly illuminates
trees entangling the sky with their conspiracies,
passes over the widow's fence
of blue bottles and river stones stuck in cement,
      then heads to sea
Selling some shuteye
to this little world

How hopeless the masts of ships in their moorings
under moonlit clouds
hardened into salt cake
in a sky that permits no one to see it

Kelp surfaces on irregular water —
the last black dots of a buried landscape

Past the point where light fails, drowned
      men's boats inch across wavelets

Making land again, the lighthouse beam
paints blank faces
on the homes of those asleep in their beds
It swings around but does not see
Yet, as an eyelid closing, ends the scene
A wave, waiting for this cue,
falls on the beach
all in a heap, exhausted

Message From the Photo-Mat

Lawrence C. Goeckel

A bit of aluminum and glass in the middle of asphalt
Paint blistering in the sun
Standing unmoved in this very second
  it has taken two billion years to form
The moon streaks across, the stars pop out,
  the drugs wear off
Nothing is to be learned from things beyond
  that already known

It is my opinion that when we say goodbye
  it means forever, that stars bring out
  the hidden sickness in the sky
We are fading…hardly here anymore
Our shadows change clothes like
  leaves twittering on weak stems behind us
Something wrong or very golden
  is unwritting us
As we try to photograph it

 Photos of a botched sunset
  over a monotonous silver green sea,
  like evidence of an adulterer
  wanting to sneak off with his loneliness
  are handed back to us in an envelope
We are a swamp of lost memories
  resurrected by the lies of photographs, the wandering
  odor of sulphur, the song of the red winged blackbird,
  cattails fading in the heat

 This world wants to
  eliminate the plurality of
  existence

Dripping like the small air conditioning unit
  hanging from the photo-mat
A rusting roof, walls protected by a yellow curb,
  radio dimly playing inside
This is the best music we have ever heard

After the photo-mat window closes
  the only characters left in this part
  of town zip up their pants
  and quickly walk off in different directions
A distant flag pole chain
  clangs in the half light   The trash heads north
  in the wind of the parking lot   A plastic lid
with a straw through its center wheels along
  like a one legged man on a unicycle
A bright, dangerous blue begins to fill in the shadows

Dust

Jaimy Gordon

When Medicine Ed finally had Little Spinoza all to his self, he told the horse: "Get ready, son. The women's gone to take your manhood." He broke the news, not like it was the end, and next come injury, bad luck, and death, but like it was a thing the horse ought to know. They were walking round and round the shedrow in a summer fog that silvered up the cobwebs and beaded the horse's eyelashes.

"Wasn't no idea of mine. I say wait, see how he do. Nothing ain't gone change that horse much at his age. I say he common, a bit of a crybaby, that's all, but easy to settle once he riled. You be surprise, I tell em. He ain't even all that interested in the señoritas compared to what you would think. They don't want to listen. They don't want to lose they edge. I say what if it change him the other direction, into a chucklehead girl? They start to laughing. Pretty soon they cackling like witches. Got me outnumbered, what it is…"

Medicine Ed checked himself. It was a stab-back and two-face thing to say about the womens. "They don't mean no harm," he added. He didn't want to be a wrong influence on the horse. What good it do if the horse love him and hate them others? Him, Maggie and Sal done bought that cheap racehorse together. They a bidness now.

"It's one thing you can count on, son. When they gone they gone. You never know what you missin. Onliest thing, you be lighter of heart. Anyhow," he say into the horse—first he spy round to see what devilborn varmint might be listening to, a crow, say, or Sal's slit-eye goat—"you know I be a little of a doctor-man. I take them things and do you good with em, you hear? You don't got to worry, you in good hands."

Little Spinoza was still looking over his shoulder into the weird blue crucifix eyes of the goat when a small commotion happened at his neck and suddenly the earth fell on him, his blood turned to warm solder, his penis dropped limp out of his body and his knees melted. He sank to the dirt. His elbows and stifles drained away. He rolled over on his side. His huge tongue went to fall out of his mouth. He was not sleepy but gravity had won a great victory and he wished never to get up again. He watched incuriously as the two men went around behind him and squatted, and one of them somehow picked up his leg and moved it a little and held the great black riverine tail out of the way. There was a pleasant tinkle of metal, a feeling of deep and strange but painless emptying, another not so agreeable snip snip, snip snip—two grayish-pink, wet, egg-like bodies, sparsely threaded with blood vessels, lay in the grass. That was it. They stood there waiting for his legs to come back under him.

The queerest thing was the long, thin, infinitely elastic tubes hanging down like spittle from the shiny balls before Haslipp snipped them away. Maggie saw Medicine Ed slide out of the tackroom and pick up the testicles out of the grass in a silver can—it could have been a soup can, nicely washed out and with the label neatly removed. And then he faded away again. She blinked. She hadn't known he was there. In fact he hadn't been there, or Tommy Hansel would certainly have called him over and made him drag away the ten-dollar goat, instead of doing that ridiculous job himself.

Medicine Ed pulled together the pink plastic curtains over the sink and sank his head and washed his hands. He must think about his dust and nothing else save his dust. All the while he is mixing it up he must think about his dust until his thinking put a kind of holy spirit on it. He had taken the jars out the wall one by one, and he was careful to bring to mind what they each contained. *He must be very deeply in earnest.* This one was a controlling powder, coltsfoot, not just dusty coltsfoot from beside any road, but the dark green velvet hand-shape leaves, soft as a lady's glove, that creep along the ruin of a stone stable deep in a woods in Vaucluse, South Carolina. In this stable his grandfather, Eduardo Picketts, greatest jockey ever known in South Carolina, born in slavery, killed in a match race in 1888, once was king.

He had hold of the dust from when he was doctoring. He knew he should get quit of it. Yet and still. It's no use crying. Evil has come out after him, and behind that evil, something must be done. Back in his crushed in trailer he make what he need. First, forward and foremost, he need speed enough to overtake and turn the wind of a horse into money. And money, too, need drawing and controlling: In this little whiskey bottle was boil of moneyplant, moneyplant gathered far from water which run itself away.

He done put away the doctoring after he lost his filly Three-Spot. Come to find out if you asked by powerful means for more than the animal had to give, you could not manage the results. Every time he had cast the powder the horse had won, but won for the last time. Twicet it was the other man's horse. Then Three-Spot, the onliest horse Medicine Ed ever loved, win for him at Hollywood Park and snapped her cannon bone in the van on the short drive home. And which was why he had let the medicine go, all except his name, which nobody up here was wise to where it come from. And that was a good thing.

In this jar was one teeninchy pinch, all he have left, of the blood of Platonic, who he rubbed for Whirligig Farm, and who give him his own bleeding ulcer. Platonic was early speed, and Cannonball was speed to close, and here, mixed in the grave dirt of Cannonball, if you scratch you find glassy, glittery things — wings of the botfly that can overtake and grab on the legs of any horse, so long as he be running.

Yesday he full of cautionary thoughts. He a owner now and a workingman too. Horse gone good. Every thing coming they way. His eyes be good, his ears good, his draggy leg no worse, remembrance still good, can't he be content to make it little by little? Yesday evening Medicine Ed was thinking let it go, put something down on the other man's horse, ony just a little — don't get greedy, don't stir up the devil, don't conjure with that old stakes horse from Nebraska, don't take his life. And then there come the sign that bad evil is lurking round and he must cover himself.

No use crying. Common judgment tell you that. It say so right in the Bible, *A horse never saved nobody.* Psalm 33. He had wished to spare that Nebraska horse. His own horse been paid good to run and stay out of it. They be of one mind on that score, Little Spinoza, Medicine Ed, and the womens. Little Spinoza is going for a walk in the park. They can save it up for another day, now that the horse got nothing down there to rile him.

Then just like that his boss Tommy Hansel have another idea. The young fool can't sit nor rest, he up and down the shedrow, in and out the stall, talking craziness to Red Dog, a big red animal, the one Joe

Dale Bigg taken from him, and which he claim back, and which he think is going to win that race for him, though he signed up for that losing money same as everybody else. He think the secret is between him and the horse. He don't even see where Joe Dale Bigg's boys are cruising up and down the dirt road watching him through the blind windows of that midnight blue gangster car.

Yesday Medicine Ed just cooling on his haybale, braiding a busted shank, when the Cadillac come grinding over the dry dirt in front of him, so slow it don't even raise no dust. The window slides down in the door and it's Joe Dale Bigg.

"You going to collect a couple dollars for losing tomorrow, Medicine?"

"Sho is, Mr. Bigg."

"I know you ladies ain't gonna turn Nebraska around. You ain't that dumb."

Medicine Ed watched the hot air wiggle over the manure pile.

"What about Tommy Hansel's horse? Whassaname of that horse?"

Medicine Ed shook his head.

"Red horse."

"Don't know his name."

"Don't know nothing, eh? I'll bet. Well, that's Red Dog. And I hear Hansel's buying up castles in Ireland from that horse. Do I hear right?"

Medicine Ed shook his head again, *I don't know nuthin bout nuthin,* and looked off at a sparrow taking a bath in the dirt. For these was the type of plans the young fool was swapping with that horse all night long.

"They say this business will drive you crazy," Joe Dale Bigg said. "The lying and the stealing and you can't be sure of nothing. Looks to me like your boss man went around that bend. Which is a sad sight to see, a talented horseman like that, but it ain't no excuse for getting in other people's business. If Hansel wants to go around with his fly hanging open, his eyes shining and his hair sticking up on end, that's his lookout. If he comes untied, that's your-all's lookout. He better not bust up my deal, you colly?"

Joe Dale practically yelling now and Medicine Ed cut his eyes up at him briefly, went on with his braiding.

"I'm putting you on that case, you hear? You old timey negroes from down around Aiken in the hunt country, I know you got your little ways. You use em, you hear me?"

"That red horse ain't gonna last in no race with Nebraska," Medicine Ed said. "He a sprinter, nemmind what the young fella say."

"I don't want him even trying," Joe Dale shouted. "I don't want no loose wheels out on that race course. I don't want no uncontrollable factors. I'm holding you responsible to stop it or let me know. You hear what I say?"

Slowly Medicine Ed raised his eyes to him. Already the purple window was riding back up in the door. Joe Dale's black sunglasses showed in the crack of it.

"Unh-huh," Medicine Ed said. "Sho is."

No use crying. Inside his pocket piece used to be anvil dust and a thumbnail of blue Getaway Goofer Powder, dressed with a drop of Jockey Club fast luck oil he order in from Lucky Heart Curios, Memphis, Tennessee. Every drugstore cunjure in South Carolina had the same. But now it's a strong Leave Alone powder in there too. He has the scooped up going-away tracks of all three of them white bosses at the Mound who like to scheme and get in your bidness, and can't be satisfied, and want it back, what anymany little bit of anything you finey lay hold of. This red racetrack dirt gave him keepaway power over the stallman, and the racing secretary, and the leading trainer, Mr. Joe Dale Bigg.

And now his boss Tommy was in there too.

Medicine Ed taken the little red flannel bag between his fingers and rub. He need speed, he need control of money, most of all he need a hand that will bend bad luck into good. He said: "In the name of the Father, Son and the Holy Ghost, I wants you to take all the bad luck off me and make it go on them, who tryna take from me, what I done rightly win, put the harm on them and let it go back to the devil where it come from." And he rubbed and listened to them clicking softly together in this strong Leave Alone powder, the carefully parched manly parts of Little Spinoza, smoked down to the size of marbles, over a dry wood fire.

On Suicides and Murders

Martin Scott

My high school debate coach, Mr. Wilkinson, was the second smartest person I knew during the first seventeen years of my life. He also taught literature and creative writing on occasion. This was South Jersey in the mid-seventies, and we were not often encouraged by *anyone* to be creative. I remember Wilkinson sitting on his old wooden desk one day after class and, with a worried-looking linoleum cutter, chopping down into the already damaged surface of the desk right between his legs, telling me it was his theory that every intelligent person had at some point in his or her life contemplated suicide. I think I was supposed to verify this hypothesis, but I just smiled. I was afraid to let him know I had, in fact, more than contemplated the issue, but I was also afraid to lie and make him feel alone. One afternoon, alone in my family's Cape Cod-style house, I had turned on an unlit propane torch in my room, hoping the gas would overwhelm all the pain I'd been accumulating like the WWII airplane models strung from my room's ceiling acoustic tiles. I had Navy fighters—Corsairs, Hellcats, Wildcats—and Army bombers—B-17s, Liberators, B-20s—and my favorite, the P-51 Mustang. I'd simulated machine gun bullet holes by heating the point of a compass in a candle flame, and piercing the plastic hulls of my favorite planes, in imitation of the way I was taking heavy flak and damage from experience.

The propane filled the bedroom, but I didn't know to seal the windows, so I didn't even get very sick. I just turned it off when it was empty and snuck it back down to the basement, then aired out my room so I wouldn't get in trouble. No one noticed anything was wrong that night, but I felt like there was an incredible difference. I did not know how to talk about this difference to anyone, not even to my mother. Every day she would go to the work that she hated at Columbia Records, or Tyco Industries, or Spectrum X-Ray, and disappear into a skin so uncomfortable it would burn her all night, all morning until she left. My family was falling apart like flesh off overcooked chicken.

And I couldn't tell anyone how lonely I was. Another time I took a whole lot of aspirin because I'd read that aspirin in heavy doses could kill you, and I didn't realize I had access to anything stronger. Actually my little brother was the biggest dope dealer in the county, but I didn't know that yet. Turns out, all those people in long hair and surplus army jackets who kept stopping by were not his friends. Turns out, all those absent nights he was sleeping on his best friend's parents' pool table in their unheated garage in the middle of winter. Maybe he was trying to die, but the mammalian heater inside the blood kept him alive despite his best efforts.

Sometimes he tries to tell me about it, but mostly he has nothing to do with me, as if another planet dictates rules directly to his head. And I'm no better; I don't know what to say to him. When we talk, I feel empty of myself, whatever that is, and I feel like I'm sliding into body armor and a Nazi-looking helmet. But other times, I feel like no one can understand me but my brother. No one else went through what we went through; no one else saw the holes he punched into the walls or the damaged model airplanes I suspended from the empty sky. We bear witness for each other.

And somehow, despite it all, despite the scratch of memory and remorse, we live on, fly on, like birds stunned by head-first contact with living room windows, but whose necks are inexplicably *not* broken. We keep trying to take ourselves out, but we're tougher than we imagined. I can't count the times I drove home across town so drunk I passed out just inside the front door. My mother tells the story of my brother speeding home one night, five police cruisers in high speed pursuit, blue lights blazing like razors, until he screeched to a stop in front of her house and roared out of the Camaro, insane on crystal meth, screaming at the cops and their drawn weapons.

Right then I was trying to take it easy, since I was the only male in my family who hadn't killed anybody. I was in college in Illinois, far away from all this. I wanted to become a Baptist minister, and somehow redeem the mess. My family either wrote me off or hoped I'd pay for their sins. So my grandfather told me about the first person he'd killed. It was an accident. Some smart-ass bully was giving him a hard time at a senior prom, so Grandpop stepped on his foot, pushed with his left, and punched him square on the nose with his right. The bully fell back fast on the curb, which would have been okay, except for the fact he smashed his head on it and died.

Despite the acquittal, there must have been some drama at the school, because my grandfather almost showed some unusual remorse while he was telling me this. Then Grandpop told me about the little Jewish guy he took on a little ride out to the country, then punched and burned with cigarettes until he signed over some valuable property—four homes in Chester, Pennsylvania. As he told me, I knew he didn't want me to know the truth about how he got rich, even as he needed me to hear it. I knew there was something shady about the old men he hung around with on the screened-in porch, with whom he traded bourbon, dirty jokes, and old stories. No one ever seemed to go to their restaurants, yet they were rich as hell. And they were all Italian and Irish who'd come up from the mean streets, still loud and rough and big as prizefighters. I started to piece it together when Grandpop told me he almost bought a machine gun once, since without it he'd be naked. Then he showed me the .32 he kept in his dresser drawer. He looked disturbed: a few of the rounds had been fired.

"Your brother must have been playing with this."

—◦—

What draws us to the self-destruction, to the ruins left after murder and suicide? When I was in college, the older brother of my roommate, having been disappointed in love, walked out one night and lay down on the Illinois Central tracks. They dedicated the next yearbook to him. Then every Halloween, someone stood out at that crossroads draped in a stained sheet, as if the ghost could not leave the campus until we all acknowledged him. I don't even remember his name, or the name of his brother. They'd both been raised in Taiwan, the children of missionaries, fluent in Mandarin and experts in Asian culture, and my roommate ended up in Yale graduate school for Chinese Studies. I don't know how he felt about his brother's death, but then, he never spoke about personal feelings. Every night he'd read his Chinese Bible and would sometimes speak about his other brother who'd named all his children after characters in Proust. We live inside these giant texts filled with figurations of the same atrocities we cannot handle in life. It's not escape to immerse yourself in the simulations of literature. It's more like bearing witness, a narcissistic martyrdom to the truth contained in the text.

—◦—

And when we write, we empty ourselves into the text, erased in memory and signified in language. Self-destruction and suicide are positive, marketable characteristics for the poet and the painter, as if being overwhelmed is a sign and symbol of genius and intensity. We can't resist the glamour of the beautiful, talented artist broken down by the very pressures the world lays upon him, the nut cracked and the meat picked out. But, on the other hand, we ignore those suicides who have nothing to offer us in terms of art or artifact, since they are inconvenient reminders of our easy oblivion. I think of Ronnie Mills, who was not an artist. One night in desperation he aimed a shotgun at himself. My mother was friends with his mother (in the same prayer group), so I heard about this when I was at college. Ronnie was one of my high school chums. He left nothing I know of, his death a sad moment only for those who loved him, his mother and brother. And then I think of Joe Bolton, a very fine poet, who put the barrel of a handgun in his mouth in Arizona when he was 28. His death was a kind of event, an opportunity for elegies and posthumous editions of his poems. As Wordsworth says in the oft-quoted lines from "Resolution and Independence":

> I thought of Chatterton, the marvelous Boy,
> The sleepless Soul that perished in his pride...
> We Poets in our youth begin in gladness;
> But thereof come in the end despondency and madness.

Yes, Chatterton and Weldon Kees, Harte Crane and John Berryman, all the merry fucked-up speaking empty oracles. I would like to believe that "By our own spirits are we deified," but it seems quite the opposite, even by Wordsworth's examples of Chatterton and Burns, or by his own. I'm not sure art redeems a life perversely lived, and I'm not sure it's healthy to think so, though of course it is valuable to have good poems left to us. I'm not sure whether we are valuing the suicide's poem, or only the frame by which we know it. The cult of personality still defines the literary world, perhaps most markedly, I must admit, in the personal essay as well as the poem. Let's face it, a text without a heartbeat is not very interesting.

What does this say about us, our culture? We want to save a few heartbeats after death, zombify the dead letter and keep it walking and working. We can't save them all, but maybe we can save a few, even if they are chosen only on talent, not character. I didn't know Ronnie at all at the end of his life, but he had always seemed like a very happy person to me in high school. Not someone you would worry about. Now he has faded into nothingness while Joe Bolton is still publishing books. I knew Joe briefly in Houston, more as an acquaintance than as a friend. Everyone in the writing program knew he was brilliant and alcoholic, the nicest guy and "the poet most likely to self-destruct." He was never without a wife, and never without unfaithfulness and the need to be alone. He dressed like Miami Vice, and carried a pint in the inside pocket of his unconstructed jacket. I only remember seeing him drink once, but it was enough to know it was his only love. He pulled the bottle out of his pocket, then passed it to his wife, and they both drank like they needed it more than air or water. People don't take communion that fervently.

Like Ronnie, no one seemed happier in my world than Joe Bolton, and that is rather frightening and says a lot about writers and suicides. I guess he knew just what he wanted, which was to mature into nothingness. Everyone else was just as insane, but we all thought we'd make it as famous writers, and then everything would be all right. When another friend finally had his manuscript taken by a publisher, his depression surprised us, but it shouldn't have. This was the beginning of the era of Kurt Cobain, and the artist who cannot stand to succeed, who works hard at making himself impossible to ignore or to deal with. This was the era of guilt; sin hadn't gone anywhere except inside the heart of behavior. All the artists I know who got what they wanted have had to pay a price, right out of flesh and spirit. Their books are finally published, and then they wind up in the hospital, the therapist's office, and the emergency ward. If you're lucky, they take it out on themselves; if not, they take it out on you.

➤ ➤

One night walking home from teaching at the local campus of the community college, someone shot at me from a passing car. There were two or three pops, and then the jingle of the expelled shells on the concrete. This was right in front of my house, so when I walked inside the living room, my (ex) wife asked me, "Did somebody just shoot at you?" I said, "Yeah!" She said, disappointed, "Well, I thought so," and went back to revising her manuscript.

I was drowning in the undertow of a bad marriage. I didn't understand you have to cut 90 degrees away from the tide's pull if you want to live, so I kept fighting directly against the pull, and lost myself deeper in the flow. And then you just relax and go out with it. The slowest but surest suicide is to surrender every interest you love, one by one, when you decide someone else knows better. You give it up like shards of pottery, or slices of papyrus cut off a scroll. Once you start, it's hard to stop. Buddy Guy and the blues, Henry James, Ezra Pound, Neil Young, my family, my friends, my writing—all these were anathema to her. I killed myself because I let her cut off everything that defined me, as if I didn't belong to myself, and needed pruning.

So I learned never to give up anything. I remember in fifth grade, how Hans, one of my special friends, pale and thin, disappeared. We used to play Time Tunnel during recess, tumbling through the warping spirals like in the TV show whenever the teachers let us do what we wanted. Then, one day, Hans didn't show up for school. Later that day we found out his father had crept into his room, and shot him with both barrels of a 12-gauge shot gun. According to the evening edition of the *Woodbury Times*, the last words of my friend were, "Oh, daddy, don't do that." Words are not good body armor. My parents used to go dancing at Hans' father's club, The Oasis, on Friday nights, because there wasn't anywhere else. They were shocked, and rather silent, about the murder. When I first heard the news that Hans was dead, I was out playing in a peach orchard, a field they'd just burned out to replant with new trees. Allison Gottshalk screamed at me from her yard that Hans was murdered. I didn't react, because I didn't know how, but it was as if I was killing him inside me. I didn't want to give up where I was: alone in a field, freshly scarred, November like a gray rag tented over the world. Then during a restroom break at school, I noted how the drinking fountain in the hall had the trademark "Oasis" embossed around the drain, a strange joke, as all jokes are.

I have some friends whose arms are plowed with scars, the razor writing of desperation on the field of the body: you cut across the vein, over and over and over, because you don't want to die, just make the acquaintance of death. You don't want to fall, just lean a little bit, and *almost* tumble over into the dark so you can see how it feels. It's cold and empty — everyone says that. So it's surprising how we have to reconfirm the obvious, over and over…Surviving is a joke and a burden, since *we're* the ones who have to go on, drag the past into the future and imagine some structure of meaning lives inside the corpse of what just happened.

We spiral down the time tunnel, ride the rifling into the flashlight beam. We're the bullet and the explosion, the powder and the wound. And for the writer, every murder is a suicide, every suicide a strange survival. Everything else smells of vanity and dead skin.

Contributors

U.N. Atana lives in Sunnyvale, California, and has been writing for several years. She was formerly an editor for Three Continents Press and is currently an M.F.A. student in creative writing at San Francisco State University. SASE is her first published story.

D.N. Baldwin was raised in Honolulu, then returned to the mainland and attended Old Dominion University. After college, he taught chemistry, then signed on at Goddard College, where he received an M.F.A. in creative writing and American literature. His short stories have found homes in *Hawai'i Review, The Washington Review, Chiron Review,* and *American Short Fiction,* where his story took second place in the annual fiction competition. Currently, he lives in a ski resort in Basye, Virginia, where he is nearing completion of his second novel.

John P. Baum III received his B.A. in English at Tulane University and his M.A. from the Center for Writers at the University of Southern Mississippi. He lives in Atlanta and teaches English at a private high school.

Shawn Behlen lives in California. His short fiction has appeared in *Press, Black Warrior Review, Puerto del Sol,* and several other publications. He is finishing a novel.

Seth Biderman will graduate this spring from the M.A. program in creative writing at the University of New Mexico, Albuquerque. He was awarded the English Department's Creative Writing Thesis Fellowship for 2000-2001, which has allowed him to write full-time while supporting a costly addiction to breakfast burritos from The Frontier.

Millicent C. Borges' recent work appears in *Laurel Review, Seattle Review, Tampa Review,* and *Witness.* In 1997 she received a poetry grant from the National Endowment for the Arts. She has been a writer in residence at Yaddo. *Boomer Girls* (University of Iowa Press) and *ClockPunchers* are anthology credits. She works as a technical writer and lives in Venice, California.

Michelle Brooks' fiction and poetry appears or is forthcoming in *Hayden's Ferry Review, Other Voices, Riversedge, Phoebe, Karamu, Poetry Motel,* and *Baltimore Review.* She has a Ph.D. from the University of North Texas and now teaches at Macomb College in Detroit.

A. Papatya Bucak teaches creative writing in the M.F.A. program at Minnesota State University, Mankato. She has recent stories and poems in *The Ohio Review, Salt Hill,* and *The Beloit Fiction Journal.*

E.G. Burrows worked for a number of years in public broadcasting before retiring to Washington State. His poems have appeared in more than 150 literary journals, most recently in *Baltimore Review, William & Mary Review, Baybury Review, Montserrat Review, Crab Creek Review, Aura, Confluence, Poet Lore,* and *White Pelican.* Poems of his were published in *Blue Mesa Review* #4 and #6.

Jeffrey S. Chapman lives in Salt Lake City, Utah, where he is working on a Ph.D. in creative writing from the University of Utah. He received his M.F.A. from Sarah Lawrence College. A previous story has been published in *Cutbank.*

Stephanie Dickinson was raised in rural Iowa and now lives in New York's Bowery. She has published in *Green Mountains Review, Gulf Stream, Mudfish, Natural Bridges,* and other journals. *Corn Goddess,* her poetry collection, was recently brought out by Linear Arts. Along with Rob Cook, she edits the new literary review *Skidrow Penthouse.*

Darrach Dolan received his B.A. from Trinity College, Dublin, and his M.F.A. from the Iowa Writers' Workshop. He is completing a book of short stories, for which he has received funding from The Arts Council of Ireland. He came to the U.S. via England, the Netherlands, and Australia. He currently lives in Carlisle, Pennsylvania, where he is an Associate Fellow of Dickinson College.

Lawrence C. Goeckel is the recipient of *Blue Mesa Review's* Graduate Poetry Contest, judged in 2000 by poet Kate Knapp Johnson. He currently runs the Electronic Warfare Section for the 58th Special Operations Wing at Kirtland A.F.B., New Mexico. Never quite able to complete the required documents, he lives in a small house on one of the dust fields south of Albuquerque, looking longingly towards the trout streams of the northern Rockies.

Jaimy Gordon's last book was *Bogeywoman* (Sun &Moon 1999). She teaches in the graduate writing program at Western Michigan University.

William Greenway's sixth poetry collection is *Simmer Dim* (University of Akron Press). He is co-editor, with Elton Glaser, of an anthology of modern poems about Ohio (also University of Akron Press). His poems appear in *Poetry, American Poetry Review, Southern Review, Poetry Northwest, Shenandoah*, and *Prairie Schooner*. He is Professor of English at Youngstown State University.

Paula Gunn Allen's poetry and prose appear widely in anthologies, journals, and scholarly publications. A recipient of numerous awards, including the 1990 Native American Prize for Literature, she is the author of seven volumes of poetry, including *Grandmothers of the Light: A Medicine Woman's Sourcebook* (1991), *The Voice of the Turtle* (1994), and *Spider Woman's Granddaughters: Traditional Tales and Contemporary Writing by Native American Women*.

Molly Hansen was born in Omaha, Nebraska, in 1976. She currently lives in Iowa City, Iowa, where she works as an editor at an educational publishing company and at a local bookstore. "Infestation" is her first published story.

Nick Hundley is a seventh year University of New Mexico undergraduate in Astrophysics.

George Kalamaras' poems appear in *Best American Poetry 1997, Boulevard, Epoch, The Iowa Review, New Letters, Sulfur, TriQuarterly*, and elsewhere. He is the author of two poetry chapbooks, *Heart Without End* (Leaping Mountain Press 1986) and *Beneath the Breath* (Tilton House 1988). His first full-length collection, *The Theory and Function of Mangoes*, won the 1998 Four Way Books Intro Series in Poetry Award and was published by Four Way Books in 2000. Among his awards are an NEA Poetry Fellowship and the Abiko Quarterly (Japan) Poetry Award. He is associate professor of English at Indiana University-Purdue University Fort Wayne.

Rosalind Lieberman was born in Philadelphia. She received her B.S. in Education from Temple University, attended the Barnes Foundation, Immaculate Heart College, C.S.U.L.A., and U.C.L.A. before moving to Albuquerque in 1995. In addition to preparing two collections of poems, she is presently at work on a historical novel set in the Frankish Empire during the eighth century.

Ada Limón is currently a graduate student at New York University where she is pursuing her M.F.A. in creative writing, poetry. She is originally from Sonoma, California, where she was raised in a community of artists and writers, including her stepfather, Brady T. Brady, and her mother, Stacia Brady. She currently teaches creative writing to second graders in the Bronx.

Lucinda Lucero is the recipient of *Blue Mesa Review's* Graduate Fiction Contest, judged in 2000 by novelist and short story writer Tom Franklin. She has a Master's in History. In her last year of teaching, Holt, Winston, and Rinehart selected her to be on the editorial review board for their textbook, *The American Nation.* In addition to her fiction writing, she volunteers at the Hispanic Cultural Center doing research and assisting patrons. She lives in Albuquerque with her husband, Lewis Real.

Glenna Luschei is the Poet Laureate of San Luis Obispo. She has been D.H. Lawrence fellow in Taos. Her latest book is *Pianos around the Cape* (Aspermont Press, San Francisco). She is publisher of *Solo,* a journal of poetry, and *Cafe Solo,* founded in Albuquerque. Recent publishing credits include *Pembroke Magazine, Prairie Schooner,* and *South Dakota Review.*

Todd Moore has had more than 80 books and chapbooks published since 1976. He is best known for writing noir poetry. His long poem *Dillinger* has appeared serially from Kangaroo Court Press and Primal Publishing. *Working on My Duende* (Kings Estate Press) is his long poem about New Mexico, Lorca, the origins of poetry, and death.

Emmy Perez, originally from Santa Ana, California, has poems published or forthcoming in *Prairie Schooner, New York Quarterly,* and *Luna: A Journal of Poetry and Translation.* Her fiction has appeared in *Story.* She received an M.F.A. from Columbia University and poetry fellowships from the Fine Arts Work Center in Provincetown and from the New York Foundation for the Arts.

Pedro Ponce is pursuing a doctorate degree in fiction at the University of Denver. His stories have appeared previously in *Ploughshares, Alaska Quarterly Review*, and *Gargoyle.*

Janice Robertson has published poetry in *The MacGuffin* and non-fiction in *Alaska Quarterly Review.*

Willa Schneberg received an Oregon Literary Arts Fellowship in Poetry and a Money for Women/Barbara Deming Memorial Fund Grant in Poetry in 1999. This summer she was a fellow in poetry at the Tyrone Guthrie Center, Annaghmakerrig, Ireland. In 2000 her poems appeared in *American Poetry Review*, *Points of Contact: Disability, Art and Culture* (University of Michigan Press), and *Knowing Stones: Poems of Exotic Places* (John Gordon Burke, Inc.). She has a poem in a soon to be released textbook *To Remember: Teaching The Holocaust* (Heinemann). She recently completed a poetry manuscript entitled *Storytelling in Cambodia*.

Zach Schomburg recently earned his M.A. in creative writing from the University of Nebraska. He has since set up camp in Akron, Ohio, where he has developed a taste for plastics and professional bowling. He has poetry forthcoming in *Onthebus* and *Rattle*.

Martin Scott took his M.F.A. from the University of Iowa and his Ph.D. from the University of Houston. He teaches at Houston Community College, a campus located in a shopping mall, and at the University of Houston. He has poems and essays forthcoming in *New York Quarterly, Southern Poetry Review, Under the Sun, Plainsongs*, and *Drunken Boat*.

Emily Spiegelman was raised in Massachusetts, where she discovered that she made a better writer than a rower. She has a B.A. in English from the University of Pennsylvania, and completed her Master's degree in creative writing at the University of New Mexico in the spring of 2000. She teaches freshman composition at UNM.

John Surowiecki works as a freelance writer in the Hartford area although he is slouching toward retirement. His work appears in or has been accepted by a number of journals, including *Cream City Review, Cumberland Review, Indiana Review, Kimera, The Literary Review Web, The MacGuffin, Nimrod*, and *Prairie Schooner*. In 2000 his poems won first place in contests sponsored by *Georgia State University Review* and *Common Ground Review*.

Arthur Sze is the author of five volumes of poetry, inlcuding most recently *The Redshifting Web: Poems 1970-1998* (Copper Canyon Press 1998), a finalist for the 1999 Lenore Marshall Poetry Prize. The recipient of a Lannan Literary Award for Poetry, three Witter Bynner Foundation Poetry Fellowships, and two Creative Writing Fellowships from the National Endowment for the Arts, Sze currently directs the Creative Writing Program at the Institute of American Indian Arts in Santa Fe, New Mexico, where he has taught for more than a decade.

Peggy Tahir lives and works in the San Francisco Bay area. She has an M.A. in English with an emphasis in creative writing from San Francisco State University and an M.L.I.S. from University of California, Berkeley. She has had one chapbook published. Her poems have appeared in local small press journals in the San Francisco area.

Luci Tapahanso is a member of the Diné nation of New Mexico and is Professor of English at the University of Arizona. She is the author of six books, including *Blue Horses Rush In: Poems & Stories* (University of Arizona 1998), which was awarded the 1998 Award for Best Poetry from the Mountains & Plains Booksellers' Association.

Stefi Weisburd has worked as a science journalist, engineer, and congressional analyst. One of her poems nested recently in *Quarterly West*. Her poems for children have appeared in *Cricket, Highlights*, and other magazines. She lives with her family in Albuquerque.

Elizabeth Ann Winslow is a recent graduate of the Iowa Writers' Workshop. She has had short stories published in *Phoebe* and *Wolf's Head Quarterly*, and translations of Arabic in *Exchanges, Banipal, Modern Poetry in Translation*, and *Mizna*. "Ablution" is part of a story cycle set in the Middle East.

Sandra Yannone teaches composition and women's studies at the State University of New York, Oswego. Her poems and reviews appear or are forthcoming in *Ploughshares, Prairie Schooner, Evergreen Chronicles, CALYX: A Journal, Connecticut Review*, and *Luna*. She is recipient of an A.W.P. Intro Award and an Academy of American Poets poetry prize.

Fredrick Zydek is the author of four collections of poetry: *Lights Along the Missouri, Storm Warning, Ending the Fast*, and *The Conception Abbey Poems*. His work appears in *The Antioch Review, The Hollins Critic, Michigan Quarterly Review, Poetry, Poetry Northwest*, and other journals. Formerly a professor of creative writing and theology at the University of Nebraska and later at the College of Saint Mary, he is now a gentleman farmer when he isn't writing. Most recently he has accepted the post as editor for Lone Willow Press.

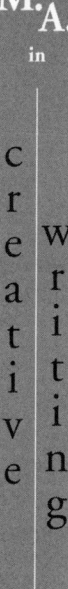